Engaging the Doctrine *of* God

Engaging the Doctrine *of* God

Contemporary Protestant Perspectives

EDITED BY

Bruce L. McCormack

Baker Academic
a division of Baker Publishing Group
Grand Rapids, Michigan

Rutherford
House

© 2008 by Rutherford House and Bruce L. McCormack

Published by Baker Academic
a division of Baker Publishing Group
P.O. Box 6287, Grand Rapids, MI 49516–6287
www.bakeracademic.com

and Rutherford House
Edinburgh EH6 7PJ
Scotland, United Kingdom
www.rutherfordhouse.org.uk

Printed in the United States of America

Library of Congress Cataloging-in-Publication Data
Engaging the doctrine of God : contemporary Protestant perspectives / edited by Bruce L. McCormack.
   p.   cm.
   Includes bibliographical references and indexes.
   ISBN 978-0-8010-3552-4 (pbk.)
   1. God (Christianity)—History of doctrines. 2. Protestant churches—Doctrines—History. I. McCormack, Bruce L.
   BT98.E54 2008
   231—dc22   2007042766

UK ISBN 978-1-904429-15-9

Contents

Contributors

Pierre Berthoud is professor of Old Testament at Faculté Libre de Théologie Réformée, Aix en Provence, France.

Henri A. Blocher is Knoedler Professor of Theology at Wheaton College.

D. A. Carson is research professor of New Testament at Trinity Evangelical Divinity School.

Oliver D. Crisp is lecturer in theology at Bristol University.

Paul Helm is teaching fellow at Regent College and professor at Highland Theological Institute.

Donald Macleod is professor of systematic theology at the Free Church of Scotland College in Edinburgh.

Bruce L. McCormack is the Frederick and Margaret L. Weyerhaeuser Professor of Systematic Theology at Princeton Seminary.

John Webster is the chair of systematic theology at the University of Aberdeen.

Stephen N. Williams is professor of systematic theology at Union Theological College in Belfast, Northern Ireland.

David F. Wright is emeritus professor of patristic and Reformed Christianity at the University of Edinburgh.

N. T. Wright is bishop of Durham, England, and author of more than thirty books.

Preface

Is there such a thing as *the* evangelical doctrine of the being and attributes of God? Many would probably like to say, "Yes, of course there is. The evangelical doctrine of God is the *orthodox* doctrine of God. It has to be because evangelicals are, by definition, committed to Christian orthodoxy." But is there even an orthodox doctrine of God? I raise the question because it is not immediately obvious what would make any doctrine of God to be orthodox in the first place. "Orthodoxy" means, quite obviously, "right teaching," and for evangelicals, the material norm for deciding what is right teaching must surely be Holy Scripture. It is conformity to scriptural teaching which guarantees the orthodoxy of any opinion. So far, all evangelicals would be in agreement. Scripture, however, has to be interpreted. Decisions must be made as to its proper meaning. In some cases, where doctrinal disputes have threatened to disrupt the peace and unity of the church, councils were called to *decide* what constitutes orthodox teaching in relation to the disputed questions. All of this is to say that "orthodoxy" is finally a church concept. It is a concept that belongs to the realm of ecclesiology because it is the Church which must make the decision as to how Holy Scripture is to be understood—not individual theologians, no matter how great their personal prestige. To be sure, since the decision of the Church is a decision with regard to the proper understanding of a material norm that is *other* than itself, its decisions on any question are inherently reformable. Still, those decisions made by the Church in the past which continue to enjoy support among the great majority of the divided churches possess a degree of ecclesial authority that is unsurpassed. The more ecumenical the council, the more its decisions shape the common faith of all the churches.

But here is the problem: no ecumenical council was ever convened to establish the limits of "orthodoxy" where the being and attributes of God are concerned. No ecumenical council has ever addressed, even in passing, the issues involved. The Nicene Creed, which did define the limits of orthodoxy where the triunity of God is concerned, certainly has *implications* for one's understanding of the being and attributes of God. But a wide range of treatments of the being and attributes of God can be shown to be compatible with the Nicene Creed. The truth of the matter is that there is no "orthodox" doctrine of God, if by that is meant an understanding of God's being and attributes.

One might well say that, for my church, the Westminster Confession of Faith serves as the sole subordinate standard for determining what constitutes right teaching in this area of doctrine. And if the reader does belong to such a church, then I would have to concede the truth of his or her claim. *For you*, the teaching of chapter 2 of the Westminster Confession stands alone in defining the limits of orthodoxy in this area of doctrine. But a defender of the Westminster doctrine of God might immediately want to ask, Is the Westminster doctrine not the doctrine of the church fathers, Calvin, and all who are "orthodox" in relation to those matters which have been treated by the church councils? This is where things get interesting! The Westminster Confession says, "There is but one only living and true God, who is infinite in being and perfection, a most pure spirit, invisible, without body, parts or passions." The insistence that God is without body or parts constitutes an affirmation of divine *simplicity*, obviously. Note also that God's being "without passions" is an affirmation of divine *impassibility*. Neither of these affirmations, however, is included in the earlier Reformed confessions.[1] In fact, these confessions give only sparse treatment to the being and attributes of God, much as Calvin did by devoting only a slim chapter to the subject in his *Institutes*.[2] This means that many Reformed churches have never

1. Simplicity and impassibility do not find expression in the articles on God in the Genevan Confession (1536), the First Helvetic Confession (1536), the French Confession (1559), the Scots Confession (1560), the Belgic Confession (1561, revised 1619), or the Second Helvetic Confession (1566). The Genevan Catechism (1545) has very little to say about God's being and attributes, choosing to turn its attention instead to divine providence and redemption, and the Heidelberg Catechism (1563) offers no treatment of the subject whatsoever.

2. Calvin's doctrine of God comprises three very brief subsections which take up but three pages in the McNeill edition. See John Calvin, *Institutes of the Christian Religion*, I.x.1–3, ed. John McNeill, trans. Ford Lewis Battles (Philadelphia: Westminster; London: SCM, 1960). Of these three sections, only the second treats the being and attributes of God. And even then, Calvin is treating how God relates to his creatures, not how God is in himself. Reflecting upon Exod. 34:6–7, Calvin writes of the name given to God there, "Here let us observe that his eternity and his self-existence are announced by that wonderful

made divine simplicity and impassibility a matter of confession. Hence the Westminster Confession defines the limits of orthodoxy in relation to the doctrine of God *only* for those churches that continue to uphold it as their sole subordinate standard of faith; it does not define orthodoxy for all Reformed churches. My point is that no ecumenical consensus exists on the doctrine of God, and there is no single creed or confession recognized across denominational boundaries that defines orthodoxy in this area for the great majority of Christians in the same way that the Nicene Creed does for the doctrine of the Trinity. That being the case, any doctrine of God which does not clearly collide with the Nicene Creed (or, we might add, if you like, the Chalcedonian Formula) might conceivably be "orthodox" and would have to be regarded as a serious possibility by doctors of all the churches.

In the nature of the case, work on the doctrine of God today—whether done by evangelicals or non-evangelicals—must be *exploratory*. In our work with the doctrine of God, we are not working in the realm of received dogma, critically analyzing it and defending it. In this particular case, we have no dogma. What we have is only the doctrines of individual teachers, past and present, whose contents often overlap but just as often diverge on important issues.

The essays contained in this volume first saw life as lectures given at the eleventh Edinburgh Dogmatics Conference, held in the city of that name from August 29 to September 1, 2005, under the sponsorship of Rutherford House. Doctrinal preaching is an important part of every Edinburgh Dogmatics Conference. The tone of this conference was set by David Wright's moving sermon—one which succeeded in introducing one of the conference's central problems, namely, the question whether God suffers and, if so, how this is possible. The papers which followed showed that evangelical exploration into the doctrine of God today is very much in flux and that opinions are divided. Contributors ranged from those deeply committed to one form of "classical theism" (Paul Helm) on the one end of the spectrum to those cautiously critical of it (Bruce McCormack) on the other end. I call my own position *cautiously* critical because I have learned so much from classical theism—and because there are evangelical options which were not represented at our conference and which would have to be located somewhere to the "left" of me. The other

name twice repeated. Thereupon his powers are mentioned, by which he is shown to us not as he is in himself, but as he is towards us; so that this recognition of him consists more in living experience than in vain and high-flown speculation." Whether Calvin is right to regard God as unknowable in himself is a question for itself. What is clear is that he wants to content himself with what God has revealed—and to say no more. Perhaps this is why divine "simplicity" and "impassibility" are nowhere mentioned in this context or in any of the confessions of faith authored or coauthored by Calvin.

contributors at our conference are to be found at various points between these two poles. If I were to divide them into groups (and this is only my opinion), I would place Don Carson, Oliver Crisp, Donald Macleod, and John Webster on the classical end of the spectrum, with N. T. Wright, Henri Blocher, Pierre Berthoud and Stephen Williams as belonging to the "progressive" end in their willingness to pose questions to concepts of divine timelessness, impassibility, and so forth (with occasional nods of agreement from the otherwise classically oriented Professor Webster). That two leading "Barthians" such as Webster and McCormack can, for the most part, appear on different ends of a spectrum of beliefs about God tells us something important about divisions within evangelical Barthianism. We do not all take the same things from Barth! Even more important, however, the range of possibilities found on this spectrum of beliefs tells us something significant about evangelical reflection on the doctrine of God today. Such consensus as may once have existed on the doctrine of God has now given way to major differences of opinion on some very important topics. It is my fervent hope that evangelicals will one day be able to build a new consensus on the doctrine of God. But that will require patience, mutual respect, careful exegetical and historical spadework, and rigorous theological argumentation. If the essays in this volume accomplish nothing more than to kick-start a conversation which leads to such a new consensus, then they will have amply served their purpose.

I would like to thank Mr. Robert Fyall, the director of Rutherford House, for his oversight of the 2005 conference and for all of his work at the House. Bob will be leaving his post as director this year. We will all miss his wise administration and his saintly spirit around the place. Thanks are also due Mr. Robert Hosack of Baker Academic. This is the second collection of essays to be published by Baker Academic.[3] Bob and his team are delightful people to work with; they are highly skilled professionals who manage to be consistently patient with the foibles of academics. I wish finally to thank Stina Busman, PhD candidate here at Princeton Seminary, for introducing uniformity of formatting into papers written by scholars from France, the United Kingdom, and the United States. Her work is deeply appreciated. And finally, thanks are due to Keith L. Johnson, another of our PhD students, for his careful editing of the final draft of the manuscript.

---

3. See Bruce L. McCormack, ed., *Justification in Perspective: Historical Developments and Contemporary Challenges* (Grand Rapids: Baker Academic, 2006).

1

Edinburgh Dogmatics Conference Sermon

The Lamb That Was Slain

DAVID F. WRIGHT

"Striving after clarity in the concept we should entertain of God," asserts Brian Gerrish, is "a fundamental mark of the Calvinistic mind."[1] The same holds, to be sure, for those who might prefer "Reformed" to "Calvinistic." It is within the broad Reformed trajectory of biblical dogmatic theology that this conference addresses its mind to the doctrine of God. Clarity is surely crucial but not the highest criterion, which must be fidelity to Scripture.

The concern of this sermon is with one aspect of the distinctively Christian character of our doctrine of God. At our particular time and place this is a critical issue. For example, do Christians worship the same God as Muslims and Jews? If not, what are the most significant differences?

Roughly the same question can be put from another angle: how complete a doctrine of God do we derive from the Old Testament alone? And again, if the Old Testament furnishes only an incomplete doctrine,

1. B. A. Gerrish, *Grace and Gratitude: The Eucharistic Theology of John Calvin* (Minneapolis: Fortress; Edinburgh: T&T Clark, 1993), 81.

what are the decisive differences? The centrality of the Trinity comes immediately to mind, but that may not be the whole answer.

Let us start with the end of the New Testament, with the apocalyptic visions of John in Revelation, a writing we may do well to regard as the climax of New Testament Scripture. Why not discern a providential hand at work in the ordering of the books of the New Testament canon in full knowledge of the details of historical development?

Central to John's visions is "the Lamb," so named almost thirty times and first introduced in Revelation 5 as "a Lamb standing in the center of the throne, looking as if it had been slain or slaughtered" (v. 6). "The Lamb," with or without further description, is the book's standard designation of the one whom it more occasionally calls Jesus, Jesus Christ, the Christ, the Word of God.

The saints have overcome their Satanic accuser "by the blood of the Lamb and the word of their testimony" (12:11). It is around "the Lamb standing on Mount Zion" that crowd the 144,000 "redeemed from humankind as the firstfruits from God and the Lamb" (14:4). They sing the song of Moses and the song of the Lamb (15:3) as they await the marriage of the Lamb, the wedding supper of the Lamb (19:7, 9). The bride, the holy city, is "the wife of the Lamb" (21:9), and the Twelve are now "the twelve apostles of the Lamb" (21:14). The temple of the heavenly Jerusalem is "the Lord God the Almighty and the Lamb"; the glory of God is the light of the city, and "its lamp is the Lamb" (21:22-23). To the very end "the throne of God and of the Lamb" is at the heart of the celestial city (22:3).

Throughout this series of visions the Lamb is surely the Lamb that looks as if it has been slain or slaughtered. It is this Lamb, the sacrificial victim, who is victorious—"because he is the Lord of lords and the King of kings" (17:14)—and who opens the seals and dispenses wrath (6:1–17).

Do we, should we, find this extraordinary? Do we expect to encounter in heaven Christ the Lord looking as if he has been killed? Didn't his wounds heal after the resurrection and become scars rather than wounds? Is John's vision compatible with believing in the glory of the exalted Christ, with the perishable having put on imperishability (cf. 1 Cor. 15:53), with our cherished convictions about how we shall be reunited with those who have died in the Lord in often distressing forms of bodily disintegration? Real questions face us, without doubt, about the coherence of the slaughtered Lamb in John's heavenly throne with the hope of our bodily renewal in the life of the world to come.

This book of Revelation is literature of a special kind, called apocalyptic, and we are called to embrace rather than dissect its riotous imagery. It certainly strains the imagination to conceive how a lamb that looked as if it had been slaughtered could be *standing* in the center of the throne and of the throng of the redeemed. One would scarcely expect a slaughtered animal to stand erect. We are given no clue what it was about the Lamb that impressed John as bearing the stamp of slaughter—what wounds, what mutilation, what bloodiness.

Much more important is what this depiction of the Lamb throughout John's visions is meant to convey to us. The answer is pertinent to the question of the distinctive Christianness of our doctrine of God, for what John's visions convey is this: that the cross is central to a Christian doctrine of God, for the victorious Christ who, ascended and exalted, stands at the heart of the Godhead is irreducibly the lamb of sacrifice. As the late and much lamented Alan Lewis put it:

> A bleeding sheep, bred for slaughter and slain for sin, must pass muster, incongruous yet somehow apt, as the first and final image of sin's victor and the world's redeemer-king.[2]

The first? John the Baptizer's acclamation in John 1:29, "Behold, the Lamb of God who takes away the sin of the world," and even earlier the prophetic word of Isaiah, "He was led like a lamb to the slaughter" (Isa. 53:7).

And the final image? Here in Revelation, of course. Were it not for this book's testimony, would we know so incontrovertibly that the exaltation of the risen Jesus Christ carried into the reality of God's being not merely the fact or memory of his once-for-all crucifixion but the whole human flesh-and-blood history of the incarnate Son? John could scarcely have expressed that message more starkly than by "seeing," with the penetration of a seer, a visionary, the conquering Christ as "the Lamb" looking like a slaughtered animal.

John makes this point with wonderful clarity at the first appearance of the Lamb in Revelation 5:

> I wept and wept because no-one was found who was worthy to open the scroll or look inside. Then one of the elders said to me, "Don't weep! See, the Lion of the tribe of Judah, the Root of David, has triumphed. He is able to open the scroll and its seven seals."
> Then I saw a Lamb, looking as if it had been slain. (vv. 4–6)

From "See, the Lion of the tribe of Judah," to "Then I saw a slaughtered Lamb." George Caird has commented,

2. Alan E. Lewis, *Between Cross and Resurrection: A Theology of Holy Saturday* (Grand Rapids and Cambridge, UK: Eerdmans, 2001), 74.

It is almost as if John were saying to us, "Wherever the Old Testament says 'Lion' read 'Lamb.'" Wherever the Old Testament speaks of the victory of the Messiah or the overthrow of the enemies of God, we are to remember that the gospel recognizes no other way of achieving these ends than the way of the Cross.[3]

But we need to go further: what is at stake here is not simply the centrality of sacrificial crucifixion in the plan of salvation but the implantation in the sphere of the eternal Godhead of the temporal life and death of the Lamb. The human experiences of Jesus, climaxing in death and burial, belong eternally to the being of God. What does this do to our doctrine of God?

We are not dependent on Revelation alone for the teaching that the exalted Son of God remains permanently and eternally the incarnate one. The Epistle to the Hebrews inculcates it repeatedly in terms of the ministry of the perfect high priest. This great high priest, able to sympathize with our weaknesses, is the one who was tempted in every way, just as we are (Heb. 4:15). It is the very one who suffered who is now able to sustain us (2:18). He has entered the Most Holy Place once for all with his own blood (9:12).

After the Lord's being raised from the dead, his wounded hands and side could still be displayed to doubting Thomas (John 20:25–27), and indeed to the rest of the disciples in their alarm that he might be a ghost: "Look at my hands and my feet" (Luke 24:39–40), for it was these which preserved the telltale stigmata of their crucified Master, both then and forever.

The hymn writers call us to exult in the confidence of access and acceptance that this dimension of Christology nurtures.

> It is my sweetest comfort, Lord,
> And will for ever be,
> To muse upon the gracious truth
> Of thy humanity.
>
> O joy! there sitteth in our flesh
> Upon a throne of light,
> One of a human mother born,
> A perfect Godhead bright! . . .

3. G. B. Caird, *A Commentary on the Revelation of St. John the Divine*, Black's New Testament Commentaries (London: A. & C. Black, 1966), 75, cited by Richard Bauckham, *The Climax of Prophecy: Studies on the Book of Revelation* (Edinburgh: T&T Clark, 1993), 179.

> For ever God, for ever Man,
> My Jesus shall endure;
> And fixed on him, my hope remains
> Eternally secure.

Thus wrote Edward Caswall, one of John Henry Newman's fellow converts to Catholicism.

From Isaac Watts's hymn "With Joy We Meditate the Grace":

> Touched with a sympathy within,
> He knows our feeble frame;
> He knows what sore temptations mean,
> For he has felt the same. . . .
>
> He in the days of feeble flesh
> Poured out his cries and tears;
> And though exalted, feels afresh
> What every member bears.

The early Methodist John Cennick has a hymn, "A Good High Priest Is Come":

> He once temptations knew,
> Of every sort and kind,
> That he might succour show
> To every tempted mind:
> In every point the Lamb was tried
> Like us, and then for us he died.
>
> He died; but lives again,
> And by the throne he stands,
> There shows how he was slain,
> Opening his piercèd hands:
> Our priest abides and pleads the cause
> Of us who have transgressed his laws.

Not every hymn writer always got it right. From the ever popular "Crown Him with Many Crowns" by Matthew Bridges:

> Crown him the Lord of love,
> Behold his hands and side,
> Rich wounds, yet visible above in beauty glorified. . . .
>
> His reign shall know no end,
> And round his piercèd feet

Fair flowers of paradise extend
Their fragrance ever sweet.

How woefully romanticized and sentimentalized! It is noteworthy that
the English hymnal *Praise!* has drastically revised that last verse:

For ever he shall reign,
And earthly princes fall
Before his throne, the Lamb once slain,
The sovereign Lord of all.

Yet I wonder whether any of our hymns does justice to what John's visions
express in their concentration on the Lamb. How does even theology
prove adequate to the task? How can it set forth the whole human history of the Lamb of God, climaxing in and focused in his death and
vindication two days later—all belonging to the trinitarian fullness of
God's being? The one who experienced so much that is common to our
human existence, apart from sinfulness of his own, abides within the
Godhead, permanently the incarnate, permanently the crucified, permanently the risen and exalted. Change, frustration, disappointment,
pain and pleasure, the whole gamut of earthly fortunes, from elation to
desolation to vindication—all, we may believe, captured forever within
the life of the God whom we worship and serve.

How far dare we go? Is there now vulnerability in God as there was
in Jesus? Was the phenomenon of growth and development which the
Son of God experienced taken up in his exaltation? Dare we exclude any
facet, any dimension of the human life of God in Christ?

Amid so many questions, one essential teaching merits emphatic
insistence, for the visions of the Apocalypse of John require it: the resurrection overcame death but it vindicated and so in a sense "preserved"
the dying one, "the Lamb as though slain." So death is indeed done away,
but the risen Christ remains still the one who died. Alan Lewis reflects
suggestively on the first question asked on the first Easter morning,
"Why are you seeking the living among the dead?" (Luke 24:5). Christ
had been removed from the place of the dead. "Yet the corollary of this
is that 'among the dead' is precisely the place where the Lord of life has
been, so that he remains forever, even in his glory, the Living One who
has been dead."[4]

It is as if after the crucifixion, and certainly after the resurrection two
days later, the human life of Christ was over with no further advance
and so no ultimate healing and no disappearance of the wounds, and

4. Lewis, *Between Cross and Resurrection*, 76.

it became eternally fixed in the frame of crucifixion, "caught" in that moment, forever, in his heavenly glory.

Let me conclude by spelling out some implications of this essential dimension of a Christian doctrine of God.

First, it invests the Gospels with special significance, for there we read, as nowhere else in Scripture, the human life of the incarnate Christ now translated in him into the eternal life of the Godhead.

Evangelical Christians have tended to be Pauline people par excellence. Do we sufficiently value the Gospels? Or are we so committed to the Christ of faith as to neglect the Jesus of Nazareth?

Second, as a focusing in of this first point, what is it about God that we derive comfort and reassurance from? An impossibly wide question! Yes, of course, but do we rest our confidence in a generalized sense of God's love and providential care and fatherly solicitude? These are, to be sure, all writ large in Scripture, yet it also unambiguously directs us to the human trials and vicissitudes of Jesus as the ground for our finding today a sympathetic ear in heaven, an understanding mind, a Lord capable, because of his experiences like ours, of coming to our aid. So again, keep close to the Gospels.

Third, evangelical Christians have generally preferred their crucifixes empty. Christ is not still hanging on the cross, and if we must wear a cross or have one on our desk or bedside, let it be empty, to bear witness to the resurrection. We steer clear of any hint of sympathy for those elements of Roman Catholic theology and piety expressed in devotion to the "sacred wounds of Jesus," to the Christ ever again sacrificed in the Mass, and in aspiring to replicate in oneself the pains of the passion of Jesus and even the stigmata themselves.

It is a sound instinct to eschew such florid excrescences of spirituality. But let us beware lest, through a discomfort with a spiritual dimension powered by meditation on the visual, we prove incapable of living with, and praying to, and gazing upon "the slaughtered Lamb" at the right hand of the Father.

It is common to lament the poverty of much evangelical spirituality, which often seems to have little to offer in the contemporary widespread pursuit of spiritual experience. Streams of evangelical spirituality issuing from different sources may be tempted to elide the scandal not so much of the crucifixion itself as of the vision of the Lamb, as it were, crucified in heaven's eternity.

The crucifixion was not pretty. The one who remains, as it were, crucified forever should not be prettified, gilded, embellished—no cosmetic makeover in or after the tomb. Whatever the women had in mind to do to the body of Jesus with their spices and scents, they were too late. The crucified one never fell into the hands of the embalmers. John saw visions of "the Lamb as though slain," and there is no reason why our sight, to say nothing of our other senses, should not be deployed in his worship and devotion.

Finally, to return to a point raised earlier as a question concerning the resurrection body—the identity we will have in the life of the world to come—listen to Paul:

> So it will be with the resurrection of the dead. The body that is sown is perishable, it is raised imperishable; it is sown in dishonor, it is raised in glory; it is sown in weakness, it is raised in power; it is sown a natural body, it is raised a spiritual body. (1 Cor. 15:42–44)

If all this is to be true of the saints, will it not be incongruous if Christ the Lord and Savior still looks as if he has been through the mill of the crucifixion? Is what Paul wrote of Christians not true also of Christ— "sown in dishonor . . . raised in glory . . . sown in weakness . . . raised in power"?

One possible answer to such questions lies along these lines and is commended to your reflection: The Son of God, when faith is swallowed up in sight, is permanently "the Lamb looking as if it had been slain" precisely in order that we shall always be reminded visibly at what price we have been made whole. Whatever the wholeness that healing may mean from person to person, we will forever behold the stripes by which we have been made new in Christ. "Those whom God justified, he also glorified"—but will glorification erase all awareness of our justification in our ungodliness? We are near to a profound insight of Martin Luther: *simul peccator, simul justus*. Will this be true in heaven also as we gather lost in wonder, love, and praise around the Lamb that was slain? Our glorification may erase all signs of weakness and dishonor while we contemplate eternally the Lamb looking as if it had been slaughtered. Praise be to God for ever and ever.

New Testament and Early Christian Origins of the Doctrine of God

2

Christian Origins
and the Question of God

N. T. WRIGHT

Introduction

The question of God is raised constantly throughout early Christianity and is routinely given the same answer: if you want to know the meaning of the word "God," look hard at Jesus of Nazareth. Indeed, much of the New Testament is written precisely to enable people of all sorts and conditions to do precisely that, and in case the point gets lost, the writers reemphasize it now this way, now that: no one has ever seen God, but the only-begotten God who is in the bosom of the Father has made him known; he is the image of the invisible God; he bears the very stamp of God's nature; or in Thomas's unforgettable confession when faced with the risen Jesus, "My Lord and my God." Not only in John (as people sometimes misguidedly suppose) but throughout the early church it is affirmed that those who have seen Jesus have seen the Father.

What this means within its historical context is an enormous topic, and to do justice to it, I really ought to discuss in detail the magnificent recent book by Larry Hurtado.[1] That, however, would give me a particular focus which is not my intention, and I leave such a review as a worthwhile

1. Larry Hurtado, *Lord Jesus Christ: Devotion to Jesus in Earliest Christianity* (Grand Rapids: Eerdmans, 2003).

road not taken on this occasion. Instead I want to look at two questions which interlock in various ways and which have come into focus and, I hope, will continue to come into focus in my own multivolume project. I do not just want to look at what the early Christians thought about the meaning of the word "God," as redefined around Jesus and (in a measure) around and indeed by the Holy Spirit. I want to dig beneath that and ask, Where did the early Christians stand on what we might call "the question of God" as it presented itself in their day, both in Judaism and in the wider pagan world into which Christianity made its way with astonishing speed? And, second, I want to ask, What does the *story of Christian origins itself* contribute to our own reappropriation of this early Christian vision of God?

Two words by way of general introduction. First, the title of my overall project, which is the title I was originally given for this essay, was a way of not settling in advance the question of whether there is something called "New Testament theology" and whether I wanted to contribute to it. The two questions of (a) what we can say as historians about the origin or origins of Christianity and (b) what we can say about God are both, in my view, perfectly valid in their own right. But whereas, from within some worldviews, these two questions might appear to exist in watertight compartments, this option is denied to the Christian at least, who is faced with the wonderfully complex and entertaining further question of how these two things overlap and interlock. The subdiscipline that has called itself "New Testament theology" (with well-known examples of the genre from Bultmann, Kümmel, and others) has come at things rather with the assumption that our task is to collect and compare the statements about central theological topics that we find in the different New Testament writers. This is important, but I sense a further set of questions underneath, which have to do with something the New Testament writers were all keenly interested in but which many in the then dominant German Lutheran world—and, to my dismay, some in today's evangelical world—are not only not interested in but downright hostile toward, namely, the events themselves through which Christianity began long before even Paul began dictating his letters. As I have said in other places, the risen Jesus does not say to the disciples that all authority in heaven and on earth is given to the books they are to go off and write. The question of God precisely as it is posed to us by the New Testament writers is one that cannot be addressed, let alone answered, by exegesis of their key passages alone but only by this exegesis in combination with the serious and sustained historical task to enquire what it was that actually happened in the reign of Tiberius and under the governorship of Pontius Pilate. Neither the Christian apologetic to the wider world nor the Christian instruction of those within the fold can confine themselves to the New Testament text alone; to do so is to falsify the text itself. This is the puzzle, the metapuzzle if you like, of the interplay between the historical study of Christian origins and the theological inquiry about the meaning and/or reference of the word "God." I decided in 1989, when roughing out my own project, that the only thing I could decently do was to set the questions out side by side as best I could and see what sparks they began to knock off one another. This work, clearly, is still in progress.

A second word of general introduction: I am very much aware that all talk about God is necessarily self-involving and that the mode of this involvement will vary according to what is being said, or at least what is being meant, about God himself. You can discuss the distant gods of Epicureanism and/or deism with a shrug of the shoulders and with your hands in your pockets. But if you mention the God of Abraham, Isaac, and Jacob and intend to take this God seriously, you are bound to adopt an attitude which some first-century Jews formalized in the way we see already in Paul: to mention this God, remind yourself that he is the one who is blessed forever, amen. And the Christian who knows what he or she is about will constantly reflect that the most natural modes of God-talk are adoration, thanksgiving, confession, supplication, and proclamation, not theorization. This is not an attempt to marginalize systematic theology—far from it. It is simply a reminder of what the greatest systematic theologians have always known and recognized—that theology is a matter of loving God with our minds and that loving does not mean merely admiring or "being intellectually interested in." This is why (to link my second introductory point to my first) it is difficult to mount a historical argument about Christian origins, because the question of God swirls around the whole project and different implicit answers to it will result in different implicit attitudes to everything else—history, of course, very much included.

Anyway, so much for introduction. I want to address my topic in three sections, which bounce off one another cheerfully all the way through: the kingdom of God, the righteousness of God, and the love of God.

The Kingdom of God

As a matter of history, it was central to the early Christian claim, belief, witness, and corporate life that the one true God had established his kingdom in and through certain events, the events to do with Jesus of Nazareth, who had been demonstrated to be Israel's Messiah and the world's true Lord. When the early Christians spoke about God's kingdom (as, by the way, they went on doing, despite the drop in references in the Pauline Letters as compared with the Gospels), they were demonstrably conscious that Jesus's constant reference to this as the major theme of his proclamation and purpose was both in line with the Old Testament celebration of YHWH's kingship, and its promise that this kingship would come to fresh expression, and in dialogue with the kingdom-expectation and kingdom-movements of the time. If we are to study Christian origins with proper historical sensitivity, we must remind ourselves constantly that neither Jesus nor his first followers had a monopoly on Jewish kingdom-of-God discourse in the first century and that the so-called revolutionary usage we associate with Judas the Galilean and other rebel groups at the beginning of that century did not suddenly disappear just because the Christians, following Jesus himself, had picked up this dangerous language and seemed to be re-shaping and remolding it. The question of God as posed in Palestine in, let us say, AD 45, certainly included the question of different visions of the kingdom of God: what would it mean, what would it look like, that God would become king? What changes would come about as a result? When would it happen—or in the case of the Christians, how was one to express one's belief that it had already happened and in another sense was still to happen? And not least important as part of that God-question, who would be vindicated when the kingdom arrived in all its fullness? How could you tell in the present time who God's true kingdom-people might be?

Already, by dipping our toe into the turbulent water of first-century Judaism, we discover the key questions that the word "God" raised at the time. They were not so much theoretical questions about attributes as practical questions about actions. What was God up to? Who spoke for God, who was acting for God, how did you know, and what should we be doing about it? We ought not therefore be surprised that the major writings which emerged over the first generation of Christian faith, the writings which the very early church, quite correctly in my view, put at the head of that extraordinarily bold and visionary thing, the emerging canon of the New Testament, were writings which dealt head-on with the question of God but did so in an utterly first-century Jewish way, *by telling a story of actual events as the story of how God at last became King.* The Gospels as wholes in their forms and intentions—and their constituent parts, large and small, in their traceable history such as it is (begging several large questions at this point)—show us a community determined to express its identity in terms of things that had actually happened, events (as we say) within history, in and through which the being they called God had become King. It is not simply, then, that the Gospels contain within themselves some remarkable pictures of God—the prodigal father, for instance, or the king who gives a wedding feast for his son; it is, rather, that by their very nature, and by what they tell us about the earliest Christianity as a storytelling and storyliving community, they point us to the God of creation and providence, the God of Israel, the God of justice, the God who, having made a good and beautiful world, has remained committed to it despite its rebellion. The Gospels have been emasculated in much of the church by being split up into small portions and never seen as a whole, rather as if a great symphony were only ever heard in twelve-bar snatches; and it is this, incidentally but importantly, that has left the door open to those who want, for quite other reasons, to suggest that works such as the so-called *Gospel of Thomas* belong in the same category as Matthew, Mark, Luke, and John. It does not; it consists of detached aphorisms, and even if they all or mostly turned out to be authentic sayings of Jesus himself, the work as a whole, and the others like it, would represent a falsification of what Jesus was saying and doing as well as a falsification of what the early church believed. Ultimately, the so-called "gnostic gospels" would be a denial of what Jesus and the church believed *about God himself* and what the canonical Gospels are inviting the rest of the world, ourselves included, to believe about God. The canonical Gospels are saying, in form and overall substance, that the word "God" properly belongs to the Creator God, the God of Israel, the God who has kept his promises to creation and to Israel *and has done so in this way*. And they are the stories told by and within the early Christian community that in its worship and witness was living by and out of the belief that these things were so.

Ironically, therefore, the evangelical imperative to believe that everything in the Gospels really happened is pushing in the right direction for, all too often, the wrong reason. The reason it matters that the events really happened is not "so that the Bible can be true after all," as though that were the bottom line, but "so that God really has become King on earth as in heaven"—a truth to which all evangelicals give lip service but not all, I fear, actually reflect on or work at in practice. More of this, perhaps, anon. My underlying point is that one of the most secure things we know about Christian origins is that the earliest Christians told these stories about Jesus not simply to reinforce (à la Bultmann) small points of doctrine or practice but to sustain the whole early Christian worldview, which necessarily expressed itself in narrative because the worldview was precisely about things that happened, about events unfolding and reaching a climax. This is why the question of the form and genre of the Gospels has proved so difficult: because the evangelists, and I assume but cannot argue here their major sources, took it for granted at point after point that the story they were telling was (at least) four different stories rolled into one. First, it was the story of the Creator God launching his project of new creation from within the womb of the old. Second, it was the story of Israel's God bringing the long story of the covenant to its appointed goal. Third, it was the story of how the life which the early Christians experienced had begun. Fourth, of course, joining all these together, it was the story of Jesus himself. No wonder the Gospels are complex documents. None of these elements can be omitted in a full account of what the Gospels actually are; and they all interact, not least in the strong implicit belief that the story of the covenant always was the story of how the Creator God had purposed to deal with the problem of evil within his creation and so to put creation itself to rights once more. All of this is implied in the very structure, layout, and narrative design of the four Gospels, different though they are. And together they all add up to a fifth story, which remains the projected title for the putative fifth volume in my own project, after the fourth volume on Paul: *The Gospels and the Story of God*. The reason the Gospels are what they are is that they are doing on a large scale what Jesus in so many parables is doing close up: they are telling these narratives in such a way as to say, "Look closely, ponder and pray your way through this story, and discover thereby who the one true and living God actually is."

And this does not mean, simply and univocally, that we should leap to the high Christology to which all the Gospels, not only John, subscribe. It does not, that is, lead simply to a one-for-one replacement, so that where before we might have said "God," now we simply say "Jesus." Things are more subtle: the Gospels, like Paul, are implicit pretheoretical trinitarians. "Who then is this?" ask the disciples, and Jesus does indeed act and speak as one who believes that he has been called to do what in Israel's Scriptures only YHWH, Israel's sovereign and saving God, can and must do. But this same Jesus prays to the one he calls "Abba, father," and sometimes that prayer is anguished and answered in the negative. And at the last the godforsaken cry on the cross, as Moltmann and others have seen so clearly, compels us to formulations of trinitarian theology with paradox at their heart and renunciation of triumphalism as their mode.

The Gospels thus offer us the narrative mode of discourse, not presumably as the only appropriate mode of God-talk but as at least a primary mode, not to be translated out into nonnarrative modes without loss. In doing so, they are reaffirming one of the central underlying themes of the Old Testament, indeed one might say *the* central underlying theme, as highlighted by John Goldingay in the first volume of his remarkable *Old Testament Theology*: Israel's story (which is itself the focal point and encapsulation of creation's story) as the story of what the one true God is up to, the story which in the Old Testament, as in the intertestamental literature, remains always a story in urgent search of an appropriate ending.[2] In reaffirming this and in offering the story of Jesus as the appropriate ending (and the appropriate beginning of another story or, if you prefer, the translation of the single-language story into the many-language story of the early church), the Gospels are standing over against the wide world of ancient paganism, which had various things to say about the creation of the world and about the interplay between divine beings and the world, not much to say about the future of the world, and several overlapping stories about divine power at work in the world through human empire. When Jesus tells his disciples that the rulers of this earth behave in one way but his disciples must behave in a different way, he is saying in a nutshell what the Gospel writers are then saying in their choice of form and mode: live within this story, and you will discover who the true God really is, what God is like, and what you must be like in consequence. The theological challenge thus constitutes for the evangelists the political challenge to live in the pagan world as the people who know Israel's God, who believe that this God has brought his covenant plan to its long fruition, and who are now living under the rule of the one who has claimed all authority in heaven and on earth. This is what the kingdom of God is all about, and the Gospel writers insist that it has been redefined around Jesus and brought to birth through his death and resurrection.

My argument so far is that the Gospels, by their very form as well as their detailed content, are stating in the strongest possible terms that the being who can properly be called God is the Creator God, the God of Israel, that he has revealed himself in decisive and climactic action in Jesus of Nazareth, Israel's Messiah, and that God has thereby called into being a people, a rejuvenated or regenerated Israel if you like, through whom his purposes for the world are now to be taken forward. What we theorize as the doctrine of creation lies at the heart of the whole thing; history matters because creation matters. When the writers we think of as constituting the wisdom tradition invite their readers to embrace wisdom and live by it, this is not a wisdom that takes you away from creation. Wisdom is the one through whom God made the world in the first place. The deep antihistorical impulse in a fair amount of Western Protestantism to this day is ultimately an anti-Judaic impulse, ultimately a step toward the gnostic rejection of creation. And along with creation goes what might be called God's justice, by which I mean loosely the utter determination of the Creator God to put his world to rights and thereby to reestablish his kingship, his sovereignty, over it. It is because of this impulse to put things to rights that God called Abraham; and

2. John Goldingay, *Old Testament Theology*, vol. 1, *Israel's Gospel* (Downers Grove, IL: InterVarsity, 2003).

this is why God's faithfulness to his covenant is also his faithfulness to creation, something which much theology and exegesis, over the last couple of generations at least, have found hard to hold together. It is this justice, this faithfulness to creation and covenant, to which the next main section now turns.

The Righteousness of God

It is with Paul, and particularly in Romans, that we meet the full-dress exposition of God's faithful covenant justice—my preferred longer translation for that impossible phrase *dikaiosynē theou*. When I talk in what follows about God's faithfulness or God's justice, it is this phrase, with its many overlapping connotations, which I shall have in mind. I have written about this at length in various places and can only here summarize what I have said elsewhere.

It is important from the outset to stress that in moving from the Gospels to Paul, we are not moving from a narrative world to a nonnarrative one. The form of Paul's writings is epistolary, not straightforward narrative, but as I and others have shown at length, understanding the underlying narratives in Paul is not simply a matter of teasing out a bit of peripheral embroidery but a way of getting to the very heart of things. Paul draws on and redeploys an almost bewildering variety of interlocking stories: the story of creation, of humankind, of Israel; of Abraham, Isaac, and Jacob; of Moses and the exodus and the giving of the law; of David and the prophets and the whole history of Israel; of Jesus himself, summarized in a dozen different ways but always so as to highlight the cross and resurrection as the events through which, as Paul says, one world is crucified and another is reborn and we with it; and, almost equally important, the stories of himself and the early church in various places and the story of what it means to be a Christian, to start as a sinner, to be grasped by God's call through gospel and spirit, to believe, to be baptized, to live the life in Christ, to work for the gospel, to die in the hope of being with Christ immediately and of being raised to new life at the last. At this point, too, the story of creation itself comes round to meet us once more, with Paul's glorious prediction that creation itself will be set free from its slavery to corruption and will share the freedom of the glory of God's children. And for Paul, as for the Gospels, whether we look at his larger arguments or his smaller summaries, it comes down again and again to the story of God: the God who made the world, the God who will judge the world and put it back to rights, the God who called Abraham, who gave Torah, who sent Jesus and condemned sin in his flesh, who raised Jesus from the dead and seated him at his right hand, who now sends the Spirit to enable the church to be the sign to the powers that their time is up. All this and much more can be said about the stories that inform and undergird the specific things which Paul says to one church after another.

All this means that Paul, like the Gospels, must be seen not least in terms of his view of God as the God of Israel—with all the problems and puzzles which this entails in terms of his insistence that God did indeed give the law and did indeed call ethnic Israel, and his equal insistence that God had now acted apart from the law and that God had called a people not from Jews only but from Gentiles also. The reason Paul faces these problems is clearly that he has no thought of abandoning the Jewish view of God, rooted in the Old Testament, as though the gospel of Jesus Christ revealed some other God. And this puts him on a direct collision course, more obviously than the Gospels because of his particular situation and the reason for his writings, with the pagan world of his day. It is in Paul that we see as clearly as anywhere else the confrontation between the God of Israel, now seen as the God revealed in Jesus and by the Spirit, and the pagan gods of the surrounding nations. For Paul, the origin of Christianity posed in a fresh way the question of God that had always been at stake between Jews and non-Jews. And when he wrote about the righteousness of God, God's saving faithful covenant justice, he was aware that it was this large theme in Jewish literature, most notably in Isaiah 40–55, which formed the basic challenge from the God of Israel to the pagan gods. The Creator will be faithful to the covenant through the work of the Servant, and the mighty gods of Babylon will find themselves tottering and crashing to the ground while God's people are rescued and the whole creation is renewed. When Paul went about his work as the apostle to the Gentiles, this image was of great importance to him. He wrote of pulling down strongholds and destroying proud systems that opposed the truth. He wrote not least of the way in which the living God had called people to know and serve him instead of their lifeless idols. And he spoke especially of the defeat of the principalities and powers through the cross of Jesus and of the folly of doing anything that would approximate to going back to serving them once more—an echo of the exodus narrative which haunts a considerable portion of his thinking and writing.

It is this exodus context which provides the two strongest and clearest examples in Paul of the redefinition of the meaning of "God" around Jesus and the Spirit. The first is Galatians 4, where he tells the story of people moving from slavery through redemption to freedom—in other words, the exodus story. The exodus was the time when the meaning of the name YHWH was first revealed; this was when the Israelites discovered who it really was that their ancestors had worshiped when he rescued them from slavery. Paul, drawing on the same Abrahamic background, describes God as the One who sends the Son and then sends the Spirit of the Son and declares that "now that you have come to know God, or rather to be known by God, how can you turn back to the *stoicheia*, the elements of the world?" (Gal. 4:9). The gospel events, in other words, have unveiled the full character of the true God; the God who made promises to Abraham is the God who now claims the whole world as his own and who does so by showing himself as the Son-sender and the Spirit-sender. Either you have the Trinity, or something remarkably like it, or you have a return to slavery. God's saving covenant faithfulness, his putting of things to rights, has been unveiled before the whole world.

The second passage is Romans 8, a more sustained exposition of the same theme and one which brings to its first great climax Paul's explicit treatment of the *dikaiosynē theou*. God's promise to Abraham, Paul had said in Romans 4, was that he would inherit the world—not just one piece of territory but the entire planet. Romans 8 describes how it is that God will be faithful to this covenant promise and thereby to the whole of his creation: God will do for the whole world, at the end, what he did for Jesus at Easter. Indeed, Easter is hereby revealed as the secret of both the future of the world and the character of God, as Paul had already said in Romans 4, describing God as "the one who gives life to the dead" (Rom. 4:17) and then as "the one who raised Jesus from the dead" (4:24). This is part of the central point of Easter, that it is the decisive work of the Creator God, who is utterly determined to put his creation to rights. (One of the many interesting things I noticed when working on my book on the resurrection was that, for the early fathers and the rabbis alike, resurrection is what you get when you insist on a strong doctrine of creation and a strong doctrine of God's justice. Conversely, for Paul, having got resurrection—the resurrection of Jesus—as his starting point, he is able to announce to the whole world that God will redeem it and to invite those who have worshiped the world rather than God to forsake their idols and meet their maker.)

In all of this Paul is not merely stressing the greatness of the salvation promised to those who are in Christ and indwelt by the Spirit, though of course he is doing this as well. Nor is he simply standing over against the kind of Judaism he had formerly taught and lived, though he is doing this too. He is deliberately outflanking the pagan worldviews, not least the views of divinity, which he knew only too well from the streets of Ephesus and Corinth. He does not need (as people used to imagine) to translate the Jewish ideas and beliefs of earliest Christianity into quasi-pagan thought-forms to make them attractive or accessible. What the world needs, Paul believed, is the God of Abraham, Isaac, and Jacob and the Messiah of Israel, who is the world's rightful Lord and coming Judge.

And though this message was sheer folly to the pagan world—a crucified Jew as the Lord of the world!—Paul discovered that when he announced Jesus as Lord, the message itself, what he called the powerful word of the gospel, did its own work and brought people to "the obedience of faith." That which paganism could not provide, a genuine humanity reflecting the image of the Creator God, was generated by the gospel. And in this generation the question of God, the central question underneath all worldviews, was given a fresh set of answers that enabled Paul to engage in debate with all comers.

This ongoing debate is brilliantly encapsulated in the Areopagus address in Acts 17. It is, of course, hugely abbreviated (there is no way that Paul would have let them off with a couple of minutes), but it demonstrates—and by its multiple links to his letters this demonstration could be considerably elaborated—that the view of God to which Paul had come by rethinking his basically Pharisaic theology afresh in the light of Jesus and the Spirit was able to trump the major answers which ancient paganism gave to the question of God.

To begin with, the classic polytheism that had left temples and images scattered all around the ancient world simply would not do. Worthless idols, Paul calls them—dismissing with a wave of the hand some of the finest ancient works of art as simply unnecessary category mistakes. Serious pagan philosophers of the time would have agreed with him. But what about the major options as catalogued a century earlier by Cicero? The Stoics believed that the world was itself divine; Stoicism is a form of monotheism, since, if everything (*to pan*) is divine, then there is only one divinity. The great strength of pantheism is that it takes seriously the signals of transcendence, of strange innate power and glory, within creation itself, but Judaism trumps this by speaking of the world as the wise handiwork of a good Creator and also offers what Stoicism cannot find, an analysis of the problem of evil with the promise that something is to be done about it. Conversely, if the strength of Stoicism is its recognition of the signs of divine life within the world, the strength of Epicureanism is its recognition that the world, as it stands, also shows signs of being, to put it mildly, other than God. But Epicurus and his great disciple Lucretius then go off into full-blown deism with a god or gods who are absent and uncaring, leaving the world to manage by itself as best it can. Judaism once more trumps Epicurus by speaking of the world as still known and loved by its Creator and of the Creator's desire that all people, instead of merely acknowledging him at a distance, feel after him and find him. The third option, that of the Academy, declared that there was not enough evidence to decide the question, but one should keep traditional religion going just in case—a position not unknown in today's Western world and church. But at this point Paul moves beyond what Judaism would have said. The devout Jew would have said that the one true and living God would, in the end, put the world to rights; some devout Jews would have said that God would do this through the coming Messiah. Paul goes one further. He knows the name of the Messiah, and the whole picture has come sharply into focus through God's raising him from the dead. The resurrection of Jesus the Messiah thus provides, for Paul, the epistemological as well as the theological fulcrum for his mission to the pagan world, for his announcement that there is a God, a Creator God, who loves the world and has remained in sustained and searching contact with it and that God will one day put it to rights. The resurrection informs the Academy a new knowledge has arrived which will settle the question after all; it informs the Epicurean that the living God has acted and is continuing to act within our world and not a great distance away; it insists to the Stoic that, though the world is full of signs of God's presence, the living God is not limited by the entropic possibilities visible within the cosmos as it is but has acted and will continue to act as its Sovereign, to judge it and to save it. The Areopagus address thus offers a concise account of the intellectual question of God as seen by the author of Romans 1 and Romans 8.

This brings us back to the larger question of God's saving, faithful covenant justice and especially to the question of Israel. Though we divide traditional Jewish belief into monotheism, election, and eschatology, the latter two are really ways of speaking about the first: there is one God, and Israel is his people; there is one God, and through the covenant he will put the world to rights. Just as the Jew further demarcates the meaning of "God" by the second clause ("and Israel is his people") and, for that matter, the Muslim substitutes an equally defining clause ("and Mohammad is his prophet"), so Paul the Christian, and with him the whole church ancient and modern when it knows its business, declares that there is one God and that Jesus is his Son. The sonship of Jesus—remembering that "Son of God" was a title for Israel as well as for the Messiah—is the climax of election as well as the fullest self-revelation-in-action of the sovereign God. Paul is thus precipitated in Romans 9–11 into a long discussion of Israel precisely because the Messiah is from Israel according to the flesh but is also God over all, blessed forever (9:5). And only when he has worked through the underlying christological logic of Israel's election can he conclude his great discussion of God's justice by speaking, doxologically, of the unsearchable depth of God's wisdom and ways. The question of election and the concomitant question of eschatology are part of the question of God because they concern God's ultimate saving faithful justice.

This in turn—though we have no time to speak of this here—flows directly into the life of the community within the larger pagan environment. Romans 12–16 is part of the logical whole, the exposition of

God's *dikaiosynē*, precisely in its appeal that the Christian community live within the present world under the rule of God's new creation, not least in its struggle for united worship across traditional boundaries. And this in turn contextualizes the appeal for obedience to authorities in Romans 13; part of the question of God in every culture is, implicitly or explicitly, the question of what obedience is owed to earthly authorities, and Paul gives the question the classic Jewish answer, that the existing powers are called into being by God (who, as the Creator, certainly does not want anarchy), even though they are constantly disobedient to their call to be agents of God's just and wise rule and must themselves be summoned back again and again to that obedience. I have written extensively elsewhere of Paul's reworking of this Jewish political theology and his quite explicit lining up of Jesus as Lord over against Caesar. I just note it here as one element, a very important one, within the overall early Christian question of God. Suffice it to say here that Paul offered the pagan world an answer to the question of whether a god, or the gods, could ever actually put the world to rights. Caesar had claimed to do so, awarding himself the titles "savior" and "lord" and claiming that Roman justice and peace would solve the world's problems. Paul called Jesus "Savior" and "Lord" and declared that it was through his gospel alone that genuine justice and peace could be found. Paul's exposition of the justice of God, the ancient Jewish doctrine reformulated around Jesus, offered a standing challenge to the powers of the world and their claims to justice, as indeed to divinity.

The Love of God

No serious reader of Paul could make the mistake one still sometimes encounters, that of supposing that his stress on God's justice was somehow antithetical to an emphasis on God's love. Once you put the terms back into Hebrew, things become far less polarized, precisely because God's "righteousness," God's justice, is his *ṣedāqâ*, whose covenantal and relational spread of meanings encloses a good deal of what our English translations are representing by the word "love." And though *agapē* has a wider meaning elsewhere in ancient Greek, including the Septuagint, than it does in the New Testament, behind it again and again stand words such as *ḥesed* and *'aḥăbâ*, Hebrew terms which speak of the constant, utterly reliable, generous, and warmhearted love of the Creator God for Israel, yes, but also for the whole of creation, not least for human beings.

The other mistake is to suppose that an emphasis on the love of God is going to lead, before too long, into a kind of mushy relativism where no lines are drawn very clearly, judgment disappears like a bad dream, and God simply becomes an indulgent grandparent. Again, no one who knows the Old Testament, not least the passages where God's *hesed* and *ṣedāqâ* are emphasized, could make this mistake. And no one who knows John's Gospel and his epistles, the documents that stake a claim to be the New Testament's central expositions of God's love, could imagine such a thing there either. The love of God, which Paul and John together insist is revealed centrally in the saving death of Jesus the Messiah, has nothing to do with an idea that evil does not really matter after all. It has everything to do with the fact that evil does matter and that it matters so seriously that nothing short of the cross will deal with it. Justice, in fact—the insistence that God will at the end put the world to rights—is itself for the early Christians a form of love, the form which God's love takes when confronted by evil. God loves the world so much that he will not allow it forever to wallow in the corruption and decay into which the rebellious human race has plunged it. Calling a halt to evil—condemning it on the cross and bringing it to a final end still in the future—is the great act of love itself.

This answer to the question of God—that the one true God is the God of love—is itself generated (from the Old Testament, it is true, but generated afresh) from within the very origins of Christianity. I return to the point at which I began. The earliest Christians were aware of the generous, healing love of God at work in Jesus. Even if he only did a quarter of the things ascribed to him in the Gospels, we would have to say that he must have been one of the most remarkable human beings of that or any age and that one of the truly remarkable things about him was his embodiment and living out of a wonderfully generous, self-giving love. When we add the other three-quarters back in and construe the gospel stories, as I believe we must, in terms of Jesus's constant implicit reference to his acting out of the vocation to do and be what YHWH himself had promised to do and be, and when we see the narrative lines all leading up to the cross, we find our conclusion strikingly stated and confirmed over and over: "Having loved his own who were in the world, he loved them *eis telos*, to the uttermost" (John 13:1); "God commends his love for us in that while we were yet sinners the Messiah died for us" (Rom. 5:8). Those who knew themselves to be traitors and yet found themselves welcomed and commissioned would have found it hard to separate their understanding of how the movement began from their knowledge of a love that had found them, forgiven them, and now equipped them. In then retelling the story of the exodus in a new way as their own story, they naturally found themselves speaking, like Moses in Deuteronomy, of a love which reached out to them and indeed to the whole world, not because of any qualities which that love found to approve but simply because it was love indeed. And with this Jewish root of the doctrine of God's love re-formed, like everything else, around the person and the death of Jesus and the power of the Spirit, they found once again that they had an answer to the question the pagan world had long asked. A glance through ancient pagan literature, or for that matter inscriptions and letters, will reveal that one of the primary attitudes of ancient pagans toward the gods was a sense of their unreliability. You could never be quite sure if this or that god was going to be pleased with you, would do something to help you, or if you were going to be let down, on the one hand, or tripped up, on the other. Over against this sense of helplessness, of not really knowing, of being tossed to and fro on a sea of theological and cosmic uncertainty, place Paul's finest paragraph on God's love, itself the central climax of a letter which has expounded God the Creator and God the faithful Judge. Who shall separate us from God's love? Neither death nor life nor angels nor rulers nor the present nor the future nor powers nor height nor depth nor anything else in all creation shall have the power to separate us from the love of God in the Messiah, Jesus our Lord. This great peroration, one of the most spectacular in all literature ancient or modern, is also the ultimate answer to the question of God as it is raised and answered afresh from within the very origins of Christianity.

Conclusion

I have written elsewhere about the detailed ways in which the early Christians drew on Jewish language about God's involvement with Israel and the world to talk of Jesus and the Spirit. Early trinitarian theology drew heavily on Jewish roots, concerned from the outset to maintain Jewish-style monotheism rather than collapse in any way into any kind of paganism, merely adding Jesus to a pantheon. Instead the early Christians drew on the Jewish language of God's word, God's wisdom, God's tabernacling presence, God's law, and God's Spirit to make it clear that what they were saying about Jesus was not destroying Jewish monotheism but fulfilling it. That is a whole other area.

The only thing I have to add here, by way of conclusion, is that by doing so they were giving Jewish monotheism the stability that it might otherwise appear to have lacked. The Jewish narrative was always open-ended, a line petering out and a hand pointing forward, a claim awaiting validation. The Christian story, while offering a new kind of open-endedness in the fresh framework of the gospel and its worldwide mission, insists that at the center of history, the history in which God's sovereign and saving purposes have been at work, the incarnate Son of God died and rose again as the condemnation of evil and the launching of the project of new creation. In these events the world can see, as never before or since, that when the powers of the world do their worst, the Creator of the world does his uttermost; that when lies and treachery and idolatry and power-games and demonic forces get together and make the world dark even at noon, then the living God comes to the heart of the darkness and takes its full force upon himself.

Thus the four great questions that collectively form the question of God received fresh answers from within the womb of Christian origins. To the question of the relationship between God and the world we know and live in, Judaism always said, against paganism, that the God of Abraham was the Creator of the whole world. Paganism, even supposing it took any notice of this absurd claim, shrugged its shoulders and wrote it off. The early Christians *were* early Christians because the event that brought them into being was the event that showed the Creator dynamically at work within his world, renewing both it and his own intimate relationship with it in incarnation and resurrection. To the question of the fact of evil, Judaism always said that evil was serious and that God's choice of Israel was designed to reverse its effects. Paganism, again if it took any notice, shrugged its shoulders and continued on its cynical way. The early Christians *were* early Christians because the event that brought them into being was the condemnation of sin on the cross and the launching of God's new, sinless creation. To the question of God and the present running of the world, Judaism always said that God wanted good earthly rulers but they would have to answer to him. Paganism sneered, persecuted the Jews, and divinized its own rulers. The early Christians *were* early Christians because in his resurrection and ascension Jesus had been enthroned as the Lord before whom all would have to bow. Finally, to the question of God and the future, Judaism always said God would put things to rights, and paganism always scoffed at such a notion. The early Christians *were* early Christians because in Jesus the Messiah Israel's God *had* put the world to rights and would complete the work on his return. The question of God emerges naturally with fresh answers from the very events that generated Christianity in the first place.

Christianity takes its origin, after all, not from fresh speculation about God or the gods, not from what the modern Western world calls religious experience, but from events through which, in their occurrence and in their continuing power when announced to the world, the question of God has been given a decisive and fathomless answer. This answer, now as then, calls forth the worship of the creature for the Creator, the work of justice to implement that of the God of justice, and the love for God and one another which is both the reflection and the reembodiment of the love of God himself, enacted in Jesus and shed abroad in our hearts by the Spirit.

3

The Wrath
of God

D. A. CARSON

Doubtless it is an honor to have this essay included among those of such an esteemed group of scholars, not least on a subject, the doctrine of God, which brooks no peers. Would it be churlish of me to admit that, had I been given my choice of topics from the advertised list, I would have chosen most of the others before choosing the one actually assigned me?

Yet my reluctance to leap at the topic of the wrath of God may merely reflect a broadly based Western sensibility that is uncomfortable with easy talk about God's anger or God's wrath, a sensibility that reads the ancient *nqm* in terms of a vengeful spirit fed by a bad temper and understands the ancient *ḥrm* in a fashion unable to be differentiated from genocide and ethnic cleansing, a sensibility that reads Jonathan Edwards in terms of Elmer Gantry. By and large, this sensibility is much too civilized to warn people about the wrath to come. Yet perhaps the old saw is true: the church, not to say the broader culture, is most in need of the biblical teachings with which it is most uncomfortable.

In what follows, I shall first of all provide a basic review, then attempt to ground discussion of the wrath of God in some exegetical and theological precision, and finally offer four theological and practical implications.

Basic Review

Words and Expressions

The raw vocabulary data are well known and frequently canvassed.[1] Here I need only mention that in the New Testament the dominant words are *orgē* and *thymos*—and their respective cognates. In the Septuagint, it is difficult to delineate an unambiguous semantic distinction between these two word groups; indeed, both render the numerous Hebrew equivalents (especially *nqm* and *ḥrm*). As in the Septuagint, so in the New Testament: *orgē* and *thymos* can each refer to both human anger and to divine anger, though the actual distribution depends somewhat on the writer. For instance, *thymos* occurs only twice in Luke, and both times the word refers to human anger, whereas in Paul, where it is used five times, it can refer both to human anger and to divine anger. In the Apocalypse, where this same word occurs ten times, the reference is almost always to God's anger (or wrath; I shall use the words interchangeably). But I shall skip further statistical observations; they are readily available and do not seem to me to have controlling interpretative significance.

More important is the range of expressions and contexts in which the wrath of God is embedded. God's anger can be depicted in dramatic metaphors: "See, the Name of the LORD comes from afar, with burning anger and dense clouds of smoke; his lips are full of wrath, and his tongue is a consuming fire. His breath is like a rushing torrent, rising up to the neck. He shakes the nations in the sieve of destruction; he places in the jaws of the peoples a bit that leads them astray" (Isa. 30:27–28; cf. Jer. 30:23–24; Ps. 2:5).[2] God's wrath is often directed against the covenant community because of the community's idolatry, apostasy, violation of God's law, or merely willful refusal to "hear" that law (e.g., Num. 25:3; 32:10; Deut. 29:25–28; Judg. 2:14, 20; Ps. 78:21; Jer. 42:18; Mic. 5:15). In such instances, God's wrath is as much an expression of rejected and wounded love (as in Hosea) as it is of just judgment. In any case, his wrath touches more than the covenant community, for it can equally lash out against individuals who defy him (e.g., Exod. 4:14; Num. 12:9; Deut. 29:18–21; 2 Chron. 19:2; 25:15), against the nations (e.g., Isa. 10:25; 13:3; Jer. 50:13; Ezek. 30:15; Mic. 5:10–15), and against all who desert him (Ezra 8:22). Yahweh repeatedly presents himself as a jealous God. As a result, the approach of sinful human beings to the holy is potentially dangerous (e.g., Gen. 32:25–30; Exod. 4:24–26; Isa.

---

1. See, e.g., H. Schönweiss and H. C. Hahn, "Anger, Wrath," in *New International Dictionary of New Testament Theology*, ed. V. D. Verbrugge (Grand Rapids: Zondervan, 2004), 1:105–13.

2. Scripture quotations in this chapter are from the TNIV unless otherwise noted.

6:5). God's wrath testifies to the living, personal response of a holy God to all that is tawdry and mean, let alone rebellious and idolatrous.

Still in the Old Testament, the wrath of God manifests itself in sword, hunger, and plague (Ezek. 6:11–14), in wasting diseases "until you perish" (Deut. 28:22), devastation (Jer. 25:37–38), scattering (Lam. 4:16), and depopulation (Jer. 50:13). God treads the nations in his winepress (Isa. 63:1–6); alternatively, God gives them the cup of his fury to drink (Isa. 51:17; cf. 63:1–2; Joel 3:13). Under the wrath of God, members of the covenant community may be "cut off" from their people (e.g., Exod. 30:33, 38; Lev. 7:20; Num. 9:13; 19:20). Nevertheless this community learns that God's anger does not necessarily last forever. God's anger is often spoken of as enduring "for a moment" (e.g., Ps. 30:5; Isa. 26:20; 54:7–8). Very frequently the display of God's wrath eventually brings the people to repentance—in which case God's anger has been the instrument that leads to restoration (e.g., repeatedly in Judges; cf. Ps. 78:38; 103:6–13).

As in the Old, so in the New Testament: the "anger" words can refer to human anger, some of it justified (e.g., the anger of the king in the parable of the wedding feast, Matt. 22:7) and some of it not (e.g., the anger of the older brother in the parable of the prodigal son, Luke 15:28). If, for the sake of our topic, we restrict ourselves to texts that speak of *God's* anger, we discover once again that his wrath is *always* justified. Although temporal judgments are far from being unknown in the New Testament (e.g., 1 Cor. 11:17–31; cf. Heb. 12:4–11, which cites Prov. 3:11–12) and some judgments partake of both temporal and transcendent elements (e.g., excommunication, 1 Cor. 5), the primary emphasis in the New Testament is on the eschatological wrath of God. Sometimes this wrath is described as already disclosed, already bearing down (John 3:36; Rom. 1:18–3:20), for all human beings are by nature "deserving of wrath" (*tekna physei orgēs*, Eph. 2:3). More frequently, however, it is the ultimate display of wrath that is in view, the wrath manifest in hell itself—dominantly so in the teaching of Jesus and in the Apocalypse. The seven last plagues are said to be an expression of God's wrath (Rev. 15:1). In language reminiscent of Isaiah, the Apocalypse declares that the rider on the white horse who is called Faithful and True, whose name is the Word of God, "treads the winepress of the fury of the wrath of God Almighty" (Rev. 19:15). Indeed, the Apocalypse gives the unavoidable impression that all earlier displays of God's wrath have been diluted, like wine cut with water, whereas those who have the mark of the beast on their foreheads "will drink of the wine of God's fury, which has been poured full strength into the cup of his wrath" (Rev. 14:10). We are even told that when the beast and the false prophet are thrown into the lake of burning sulfur, they "will be tormented day and night for ever and ever" (Rev. 20:10).

This is, of course, the merest sketch of a handful of texts. It is not possible to feel the weight of the biblical emphasis on God's wrath without taking the time to scan, perhaps with the aid of concordances, the many hundreds of passages that bear on our topic. It is a humbling and frightening experience. To be included in such scans are not only the passages that speak explicitly of "anger" and "wrath" (in English translations), with the diversity of their underlying Hebrew and Greek words, but the many passages that describe or threaten or predict or reflect on the judgment of God, even when such words are not used. For instance, one must reflect on the many references to God's "vengeance." In his magisterial study, H. G. L. Peels shows that whether judgment is meted out on the covenant community or on those who afflict the covenant community, "God's justice is on trial." Indeed,

> throughout all of history [God] shows himself to be a God who acts according to his covenant, forgiving and avenging (Ps. 99). Furthermore, the notion of vengeance is closely related to that of justice; God's vengeance is the enactment of his punishing judgment, whether in a personal situation (1 Sam. 24; 2 Sam. 4), or in a matter concerning the nations (Judg. 11). Also, when God makes use of human instruments, he does not pass off responsibility for the vengeance. Especially Psalm 99 gives the context in which the vengeance of God functions: God's kingship and judgeship; his holiness and covenant. Thus, the vengeance of God has a firm place in the revelation and the confession of God in the Old Testament.[3]

The Story Line

Yet there is a sense in which, as important as a detailed survey of that sort might be, it cannot compete in importance with the way the theme of God's wrath—however denoted in displeasure, judgment, vengeance, historical catastrophe, or eternal fury—works its way through the biblical story line. Genesis depicts the original creation as "good," indeed "very good" (Gen. 1:31). God threatens his image-bearers, the first humans, with death if they disobey the one prohibition (2:17). The temptation to flout this prohibition was an enticement to more than the transgression of a legal requirement; it was an incitement to be "like God" (3:5), to run competition with God, to become God— and thus to de-god God. Here is the beginning of all idolatry, and with it banishment from Eden, curse upon the created order, the onset of death—the latter element dramatically underscored in the refrain of the first genealogy: "and then he died . . . and then he died . . . and then

3. H. G. L. Peels, *The Vengeance of God: The Meaning of the Root* NQM *and the Function of the* NQM-*Texts in the Context of Divine Revelation in the Old Testament*, Oudtestamentische Studiën 31 (Leiden: Brill, 1995), 264.

he died" (Gen. 5). The first murder brings its own judgment precisely because it is God who is displeased (Gen. 4). When the wickedness of the race multiplied to the point where "every inclination of the thoughts of the human heart was only evil all the time" (Gen. 6:5), it is God who sends the flood to destroy all but a remnant. The hero of this dramatic cleansing, Noah, promptly gets drunk (Gen. 9). When the race multiplies again and shapes its hunger to compete with God and to escape his judgment into the tower of Babel, it is only God's vow not to destroy the race with another flood that prevents his judgment from repeating itself; but even so, judgment and mercy together work out in the multiplication of languages. God's choice of Abram is an act of grace, but the Abraham cycle itself recounts the destruction of Sodom and Gomorrah (Gen. 19), a decisive act of divine wrath.

It would be tedious to survey every instance of divine wrath. Nevertheless, it is important to remember that the God who pours out his anger on the Egyptians, in the plagues and the destruction of the Egyptian forces at the Red Sea, because they will not let his people go to worship him is the same God who pours out his wrath on his own covenant people because, even after so magnificent a display of his power and his gracious, covenantal commitment to them, they so rapidly turn to syncretism while Moses is on Sinai (Exod. 32) and fail so abysmally at Kadesh Barnea (Deut. 1), not to mention numerous intervening episodes (e.g., the bronze snake, Num. 21). The cycles of rebellion spiral downward in Judges and are so depressing that the last three chapters of that book can scarcely be read in public: even the "good guys" are so appallingly evil that the judgments that befall the people do not seem unmerited. In due course, God's judgment falls on King Saul, on David, on the Davidic dynasty (even though the Davidic line is not wiped out, as Saul's was), on the northern kingdom and its numerous short-lived dynasties, and on the people of both north and south, culminating in the exile. The detailed declarations of judgment on both the covenant people and on the surrounding nations in Isaiah, Jeremiah, and Ezekiel fill many pages. The cycle of judgments poured out on the surrounding nations, on the northern kingdom, and finally on Judah itself in Amos's dramatic opening repeatedly tie these judgments to sin. Paul's declaration of the wrath of God on Jew and Gentile alike in Romans 1:18–3:20 is of a piece with this heritage, which is why he can end this section with a catena of Old Testament quotations to this effect. Small wonder that Jesus's anger is carefully recorded no less than his compassion (e.g., Mark 3:5; cf. Matt. 23).[4] Moreover, if it is the last book of the

---

4. See the useful summary in Andrew D. Lester, *The Angry Christian: A Theology for Care and Counseling* (Louisville: Westminster John Knox, 2003), esp. 150–68.

Bible that speaks most often of God's eschatological wrath per se, it is Jesus himself who introduces the most varied and repeated depictions of gehenna.

Some Attempts at Exegetical and Theological Precision

So much for the basic review. I offer here six attempts at exegetical and theological precision.

1. *It is exegetically unwarranted to depersonalize God's wrath, reducing it to an abstract and impersonal manifestation of irrevocable and implacable justice.* Many have attempted this. Klaus Koch's seminal essay half a century ago argued that in the Old Testament the fate of both the good and the wicked is frequently depicted as the inevitable consequence of their own choices and actions. Yahweh's role is little more than overseeing and energizing the process so as to ensure a proper nexus between actions and consequences. Koch argues that in general the Old Testament writers conceive of the world as a kind of moral force field in which every action finally generates its appropriate reaction (*schicksalwirkende Tatsphäre*).[5] More recent writers, even when they have not wanted to abandon Koch's *Tatsphäre*, have argued that this moral force field is not quite as mechanistic as Koch supposes. For a start, the field is distorted by the network of complicated human relationships, which are far from being invariably reciprocal. The result is that the good and the wicked do not always get what they deserve. Claudia Sticher goes further. After analyzing twenty psalms and Proverbs 1–9, she argues that Yahweh is presented as standing behind the good in typically direct terms whereas he stands behind the evil in typically indirect terms. For instance, active verbs are more typically used to describe Yahweh as he furthers or causes or energizes the fortunes of the righteous, but when one reads analogous descriptions of the wicked, passive verbs are more common to describe what has befallen them, leaving the agent in some doubt. Indeed, many of the texts Sticher studies are psalms of complaint, in which God is petitioned to intervene against evildoers who are the real source of mischief.[6]

Some part of Sticher's conclusions is surely right. I have elsewhere argued at some length that in the Bible, though God stands behind

5. Klaus Koch, "Gibt es ein Vergeltungsdogma im Alten Testament?" *Zeitschrift für Theologie und Kirche* 52 (1955): 1–42.

6. Claudia Sticher, *Die Rettung der Guten durch Gott und die Selbstzerstörung der Bösen: Ein theologisches Denkmuster im Psalter*, Bonner biblische Beiträge (Berlin and Vienna: Philo, 2002).

good and evil, by and large he does so asymmetrically, so that the good is finally credited to him but the evil is ultimately credited to secondary causalities.[7] Yet as it stands, Sticher's argument fails to convince. Psalms of complaint in which appeal is made to God to rescue the supplicant from external dangers or evils cannot be taken as the dominant, still less the exclusive, way in which God's wrath is said to manifest itself in the pages of the Old Testament Scriptures. In other words, her choice of texts guarantees a particular outcome, which cannot be projected on the entire Hebrew canon. Again, when she appeals to several chapters of Proverbs, she is dealing with a genre that tends to polarize reality: one follows Lady Wisdom or Dame Folly; there are only two ways, and God's way is only one of them. Sticher's problem is that she draws outsize conclusions from a carefully selected and limited number of texts. Narrative and especially prophetic texts paint a rather more complicated picture. It is because God's anger burns against Israel that he incites David to take a census (2 Sam. 24:1)—and of course the verb is active. It is not clear that the Chronicler's parallel, in which Satan incites David (1 Chron. 21:1), would be seen as a necessary contradiction: consider the opening chapters of Job. But more telling yet are numerous prophetic texts where Yahweh wants to make it very clear that he himself is the One who sovereignly brings about the catastrophic judgment, even when an imperial party such as Nebuchadnezzar is the historical agent. One of the purposes of Ezekiel 8–11, where the prophet is, in his vision, transported seven hundred miles from the banks of the Kebar River to witness the grotesque idolatry of Jerusalem and to witness God's abandonment of the temple and the city (the glory leaves on the mobile throne chariot and takes up a watch on the Mount of Olives), is to make it clear to Ezekiel and to the exiles with him that when Jerusalem does actually fall (Ezek. 33) it is not because God has lost a battle with other gods or with the Babylonian Empire but because God in his anger has brought this about: "Have you seen this, son of man? Is it a trivial matter for the house of Judah to do the detestable things they are doing here? Must they also fill the land with violence and continually arouse my anger? . . . Therefore I will deal with them in anger; I will not look on them with pity or spare them. Although they shout in my ears, I will not listen to them" (Ezek. 8:17–18).

More striking yet is Isaiah 10:5–19. There God speaks of the Assyrian Empire as the club of his wrath that he has deployed "against a godless nation"—that is, against his own covenant people, especially the southern kingdom: "I dispatch him against a people who anger me, to

---

7. D. A. Carson, *Divine Sovereignty and Human Responsibility: Biblical Themes in Tension* (London: Marshall, Morgan & Scott, 1981).

seize loot and snatch plunder, and to trample them down like mud in the streets" (10:6). This, of course, is not what Assyria thinks. The Assyrian leadership boast extravagantly of their military prowess (10:7–11), arguing that Israel's cities and Israel's gods are no better than the cities and gods of others they have crushed. So Isaiah says that when Yahweh has "finished all his work against Mount Zion and Jerusalem" (10:12), he "will punish the king of Assyria for the willful pride of his heart and the haughty look in his eyes" (10:12). In what does this pride consist? How is it demonstrated? It displays itself in the arrogance that thinks its own strength and prowess have produced all the military success. The king of Assyria is condemned for saying, "By the strength of my hand I have done this, and by my wisdom, because I have understanding. I removed the boundaries of nations, I plundered their treasures; like a mighty one I subdued their kings. As one reaches into a nest, so my hand reached for the wealth of nations" (10:13–14). Isaiah indignantly responds, "Does the ax raise itself above the one who swings it, or the saw boast against the one who uses it? As if a rod were to wield the person who lifts it up, or a club brandish one who is not wood! Therefore, the Lord, the LORD Almighty, will send a wasting disease upon his sturdy warriors; under his pomp a fire will be kindled like a blazing flame" (10:15–16).

In this passage there is no textually faithful way of domesticating the personal nature of God's wrath. God himself is using the Assyrian Empire as a tool—a club, an ax, a saw. This is *Yahweh's* work; it is *his* decision to "dispatch" the Assyrians against the people who "anger" him; it is *his* intention to "trample them down like mud in the streets." The Assyrians may complete all their looting and pillaging, their "work," but it is God's work they are accomplishing. Nor will it do to suppose that this passage is unique, a theological aberration, for similar declarations of God executing judgment in this way are not uncommon. As God has used the Assyrians, so he uses the Babylonians (frequently in Ezekiel; cf. Jer. 27:8–9) and the Persians (e.g., Cyrus in Isa. 45:1). Thus readers of the Bible are told that, after using the Babylonian superpower to effect his judgments and pour out his anger in punishment, God in due course punishes the Babylonians for their sins. When he does so, the Lord opens "his arsenal and [brings] out *the weapons of his wrath*, for the Sovereign LORD Almighty has work to do in the land of the Babylonians" (Jer. 50:25, emphasis added). Elsewhere, because Habakkuk recognizes that it is Yahweh himself who is using a more corrupt pagan superpower to chasten a less corrupt but nevertheless guilty covenant community, Habakkuk agonizes over the implicit moral dilemma. His problem could not be real if God were not somehow personally bringing about the judgment, if God were not through these military means pouring out his wrath, if God were merely administering a large and impersonal system so as to guarantee the proper nexus between actions and consequences.

In the New Testament, when Jesus tells parables in which God brings in final judgment, the picture he paints is never characterized by mere impersonal inevitability. The wrath of the king signals the king's being slighted. Similarly, the depictions of final wrath in the Apocalypse have nothing of the flavor of impersonal justice grinding its inevitable way to a satisfactory conclusion, with God doing no more than supervising the system. Even the cries of the condemned recognize the ultimate cause of their destruction. They call to the rocks and the mountains, "Fall on us and hide us from the face of him who sits on the throne and from the wrath of the Lamb! For the great day of their wrath has come, and who can withstand it?" (Rev. 6:16–17).

In short, there is no exegetically responsible way to dissolve the personal nature of God's wrath throughout the canonical Scriptures. Our incentive to make this move may spring, in part, from certain Western cultural biases. In Western jurisprudence, the criminal offends against the state, or the law, or the Crown, or the people. Correspondingly, the judge is not the one who has been harmed by the criminal; rather, the judge is supposed to be a more-or-less neutral administrator of the system. Judges who have suffered at the hand of defendants are supposed to recuse themselves. Moreover, as important as the role of the judge may be, it pales into insignificance compared with the majesty ascribed to the state, the Crown, the law, and the people. So our mental image of a judge is that of one who serves large ideals and maintains impartiality as he or she seeks to discover the truth and administer the law fairly. But God as Judge is never the mere administrator of a system that is greater than he. The law is his law, and he is offended when it is ignored or contravened; he himself is always the offended party. But far from disqualifying him from acting as Judge, this fact—that he is the offended party—cannot be used to disqualify him from exercising judgment, for his perfections ensure that his judgments are invariably just. He has no need to recuse himself. The impartiality of the human judge is maintained by preserving a distance between the judge and the offense as the judge deploys the system to determine what happened. But God's impartiality does not depend on *not* being the offended party but on the perfections of his knowledge and justice. He makes no mistakes in judgment not because he is never the offended party (since in one sense he is always the most offended party) but because his perfections preclude errors of judgment or accident. In this case, our cultural reasons for preferring an aloof judge uninvolved in the crime are no longer relevant.

It appears unwarranted, then, to depersonalize or impersonalize the wrath of God.

2. *It is equally unwarranted to limit God's wrath by several other clever maneuvers.* For example, regarding the passage in Isaiah 10 already discussed, where God in his wrath uses the Assyrians to chasten his covenant people yet holds the Assyrians accountable, Terence E. Fretheim suggests that God had not foreseen how awful their carnage would be. They prove to be more extreme and cruel than he had envisaged, and this is why he punishes them after the fact.[8] But this is not what the text says. God is not depicted as saying, "Hold on, there! I wanted you to give them a little spanking, but since you have given them a whopping big spanking, therefore I'm going to have to spank you." Rather, the punishment is explicitly tied to God's purposes. The reason God turns on the Assyrians is not because they went over the top but because they think they have achieved all their conquests themselves, utterly ignoring God.

It is possible to read Zechariah 1:14–15 the way Fretheim proposes. There God says, "I am very jealous for Jerusalem and Zion, and I am very angry with the nations that feel secure. I was only a little angry, but they added to the calamity." In other words, it is possible to understand this to mean that God's "little" anger with his people authorized the nations to chasten them, but on their own "they added to the calamity." Yet the only specific substance that describes the shortcomings of the nations is that they "feel secure." In other words, this sounds very much like the arrogance of the Assyrians in Isaiah 10. Perhaps it is this that added to the calamity.

Fretheim rightly reminds us that the apostasy of the people can elicit a portrait of God being wounded as much as God being angry: witness Hosea. Indeed, God's sorrow over the punishment that he himself has inflicted is a not uncommon theme (e.g., Jer. 42:10: "If you stay in this land, I will build you up and not tear you down; I will plant you and not uproot you, for I have relented concerning the disaster I have inflicted on you"). Yet it is not entirely clear that the biblical writers mean to "soften" God's wrath by such depictions, any more than that the juxtaposition of wrath and love means to mitigate the love. However imperfectly, parents may glimpse something of the place that both wrath and love rightly enjoy. In sum, I doubt that we will make the best progress in our reflections on the wrath of God if we attempt to dissipate the stark frankness of the countless texts bearing on this theme by prematurely appealing to complementary themes.

Many writers attempt to domesticate the biblical portrayal of the wrath of God rather less by exegetical means than by theological arguments. Much in line with Koch, to whom I have already referred, Eberhard

8. Terence E. Fretheim, "'I Was Only a Little Angry': Divine Violence in the Prophets," *Interpretation* 58 (2004): 365–75.

Jüngel denies that punishment is ever *inflicted* by God: so-called punishment is never more than the harvest of what is sown, the consequences and outworking of the inner logic of sin.[9] Yet not only does this stance not wrestle with the many highly personal texts to which I have already referred (and they represent but a tiny percentage of the whole); even those that speak of sin and its consequences in terms of "sowing" and "reaping" do not see this as a quasi-mechanical process one step removed from God, for they preface the analogy by a firm "God cannot be mocked" (Gal. 6:7). The effort of Paul Ricoeur[10] is no more successful.[11]

None of this means that we can afford to ignore what *other* things the Scriptures say about God—things that may evoke prolonged reflection on how the wrath of God should be integrated with these other things that are found in the same documents. Nor are these observations meant to sidestep texts that speak of innocent suffering (e.g., Job). It means only that steps to depersonalize or impersonalize the wrath of God find little sanction in Scripture.

3. *Perhaps it is here that I should venture a few comments on the doctrine of the impassability of God.*[12] In recent decades, this doctrine has increasingly been called into question, especially in treatments of the suffering of God or of the love of God. Attempts to reduce God's love to a subset of his will—God's willed determination of the other's good, for instance—do not stand up to either lexical semantics or responsible exegesis. If impassability is too deeply shaded by the categories of Stoicism, Platonism, or other forms of Greek metaphysics,

9. Eberhard Jüngel, *Das Evangelium von der Rechtfertigung des Gottlosen als Zentrum des christlichen Glaubens: Eine theologische Studie in ökumenischer Absicht* (Tübingen: Mohr Siebeck, 1998), 113.

10. Esp. in Paul Ricoeur, "Interprétation du mythe de la peine," in *Le conflit des interprétations: Essais d'herméneutique* (Paris: Seuil, 1969), 348–69.

11. See esp. the succinct but penetrating discussion by Henri Blocher, "Justification of the Ungodly (*sola fide*): Theological Reflections," in *Justification and Variegated Nomism*, vol. 2, *The Paradoxes of Paul*, ed. D. A. Carson, Peter T. O'Brien, and Mark A. Seifrid, Wissenschaftliche Untersuchungen zum Neuen Testament 2/181 (Tübingen: Mohr Siebeck; Grand Rapids: Baker Academic, 2004), esp. 475–78.

12. This movement has come from many sources, but perhaps best known in recent decades are the works of Jürgen Moltmann (esp. *The Crucified God: The Cross of Christ as the Foundation and Criticism of Christian Theology* [New York: Harper & Row, 1974]) and Eberhard Jüngel (esp. *God as the Mystery of the World: On the Foundations of the Theology of the Crucified One in the Dispute between Theism and Atheism*, trans. Darrell L. Guder [Grand Rapids: Eerdmans, 1983]). See the treatment by Henri Blocher, "God and the Cross," in chapter 7 of this collection. One thinks also of the influence of the "openness" theologians (nicely documented by Bruce L. McCormack in chapter 10 of this volume, "The Actuality of God"). Perhaps the most important book on the subject in recent times, from a classical perspective, is Thomas Weinandy, *Does God Suffer?* (Edinburgh: T&T Clark, 2000).

it is difficult to square the resulting picture of God with the biblical emphases.

But this is not the only framework in which to think about impassability. Most who today defend some form of impassability begin by insisting that God never changes his character in all his relations with his people. This is true, but such a formulation speaks rather more to immutability than to impassability. Perhaps one may go a little further by observing (as many have done) that although the Bible frequently speaks of God's love, it never projects an image of God "falling in love" or the like. In English, "falling in love" conjures up a lover so much under the sway of overwhelming emotions that all other considerations— considerations of right and wrong, of responsible commitment to others, of the place of reason and will and knowledge—are swept away. In this sense, it is impossible to think of the God of the Bible "falling in love." It is surely far better to think of God's love being displayed in the context of the display of all his other perfections. If God loves, his love cannot be divorced from his knowledge, his sovereignty, his will, his aseity, his immutability, his omniscience—indeed, it cannot be divorced from his choice to love. On the other hand, if God wills or chooses something, he never does so in a fashion divorced from his own intrinsically loving nature. It seems proper, then, to confess that God is impassable in the sense that he is never so controlled by his "passions" that the other perfections of his very being as God are somehow swept away or in any sense jeopardized. All the more must we insist on this point when we draw the parallel with human passions, which are so frequently ignited by people or circumstances outside ourselves. God is impassable in the sense that he sustains no "passion" over which he has no control, no passion disconnected from all his other perfections.[13] In short, we need not label each instance of God suffering or loving (as, say, in Hosea) a mere anthropomorphism (or, more properly, a mere anthropopathism), so that we construe God's love as devoid of affective elements. There is ample biblical reason to think that God has a rich and intense emotional life, even though, since God is incorporeal, infinite, and perfect, his emotional life must not be thought of as being exactly like ours. In this highly attenuated sense, one may still, I suppose, speak of anthropomorphism or anthropopathism.

The same sort of reflection pertains to what the Bible says about God's wrath. Just as God does not "fall in love," so he does not "lose his temper." Just as one must be suspicious of a version of impassability that dissolves

---

13. I have discussed this at slightly greater length, not least with respect to current debates on the immanent and economic Trinity, in D. A. Carson, *The Difficult Doctrine of the Love of God* (Wheaton, IL: Crossway, 2000), 58–64.

God's love in willed altruism, so one must be suspicious of a version of impassability that dissolves God's wrath in impersonal and implacable justice. What is missing, in both instances, is a fundamentally personal and affective component. Yet just as one must avoid notions of God's love that ultimately make him the victim of his own passions, so one must take similar precautions when reflecting on his wrath.

This comparison between the love of God and the wrath of God has a certain utility when we try to understand in what way it may be appropriate to speak of the impassability of God. But it would be quite wrong—indeed, deeply misleading—to press such a comparison too far. God is always loving; the Bible can say that "God is love" (1 John 4:8). But it is mistaken to think of God as always wrathful; there is no passage that affirms that "God is wrath." Even an affirmation such as "God is a consuming fire" (Heb. 12:29, citing Deut. 4:24) lies within the context of encouraging faithfulness and perseverance, of warning against apostasy, unbelief, and disobedience. In other words, God's wrath is the response (including an affective element) of his holiness to sin. It is a response to creatures external to himself, even if this response is entirely shaped by who God is in his own character. Insofar as God's wrath reflects God's holiness, it is grounded in the very Godness of God; insofar as it is impossible to think of God's wrath absent sin, it is no more ultimate than sin itself. In this respect, then, God's wrath is fundamentally different from God's love.[14] But I shall return to and build on this point later.

4. *Serious reflection on the wrath of God is a necessary element in any faithful understanding of what the fundamental human problem is.* This is becoming more and more of a challenge when Christians try to articulate the gospel in the Western world. For unless we gain agreement on what the problem is, how can we in any way gain agreement, much less clarity, on what the solution is?[15]

The severity of the challenge is starkly displayed in the most recent book by Christian Smith, who has undertaken a major study of the beliefs

14. Some traditions of systematic theology would at this juncture introduce discussion about God's "essence"—i.e., God's perfections and essential attributes (characteristics which *could not* have been otherwise) over against his contingent properties (characteristics which *could* have been otherwise). For a useful discussion of this strand of philosophical theology, rendered important because it is ignored or downplayed by process theology, see Jay Wesley Richards, *The Untamed God: A Philosophical Exploration of Divine Perfection, Simplicity and Immutability* (Downers Grove, IL: InterVarsity, 2003).

15. The converse—that if we do not have agreement on the solution, we are unlikely to agree on the nature of the problem—is no less true but is not the point I am making here. In other words, I am concerned to establish the ineluctable nexus between the two, not necessarily the sequence in which knowledge of each must be achieved.

of American teenagers.[16] His findings may reflect the more extreme case, but they resonate with our impressionistic perceptions of the direction the culture is taking. Of those who identify themselves as "Christian" (Catholic, Protestant, Orthodox, or whatever), the majority clearly belong to what Smith calls the dominant American religion, namely, "Moralist Therapeutic Deism," or MTD. The five dominant beliefs of MTD are:

a. A God exists who created and orders the world and watches over human life on earth.
b. God wants people to be good, nice, and fair to each other, as taught in the Bible and by most world religions.
c. The central goal of life is to be happy and to feel good about oneself.
d. God does not need to be particularly involved in one's life except when God is needed to resolve a problem.
e. Good people go to heaven when they die.[17]

Thus God becomes distant, and the summum bonum is a strange brew comprised of equal parts works righteousness and pop therapeutic "feel good" psychology. By any reading, this religion takes the hard edges off a more biblically informed Christian faith. It makes us comfortable with a sentimentalized reading of, say, John 3:16 ("For God so loved the world . . ."); it makes it unthinkable to dwell on, for example, John 3:36, a bare twenty verses later ("Whoever believes in the Son has eternal life, but whoever rejects the Son will not see life, for God's wrath remains on them"). This sort of passage makes wrath the default situation, as it were—equally presupposed in Jesus's words to those who wanted to draw the wrong theological conclusions from public disasters (Luke 13:1–5): "Unless you repent, you too will all perish."[18]

16. Christian Smith, *Soul Searching: The Religious and Spiritual Lives of American Teenagers* (New York: Oxford University Press, 2005).
17. Ibid., 162–63.
18. At the conference where this paper was read, one of the participants came up to me after the session and said that this rendering leaves out the most important word: "Unless you repent, you will all *likewise* perish." Just as the tower fell on the people of Siloam, so walls would come crashing down on the people of Jerusalem. The reference, then, is not to the judgment of the last day but to the destruction of the temple in AD 70. A few commentators have indeed made the connection with the fall of Jerusalem, but this seems to bleed "likewise" (*hōsautōs* in Luke 13:5 and *homoiōs* in 13:3, plus or minus textual variants in both passages; it is difficult to detect a semantic shift) rather badly. If the "likewise" in 13:3 is taken with equal severity, we must envisage more people dying in such a way that their blood is mingled with that of their (animal) sacrifices under the barbaric decree of a Roman governor. In any case, the context of discussion is not *when* the parallel judgment will occur absent repentance but that there is no ground for feeling morally superior to those who die tragic deaths (whether caused by a wicked tyrant or by

The general point might be clarified by three observations.

First, precisely because God's wrath is *not* arbitrary but is the willed and principled response (however affective) of his holiness when it confronts the rebellion of his creatures, not least those of his creatures who have entered into covenant with him, sin itself gains a certain transcendental significance. It is not mere peccadillo, not mere unfortunate preference, not mere social product (though it may be all three of these things); it is defiance of the living God, which, because God is God, attracts God's wrath. Although many things are said to bring down God's wrath, the one transgression most frequently said to do so is idolatry. For the same reason, because the first commandment is the commandment to love God with heart and soul and mind and strength, the first sin is breaking the first commandment; that is, it is *not* to love God with heart and soul and mind and strength. It is the one sin that is always committed every time any other sin is committed. To venture an aside: We sometimes try to prove the relevance of Christianity to a skeptical world by talking about failure and evil in exclusively social, horizontal categories in the hope of winning some well-intentioned people to our side. But if sin is defined with reference to God, if the primal sin is defiance of God, it is highly doubtful that we shall be at all successful in getting across much of a biblically coherent worldview unless we learn to explain to our biblically illiterate generation who *God* is and what our sin looks like to *God*.

Second, this nexus between God and sin, looked at from the other end, tells us important things about God. Here are two of them.

(a) God is passionately (if I dare use this word) concerned for his own glory. His glory is something God does not yield to any other (Isa. 42:8; 48:11). God must be true, so that all who contradict him are necessarily liars (Rom. 3:4). To put the matter more broadly: God must be God. What is sin, not least the fundamental sin of idolatry, but the attempt to promote ourselves to the status of God or to demote God to our own level? What is it but the de-godding of God? And God will not have it; he is passionately against it, for in the first instance it means denying who he himself is.[19] It means overturning the fundamental distinction between Creator and creature.

Perhaps I may be permitted a personal aside. Although I have been thinking about these themes for many years, the importance of this reflection was borne in on me a few years ago by an undergraduate

---

an "accident" such as a falling tower), since we are all guilty and, apart from repentance, we will all perish. The "likewise" almost certainly refers to the *fact* of perishing, not the *mode* of perishing.

19. Cf. John Piper, *The Pleasures of God: Meditations on God's Delight in Being God*, 2nd ed. (Portland, OR: Multnomah, 2000).

interlocutor. I have engaged in sporadic university missions for more than thirty years, and after a while one has heard most of the common questions and objections. But in the last few years I have faced a question that had never been raised to me before. It was first put to me by this student, who said something like this: "In human relationships, we learn to distrust and despise anyone who always wants to be number one, who is offended if he or she is not number one. So why should we not take umbrage at a God who wants to be number one, who is offended if he is not number one?" I could have given a long answer about God's compassion, about the humility and self-negation of the Son of God in the incarnation, about the cost to God of the cross itself—and, indeed, as part of a satisfying answer, all these things and more must be said. Yet in a sense, the measure of God's condescension, compassion, and self-humiliation found in the incarnation and in the cross can be taken only if the sheer blindness of my interlocutor is glimpsed: God is God; he is number one. The very angels hide their faces before the brilliance of his glory. The fundamental answer to my interlocutor's question, then, is this: God is God. He is not to be compared with human beings, even if he sent his Son to become one. The question itself betrays the heart of the question: it supposes that God ought to be like us, perhaps slightly souped up. What Jesus calls the first commandment makes sense only if God is God, our Creator, Sustainer, providential Ruler, and final Judge. Breaking this first commandment, that is, failing to love God with heart and soul and mind and strength, calls forth his wrath precisely because he alone is God.

In answer to the deist's claim, we sometimes argue that a God who is indifferent to, for example, the butcheries of a Pol Pot, an Idi Amin, a Joseph Stalin, an Adolf Hitler cannot be thought of as being morally superior to a God who is outraged at their barbarisms. This is true, of course, and conforms to the way that God is outraged at social injustice in Amos and parts of Isaiah, but in a sense, it is also secondary. God is outraged, in the first instance, at the fundamental barbarism: the outrage of stripping him of his glory. The same point can be seen from another angle in a text such as Leviticus 19. In this remarkable list of commandments, running from the prohibition of slander to the prohibition of divination and idolatry, from the commandment not to plant two kinds of seeds in one field to the commandment to love your neighbor as yourself, the ultimate warrant is repeatedly applied: "I am the Lord."

It follows, then, that God's wrath is personal, for the offenses are not against some mere principle, some abstract system, some law that is independent of God's identity, of his very being as God. To the extent, then, that this world, the world that God created and which depends on him for its very existence, is broken, anarchic, and God-defying, to this extent God's wrath is as personal and as ultimate as his holiness, for it is an expression of it in the face of sin.

(b) It follows therefore that the fundamental human problem is that God is against us. I hasten to add that it is also gloriously true that God is for us, that while we were yet sinners, Christ died for us, that God loves us not because we are so very intrinsically lovable but because he is that kind of God. These sorts of themes are treated in other contributions to this volume. But if the nexus between sin and wrath that I have briefly sketched is a fair representation of Scripture, it follows that our most fundamental problem is that God stands over against us. Granted what God is, granted what sin is, it could scarcely be otherwise. Whatever "salvation" means, in all its dimensions, it must deal with our profound alienation from the God who made us and to whom we must give an account, the God we de-god by our thoughts and words and deeds; otherwise it is "salvation" in only the most superficial senses. That this salvation comes about because the God who is against us is also the God who, full of compassion, is for us is almost too wonderful to take in.

Third, the fact that these are constantly reiterated themes in Scripture ought to influence the way we understand a substantial number of texts. For example, in recent times it has often been pointed out that the great atonement passage in Paul's letter to the Romans (3:21–26) immediately rushes on to assert that God is the God of both Jews and Gentiles (3:29). Romans 4, then, by this reading, talks about God's faithfulness to the covenant with Abraham and about his creation of a new humanity from both halves of sinful humankind.[20] This is not so much wrong as a confusion of what the text foregrounds and backgrounds.[21] Paul's dominant purpose from Romans 1:18 to 3:20 is to prove that all human beings are guilty of sin and fall under the righteous wrath of God. In this context, there is considerable discussion of the different ways in which Jews and Gentiles fall afoul of God's demands, but the unit ends with a blistering catena of Old Testament quotations that confirm the universal guilt of human beings. The great atonement passage therefore provides a remedy for Jews and Gentiles alike, for *all* have sinned and fall short of the glory of God (3:23).[22] In other words, the atonement is a remedy

20. So, e.g., N. T. Wright, "Romans," in *The New Interpreter's Bible* (Nashville: Abingdon, 2002), 10:464–507.

21. This judgment, regarding the confusion of background and foreground, is a major plank in the perceptive essay by Douglas J. Moo, "Israel and the Law in Romans 5–11: Interaction with the New Perspective," in *The Paradoxes of Paul*, ed. Carson, O'Brien, and Seifrid, 185–216.

22. Elsewhere I have tried to show how this "all" has an important and frequently overlooked bearing on how we understand the *pisteōs Iēsou Christou* expression in Rom. 3:22; see D. A. Carson, "Atonement in Romans 3:21–26," in *The Glory of the Atonement—Biblical, Theological and Practical Perspectives: Essays in Honor of Roger R. Nicole*, ed. Charles E.

for sin and thus a way to handle the well-deserved wrath of God (1:18) upon Jews and Gentiles alike rather than a remedy for the disunity of Jews and Gentiles, who both happen to be sinful—this is a confusion of foreground and background. That God is the God of both Jews and Gentiles (3:29) is established both by creation and by the Abrahamic covenant itself, since this covenant promises that in Abraham and his seed all the nations of the earth will be blessed. What one must not overlook in Romans 4 is that when the justification of Abraham is introduced, it is introduced as justification by faith and therefore, Paul argues, cannot be something that Abraham has earned, and this fact demonstrates that it must be the justification of the wicked, not the righteous; we are back to the centrality of sin and the curse (the expression of God's wrath) in Paul's argument.[23] This sort of argument requires that readers think very carefully about what roles the law plays in the history of the Jews and in the history of the human race, but it does not lose sight of the dominant point in Paul's argument.

The point becomes clear once again when we consider the way Paul quotes Hosea 1:10–11 and 2:23 in Romans 9:24–26. In the context of Hosea, the people who are addressed, "You are not my people," and who are thereafter called "children of the living God" are not Gentiles but sinful and alienated Jews. So what is Paul doing when he applies the Hosea texts to Gentiles? Closer reflection suggests why Paul can make the leap without distorting the prophetic context. Hosea 1:19 has already established that the Lord has disowned the northern kingdom because of its apostasy, its spiritual adultery with other gods. Hosea 1:11 demonstrates that Judah is sliding down the same slippery slope and will join her adulterous sister in her adultery. Hosea is to name his child Lo-Ammi (1:9, "not my people") because the covenant community is about to lose its privileged covenantal status as the people of God. Mercifully, this sweeping denunciation is then followed by a promise, "In the place where it was said to them, 'You are not my people,' they will be called 'children of the living God'" (1:10). As one of my doctoral students has nicely put it:

A sequential unfolding of these two pronouncements might look like this:
(1) Ephraim and Judah will be cut off from the covenantal promises of God;
(2) this is announced to them while they are still in the Promised Land;

Hill and Frank A. James III (Downers Grove, IL: InterVarsity, 2004), 119–39. See also the important discussion by Moisés Silva, "Faith versus Works of Law in Galatians," in *The Paradoxes of Paul*, ed. Carson, O'Brien, and Seifrid, 217–48, esp. 227–34.

23. Cf. D. A. Carson, "The Vindication of Imputation: On Fields of Discourse and Semantic Fields," in *Justification: What's at Stake in the Current Debates*, ed. Mark Husbands and Daniel J. Treier (Downers Grove, IL: InterVarsity, 2004), 46–78.

(3) as a result, they will go far away into exile for a period of time; (4) one day in the future a remnant will be regathered to the land from which they left; and (5) it will be said to them at that time and in that place, "you are my people" (Hos. 2:23), the "sons of the living God" (Hos. 1:10).[24]

If, then, the apostle Paul takes seriously God's pronouncement that Israel will no longer be his people because of their sin, we begin to see why the apostle argues as he does. One of the fundamental promises of the covenant was, "I will be your God, and you will be my people," and so if this is now being disowned by God himself, then Israel is being relegated to the status of a pagan Gentile nation (cf. further Hos. 8:8; 9:17; Zeph. 2:1).[25] Yet a remnant from this newly declared Gentile nation will one day again be called "my people." Paul understands that if such a restoration from Gentile status to covenant community is possible for Israel, there is no fundamental reason Gentiles who have always been Gentiles cannot be taken up into the covenant community and be called "my people." In other words, from Paul's perspective, all those who are taken up into the new covenant community were in fact Gentiles, whether they were born Gentiles or not; all are equally sinners and under the wrath of God. There is thus a profound sense in which Israel's loss of her privileged status opened the way for the privilege of new covenant blessings to be poured out on all Gentiles. Of course, if this reading is right, the crucial assumption, once again, in Paul's argument is the universality of sin and concomitantly the universality of being under the righteous wrath of God.

Time does not permit detailed exploration of these passages and numerous others like them. But perhaps enough has been said to recognize afresh that serious reflection on the wrath of God is a necessary element in any faithful understanding of what the fundamental human problem is. It is difficult to imagine that we will be able to gain substantial agreement on what the solution is unless we gain substantial agreement on what the problem is—or to put it more bluntly and less enigmatically, it is doubtful that we will enjoy a shared understanding of what the gospel is unless we share an understanding of the problem the gospel addresses. Although this problem has many parameters, including social injustice, alienation among many races (the tension between Jews and Gentiles is not the only one), defeat before Satan's power, the physical deterioration climaxed by death itself, and the threat of eternal punishment, at the

24. Thomas R. Wood, "The Regathering of the People of God: An Investigation into the New Testament's Appropriation of the Old Testament Prophets concerning the Regathering of Israel" (PhD diss., Trinity Evangelical Divinity School, 2005), 297–98.

25. See, e.g., Hans Walter Wolff, *Hosea*, Hermeneia (Philadelphia: Fortress, 1974), esp. 21–23.

heart of our lostness is the guilt we have incurred by our de-godding of God, by our passionate devotion to idolatry, and therefore of the wrath we have rightly attracted.

This inevitably brings us to the fifth theological reflection.

5. *The wrath of God bears, in several ways, on how we understand the cross.* This subject demands a great deal more research. I have space only to begin to tease out the argument.

I must begin with a caveat. My assigned topic is "the wrath of God," and I must now say something about the connections between God's wrath and the cross. But a more comprehensive treatment of the cross would soon speak of God's ineffable love in sending his Son to the cross, of his immeasurable compassion, of his condescension. If I do not here focus on such truths, it is most certainly not because they are somehow less important to our understanding of the cross than is God's wrath but because I must lay primary emphasis on the subject assigned me.

The heart of the issue may be put this way: if the human plight is our sin and its effects, not least the fact that we stand alienated from God and rightly under his wrath, then, granted the place of the cross in the Bible's story line, whatever else the cross accomplishes, it must reconcile us to God, it must remove the ground of our alienation, it must set aside God's wrath—or it does not meet the plight that the Scriptures themselves set forth. Of course, this is a hopelessly inadequate summary of some extraordinarily intertwined themes. Countless passages in both Testaments picture human lostness not only in terms of guilt, condemnation, and wrath but also in other terms: sin is so social that others are caught up in anyone's sins, with the result that there are victims, broken people, isolated people, morally enslaved people, and dying people—and in all these horrible realities, we are met by God's compassion, even as our idolatry is met by his wrath. In sum, we find ourselves fighting the Bible's entire story line if we do not recognize that our deepest need is to be reconciled to God (cf. 2 Cor. 5:11–21).[26] If this reconciliation turns, in substantial measure, on the setting aside of God's deserved wrath, we have arrived unavoidably at sacrifice, expiation, propitiation—in short, at penal substitution.[27]

26. Among recent works that probe many of sin's dimensions without losing its primary focus as revolt against God are Cornelius Plantinga Jr., *Not the Way It's Supposed to Be: A Breviary of Sin* (Grand Rapids: Eerdmans, 1974); and Marguerite Shuster, *The Fall and Sin: What We Have Become as Sinners* (Grand Rapids: Eerdmans, 2004).

27. It is still salutary to ponder J. I. Packer, "What Did the Cross Achieve? The Logic of Penal Substitution," *Tyndale Bulletin* 25 (1974): 3–45. Cf. also Steve Jeffery, Mike Ovey, and Andrew Sach, *Pierced for Our Transgressions: Rediscovering the Glory of Penal Substitution* (Wheaton, IL: Crossway, 2007).

It may be helpful to present the argument in five brief steps.

(a) In a useful essay, Paul Wells summarizes five of the most common objections to penal substitution. This understanding of the atonement is unacceptable, its detractors insist, because it is

> ontological and objective, not demonstrative or subjective (liberalism); unethical, as sin and guilt are personal and non-transferable (Socinianism); untrinitarian, or implies tri-theistic divisions in God; self-contradictory, since God the Father cannot act for and against Christ at one and the same time; finally, a wrong interpretation of the Biblical data. Sacrifice does not imply penal substitution. Various images are merged in a totalising way and the legal model is given a non-biblical pre-eminence.[28]

In the most extreme cases, the criticism is exegetically bizarre. J. Denny Weaver, for instance, argues that Jesus's death was not the will of God, formed no part of Jesus's God-given mission, and played no necessary part in our salvation. Weaver thinks he can avoid the many references to wrath in the Apocalypse by simply labeling them "apocalyptic." He manages to write his entire book on this subject without once referring to a series of texts that are classical loci for the doctrine, including Mark 10:45, Acts 4:28, Romans 3:25, all of John's Gospel, and 1 John 4:10.[29] It is true that there are forms of argument that, at least initially, strike many contemporary readers as more believable than Weaver's approach, such as Goldingay's analysis of Old Testament sacrifice. Goldingay argues that sacrifice can be a way of giving a gift, a way of cleansing and restoration, a bridge between this world and the holy, a way of handling violence in the community[30]—and he concludes that insofar as Jesus's death was punitive, it satisfied human justice, not divine.

(b) It is not possible in short compass to respond to all of these criticisms. But one rather startling fact is that many of them do not wrestle seriously with the theme of the wrath of God. Pierre Berthoud's contribution to this volume, "The Compassion of God: Exodus 34:5–9 in the Light of Exodus 32–34," rightly draws attention to the extreme tension between God's well-deserved wrath and his totally underserved compassion in Exodus 32–34. What follows next in the book of Exodus is the detailed stipulations for the construction of the tabernacle,

28. Paul Wells, "A Free Lunch at the End of the Universe? Sacrifice, Substitution and Penal Liability," *Themelios* 29/1 (2003): 43–44. Cf. also Henri Blocher, "The Sacrifice of Jesus Christ: The Current Theological Situation," *European Journal of Theology* 8/1 (1999): 23–36, including penetrating criticism of J. Goldingay, ed., *Atonement Today* (London: SPCK, 1995).

29. J. Denny Weaver, *The Non-violent Atonement* (Grand Rapids: Eerdmans, 2001).

30. J. Goldingay, "Old Testament Sacrifice and the Death of Christ," in *Atonement Today*, ed. Goldingay, 3–10.

the organizing of the priestly system, and the ordering of the feasts. True, not all sacrifices were sin offerings, but many were, none more trenchantly than what was offered on *yôm kippurîm*. When Solomon dedicates the temple, he sees this place of sacrifice as the rallying point for repentance and return after the people have turned away from God and in consequence face his wrath. Moreover, if we read the Bible canonically, we will reflect on how Hebrews 7:11–19 insists that it is the priestly sacrificial system of the Torah that lies at its heart (not, in this context, moral law), such that when there is an announced change in the priesthood (as, implicitly, there is in Ps. 110), there must be a change in the entire law-covenant.[31] What replaces it is the prophesied new covenant (Heb. 8), which has a better sacrifice, a better tabernacle, a better priest, and better blood (Heb. 9)—"the blood of Christ, who through the eternal Spirit offered himself unblemished to God, [to] cleanse our consciences from acts that lead to death, so that we may serve the living God" (9:14). And it is not for nothing, as we are reminded in this collection of essays, that the closing book of the canon is nothing other than the triumph of the Lamb, the Lamb who is both the apocalyptic warrior and the slaughtered sacrifice, slain so as to purchase with his blood a people for God—"members of every tribe and language and people and nation" (Rev. 5:9).

(c) Some scholars advocate readings of the Gospels that treat the passion narratives climaxing each as detachable accounts that have little affect upon the interpretation of each Gospel read as a whole. I confess I prefer the older school that thinks of the Gospels as passion narratives with extended introductions. Once again, the topic is too substantial for a brief paper, but one might well begin by reading Peter G. Bolt's sometimes moving treatment of how the sacrificial death of Jesus shapes the entire presentation of Mark's Gospel.[32] In John's Gospel not only is Jesus

31. The explanatory expression *ho laos gar ep' autēs nenomothetētai* in Heb. 7:11 is rightly (if slightly paraphrastically) rendered by the NIV as "for on the basis of it [the priesthood] the law was given to the people," taking *autēs* to refer to *hierōsynēs*, as most commentators do, and not *teleiōsis*. See the discussion in Paul Ellingworth, *Commentary on Hebrews*, New International Greek Testament Commentary (Grand Rapids: Eerdmans, 1993), 372. The TNIV has it exactly wrong: "and indeed the law given to the people established that priesthood." The author of Hebrews is not saying that the law-covenant established the priesthood but that the law-covenant was established *on* the priesthood—i.e., the dependence goes the other way—with the result (as 7:12 shows) that when the priesthood changes, the law-covenant itself must change. The ESV's "for under it the people received the law" is a slightly strange way to understand the force of the preposition *epi* and ill prepares the ground for the argument of 7:12.

32. Peter G. Bolt, *The Cross from a Distance: Atonement in Mark's Gospel*, New Studies in Biblical Theology 18 (Leicester, UK: Inter-Varsity; Downers Grove, IL: InterVarsity, 2004).

announced as the Lamb of God who takes away the sin of the world;[33] he is the Good Shepherd who gives his life for his sheep, the grain of wheat that falls into the ground and dies that others may live. In John 6, he is the bread of life—not merely the antitype of the Old Testament manna and the real significance of the feeding of the five thousand but something more. The graphic language (of John 6:51–58) reminds us of what everyone in an agrarian culture knew, something we so easily forget when we buy food in cardboard boxes, plastic containers, and tin cans: we live only because other living things die. If no other living thing dies, we do not eat: the cow and the cod, the carrots and the parsnips must die; otherwise we will. We feed on Jesus: he dies, or we do. And with the Old Testament curses lying in the background, the odious death of a man hanging on a tree bespeaks not merely the most cruel of the three Roman modes of execution but the curse of God. But because the death of that God-damned man tore the veil of the temple (Matt. 27:51; cf. Heb. 9:3, 8; 10:19–20) and opened the way into the Most Holy Place, we see, too, that either we would be cursed or he would be.

(d) But perhaps the locus classicus remains Romans 3:21–26. I have already brought attention to the portrait Paul draws, in the preceding two and a half chapters in Romans, of universal guilt and universally distributed wrath. There is another reading of 3:25–26, amply discussed elsewhere.[34] But I remain convinced that the more traditional reading is the correct one: the passage unpacks what some have called the internal mechanism of the atonement. God set forth Jesus as the *hilastērion* "to demonstrate his justice"; justification is as much about the vindication of God as about the vindication of sinners. He did this because all the temporal punishments that had been meted out on men and women in past centuries were not the full measure of his wrath. He had graciously left their sins, in very substantial measure, unpunished as he waited patiently and compassionately for the culmination of his redemptive purposes. But now, "at the present time," in the death of Jesus, God shows forth his justice while justifying those who have faith in Jesus.

33. The view that John the Baptist meant by this announcement (John 1:29) that Jesus would be the warrior-lamb "taking away" the sin of the world by his sweeping authority has many attractions. Even so, John the evangelist, by this reading of the Baptist's intentions, is nevertheless insisting that the Baptist spoke better than he knew: the manner of Jesus's "taking away" the sin of the world would not be as expected by the forerunner. After all, the evangelist fairly frequently notes how people speak better than they know, none more so than Caiaphas, who, like the Baptist, utters words whose ultimate referent must, in the evangelist's understanding, be the substitutionary redemptive work of the cross (11:51–52).

34. See, e.g., Douglas J. Moo, *The Epistle to the Romans*, New International Commentary on the New Testament (Grand Rapids: Eerdmans, 1996), esp. 227–43.

Is it really necessary to say once again that this portrait does not picture an angry God and a soft Jesus? This would be a tragic distortion of trinitarian thought. Rather, the Bible pictures an angry God and a loving God or, better put, one God who is both angry and loving; the Gospels present an angry Jesus and a loving Jesus or, better put, a Jesus who is both wrathful and loving—a Jesus, for instance, who denounces in blistering terms the hypocrisy of some religious leaders (Matt. 23) but who weeps over the city (Luke 19:41). Here, at last, sin is expiated, God's wrath is propitiated, God is vindicated, and those who have faith in Christ Jesus are declared just. Here is *substitution*: "Very rarely will anyone die for a righteous person," Paul explains two chapters later, "[but] . . . while we were still sinners, Christ died for us" (Rom. 5:7–8). "One died for all, and therefore all died" (2 Cor. 5:14). Here is *punishment*: New Testament believers loved to quote Isaiah 53:5, "He was pierced for our transgressions, he was crushed for our iniquities; the punishment that brought us peace was on him, and by his wounds we are healed." In Paul, Christ bears our sin; he becomes a curse for us; he even becomes sin for us: "God made him who had no sin to be sin for us, so that in him we might become the righteousness of God" (2 Cor. 5:21). "For what the law was powerless to do because it was weakened by the sinful nature, God did *by sending his own Son in the likeness of sinful humanity to be a sin offering*. And so he condemned sin in human flesh, in order that the righteous requirement of the law might be fully met in us, who do not live according to the sinful nature but according to the Spirit" (Rom. 8:3–4, emphasis added). Peter adds his voice: "He himself bore our sins in his body on the tree. . . . By his wounds you have been healed" (1 Pet. 2:24 RSV).

(e) In the past, many scholars have set forth the various theories of the atonement that have been developed over the centuries—the *Christus Victor* theory, the satisfaction theory, the moral example theory, and so forth—and sometimes treated them as equally valid interpretations of the cross. After all, something of their voice can be heard somewhere or other in the New Testament, and each one has been defended by various voices in the great atonement traditions that have come down to us. But this pick-and-choose approach is methodologically and theologically bankrupt. We will be more faithful to Scripture if we seek to determine when and where each atonement emphasis is taught in the text and then determine how they hang together (see, e.g., the careful linking of substitutionary penal authority and exemplary ethical model to constrain conduct in 1 Pet. 2). But on two grounds, I suggest that if any of the atonement models (I do not much like the word "models," but it has become traditional) must have precedence, it must be substitutionary atonement. First, only this model adequately handles the massive biblical insistence on the righteous wrath of God, which is so much a part of the Bible's story line. Otherwise put, only this preserves the centrality of God, the raw fact that whatever else the cross achieves, it must reconcile us to God while vindicating God's justice. Second, I think it can be shown that all the other atonement models can be derived from this understanding of the cross and can add their own perspective and coherence; I doubt that this can be done by placing any other model at the core.[35]

6. *There will come a time, in the consummation of all things, when the wrath of God will no longer hang over us in any sense.* John tells us, "Perfect love drives out fear, because fear has to do with punishment. The one who fears is not made perfect in love" (1 John 4:18). In one profound sense, we have already escaped God's wrath: "Therefore, there is now no condemnation for those who are in Christ Jesus" (Rom. 8:1). Yet several New Testament writers not only continue to warn us against apostasy; they remind us of God's temporal judgments, the chastening of a wise Father (e.g., 1 Cor. 11:30–32; Heb. 12:4–11). Precisely because each of us is *simul justus et peccator*, God's wrath and our fear are both salutary.[36]

When this wrath is preached *in the context of the gospel*, however, we are rightly reminded of the central problem we face in this fallen and broken world and simultaneously hear words of forgiveness and hope. But one day we will be made perfect in love, and we will never fear punishment; we will never fear the wrath of God in any sense ever again. If wrath is the expression of God's holiness when it confronts sin, wrath will not be found when sin is not found. In this still compromised, sin-tarnished, double-standard world, the mere words, the truth that "perfect love drives out fear" (1 John 4:18), could easily become yet one more excuse for the most egregious sin: in the name of "love," what odious things may be baptized? But one day, one day, we will love without restraint and without compromise. We will understand exactly how perfect love drives out fear. Even so, come, Lord Jesus.

35. Among various treatments of this theme, see Alan Spence, "A Unified Theory of the Atonement," *International Journal of Systematic Theology* 6 (2004): 404–20.

36. Some scholars, influenced perhaps by Romans 8:1, argue that believers living this side of the cross must surely be thought of as escaping God's condemnation, escaping God's wrath. When believers suffer, we must think of their suffering in some other category: it is not the product of God's wrath, we are told, but merely the residue of the curse. But surely this is a false antithesis. In biblical thought, is it possible to think of the curse apart from God's pronouncement of it? Moreover, this line of thought does not adequately address the complexities of the inaugurated eschatology that is ubiquitous in the New Testament. All the blessings that will one day be the heritage of believers, including resurrection life in the new heaven and the new earth, are secured by the cross, but this does not mean that we experience all of them in their fullness just yet.

Further Theological and Practical Implications

I briefly mention four theological and practical implications.

1. *Although it would take us into a domain we cannot possibly pursue here, there must be some sense in which we should be wrathful as God is wrathful.* Andrew Lester is not overly forceful when he insists that "not being angry at evil in all its manifestations is sinful."[37] This is rarely an easy thing to get right, for human wrath easily degenerates into bitterness, one-upmanship, and condescending arrogance. Still, parents are often afforded small glimpses as to how wrath and compassion are not necessarily mutually antithetical. We catch other glimpses in some of the psalms of imprecation and in the Pastoral Epistles, where, on the one hand, readers are advised to avoid wrangling, to respond to people gently, and to cast a godly example and, on the other, they are informed that Paul has handed Hymenaeus and Alexander over to Satan that they might be taught not to blaspheme.

2. *Rightly integrated into Christian theology, the wrath of God enhances our grasp of God's love; it does not diminish it.* The point has often been made but not often more tellingly than by J. Gresham Machen in a passage I stumbled across recently:

> It is a strange thing that when men talk about the love of God, they show by every word that they utter that they have no conception at all of the depths of God's love. If you want to find an instance of true gratitude for the infinite grace of God, do not go to those who think of God's love as something that cost nothing, but go rather to those who in agony of soul have faced the awful fact of the guilt of sin, and then have come to know with a trembling wonder that the miracle of all miracles has been accomplished, and that the eternal Son has died in their stead.[38]

3. *There must be some sense in which God is praised for his wrath.* If I began this essay by intimating that the wrath of God is a "problem," in certain respects this intimation must be seen as an exercise in misdirection. God's wrath is a "problem" in that people withdraw from the category and often refuse to face realistically its prevalence in Scripture. But the biblical writers are not embarrassed when they treat the theme. This is surely because, for

37. Lester, *The Angry Christian*, 207.
38. J. Gresham Machen, *Selected Shorter Writings*, ed. D. G. Hart (Phillipsburg, NJ: P&R, 2004), 32.

them, the wrath of God is an entirely just and therefore admirable display of holiness as it confronts sin. To be embarrassed by what Scripture so clearly and repeatedly sets out as belonging to the character of God when he deals with rebels is not the stance of sophistication and moral superiority. Rather, it is the stance of arrogant disbelief. What right does the creature ever have to be embarrassed by the Creator? To disown the theme of judgment is to slouch toward the very first reported instance of doctrinal disavowal—the insistence of the serpent, "You will not certainly die" (Gen. 3:4). Far better and wiser is it to see that the theme of God's wrath provides, inter alia, another angle into who God is, into the blinding brilliance of his holiness (cf. Isa. 6). And this must end in worship.

4. *Try tears*. In his contribution to this volume, Pierre Berthoud reminds us that Moses interceded for the covenant community with such self-identification with them that he could pray, "But now, please, forgive their sin—but if not, then blot me out of the book you have written" (Exod. 32:32). Paul could wish himself accursed for those of his own race (Rom. 9:3). To speak faithfully of the wrath of God, very often what we most urgently need are tears.

A few years ago on a radio talk show with a large audience in Chicago, the host asked several guests to discuss whether anyone could be saved apart from Jesus. Three pooh-poohed the idea in graphic terms. The fourth was a Jewish-Christian believer on the faculty of Moody Bible Institute. His ethnic background was known by everyone there, so when it was his turn to speak, the host baited him by asking him if he thought his fellow Jews could be saved apart from Christ. This Christian brother began to weep, and then to sob quietly, uncontrollably. After a minute or two, the host said that he had never heard a more compelling reason to become a Christian.

So we teach the wrath of God, for faithfulness to Scripture demands it; and we follow Jesus and learn to weep over the city.

Historical
Perspectives

4

John Calvin
and the Hiddenness of God

PAUL HELM

Preliminary

In *John Calvin's Ideas* I denied myself the pleasure of examining Calvin's view of predestination in order to emphasize opposition to the idea that Calvin's entire theology is governed by this concept, that predestination is the "central dogma" of his theological system.[1] Having made this point, I now feel free to indulge myself! So this essay will consider some aspects of Calvin's doctrine of predestination—not, however, the "usual suspects," such as the sense in which it is absolute predestination, or whether it is single or double, or its relation to providence, but rather the doctrine of God implied by his view. Nor will this contribution be only an exercise in historical theology.

I want to engage with what I think is a terrific article by Bruce McCormack on Karl Barth's doctrine of election.[2] McCormack raises with Celtic clarity the sharpness of Karl Barth's departure from Calvin and the Reformed tradition on the place of the divine Logos in election and

1. Paul Helm, *John Calvin's Ideas* (Oxford: Oxford University Press, 2004).
2. Bruce L. McCormack, "Grace and Being: The Role of God's Gracious Election in Karl Barth's Theological Ontology," in *The Cambridge Companion to Karl Barth*, ed. John Webster (Cambridge: Cambridge University Press, 2000), 92–110. Page references in the main text are to this article.

predestination. He says that Calvin and Barth are in "collision" (98) over the matter and clearly shows at least some features of what worried Barth about Calvin's views in this area and of the nature of Barth's own response. Paradoxically, McCormack also suggests a way in which Calvin could have effectively replied to Barth. I shall show that this suggestion is close to what Calvin did in fact say, and it makes one wonder whether the problems that Barth had with Calvin in this area were not largely of his own making. So there was a collision, but fortunately Calvin was not in the car at the time.

This essay will focus on the relation of the Logos to human redemption and in particular on the relation of the preincarnate Logos to the person and work of Jesus Christ. There are two areas of concern here. The first is how we are to understand the character of the Logos when considered as logically prior to the incarnation. The second concerns what, if anything, we can say positively about the character of this Logos in relation to what, in the incarnation, this character comes to be. These are abstruse issues, certainly, and it may be thought that they are of merely theoretical interest, merely "theological" matters in the pejorative use of this word that politicians have given it. Neither Calvin nor Barth thought so, however, and we shall see that Calvin's and Barth's answers contain implications for the doctrine of God as a whole and have an impact on such perennial practical concerns as the assurance of salvation. So I hope that you will not get the impression that this is merely a game of theological ping-pong.

So, prompted by what McCormack says about Barth and Calvin, I shall address two questions to John Calvin:

1. According to Calvin, in the Triune God of the *decretum absolutum*, is the Second Person a *logos asarkos* and logically prior to the divine decree that the *logos* become incarnate? I shall show that the answer is "yes."
2. According to Calvin, is the Logos of the *decretum absolutum* "hidden" or "undetermined"? I shall try to show that in any clear sense of the question, the answer is "no."

These questions will be considered in the light of what Barth says about them. However, not being a Barth expert, I shall not only make use of McCormack's own comments on Barth but also rely on him for the interpretation of Barth.

Before we proceed to our questions, it is necessary to say something about some of the terms appearing in them. The *decretum absolutum* refers to the divine decree of predestination, absolute because (according to Calvin) it is not conditioned by God on anything meritorious that is foreseen in the one predestined. The phrase *logos asarkos* refers to the divine Logos considered apart from his incarnation as Jesus Christ. It is often contrasted with *logos ensarkos*. Logical priority is contrasted with temporal priority. Both Calvin (certainly) and Barth (I think) held that there was no time when the Logos was *asarkos*. But as the cup is logically prior to its rim but not temporally prior, so the *logos asarkos* is logically prior to the *logos ensarkos* but not temporally prior. There are other terms to be introduced that also require clarification, which I shall offer as we proceed. To our questions, then.

Calvin and the *Decretum Absolutum*

> 1. According to Calvin, in the Triune God of the *decretum absolutum*, is the Second Person a *logos asarkos* and logically prior to the divine decree that the *logos* become incarnate?

There can be no real debate about Calvin's view. According to him, the Logos remains *asarkos* even while he is incarnate, and a fortiori he is *asarkos* prior to the incarnation.[3] This follows from Calvin's commitment to the *extra Calvinisticum*, the view that in the incarnation God the Son, being *autotheos*, retained all essential divine properties, including immensity and omnipresence, and therefore could not be confined within the limits of a human person. It is disputed whether this view is unique to Calvin. In an excellent study, E. David Willis shows that the *extra Calvinisticum* might equally well be called the *extra Catholicum*, citing statements of it (or of its equivalent) from a host of Christian writers from Athanasius to Aquinas.[4] So, at least on the strength of this evidence, the position that we shall discuss represents an important strand of Christian orthodoxy.

In the *Institutes* Calvin refers explicitly to the *extra* in two places. First, in his discussion of the incarnation in book II:

> They thrust upon us as something absurd the fact that if the Word of God became flesh, then he was confined within the narrow prison of an earthly body. This is mere impudence! For even if the Word in his immeasurable essence united with the nature of man into one person, we do not imagine that he was confined therein. Here is something marvelous: the Son of God descended from heaven in such a way that, without leaving heaven, he willed to be borne in the virgin's womb, to go about the earth, and to

3. *Asarkos* is not a term used by Calvin, but I shall follow McCormack in this usage. Insofar as *asarkos* means "not at all enfleshed," then Calvin cannot be said to hold that Jesus Christ is *asarkos*. Calvin's point here, whatever the precise terminology, is that the Logos, when incarnate, was not encompassed or bounded by his human body.
4. E. David Willis, *Calvin's Catholic Christology* (Leiden: Brill, 1966).

hang upon the cross; yet he continuously filled the world as he had done from the beginning![5]

And, second, in his discussion of the nature of the Lord's Supper in book IV:

> But some are carried away with such contentiousness as to say that because of the natures joined in Christ, wherever Christ's divinity is, there also is his flesh, which cannot be separated from it. . . . But from Scripture we plainly infer that the one person of Christ so consists of two natures that each nevertheless retains unimpaired its own distinctive character. . . . Surely, when the Lord of glory is said to be crucified [1 Cor. 2:8], Paul does not mean that he suffered anything in his divinity, but he says this because the same Christ, who was cast down and despised, and suffered in the flesh, was God and Lord of glory. In this way he was also Son of man in heaven [John 3:13], for the very same Christ, who, according to the flesh, dwelt as Son of man on earth, was God in heaven. In this manner, he is said to have descended to that place according to his divinity, not because divinity left heaven to hide itself in the prison house of the body, but because even though it filled all things, still in Christ's very humanity it dwelt bodily [Col. 2:9], that is, by nature, and in a certain ineffable way. There is a commonplace distinction of the schools to which I am not ashamed to refer: although the whole Christ is everywhere, still the whole of that which is in him is not everywhere. And would that the Schoolmen themselves had honestly weighed the force of this statement. For thus would the absurd fiction of Christ's carnal presence have been obviated. Therefore, since the whole Christ is everywhere, our Mediator is ever present with his own people, and in the Supper reveals himself in a special way, yet in such a way that the whole Christ is present, but not in his wholeness.[6]

That is, the whole Christ is present with his people but not in every respect in which he is the Christ. As the Christ, he is embodied; nevertheless, he is wholly present even when not bodily present. The oddity and obscurity of this cannot be denied, any more than can the influence of Calvin's pronounced body-mind dualism upon his Christology.

In expounding this view, McCormack says that, for Calvin, "the second person of the Trinity was, at one and the same time, completely within the flesh of Jesus (spatially circumscribed) and completely without the flesh of Jesus (not limited by space)" (95). That is, at the incarnation the Second Person of the Trinity was both spatially circumscribed and not limited by space. Calvin does not say this, however, nor would he have

5. John Calvin, *Institutes of the Christian Religion*, II.13.4, ed. John McNeill, trans. Ford Lewis Battles (Philadelphia: Westminster; London: SCM, 1960).
6. Ibid., IV.17.30. For further discussion see Helm, *John Calvin's Ideas*, ch. 3.

said it, because he is too sensitive to the theological danger of uttering manifest self-contradictions, and this expression of McCormack's is manifestly self-contradictory. But it is not just Calvin's sensitivity to logic that forces him to dissent from this; he also has a strong theological reason. God is an infinite being and so cannot be spatially circumscribed. The Son of God, being God, is simple and indivisibly God and so cannot be circumscribed.

It is not this aspect of things, however, that troubles Barth. This is what he says about the *extra Calvinisticum*:

> We may concede that there is something unsatisfactory about the theory [viz., of the *extra Calvinisticum*], in that right up to our own day it has led to fatal speculation about the being and work of the *logos asarkos*, or a God whom we think we can know elsewhere and whose divine being we can define from elsewhere than in and from the contemplation of His presence and activity as the Word made flesh.[7]

Barth suggests a connection between what he takes to be Calvin's position and something he calls "fatal speculation," because it entails a God whose being we can "define" (note Barth's word) apart from the incarnation. But shortly we shall see that this charge goes against both the spirit and the letter of what Calvin says.

A second aspect of the question, the question of divine freedom, though it involves matters that are far from straightforward, can be straightforwardly answered. Calvin was an eternalist. He believed, along with his mentor Augustine, that God is outside time. So there was never a time in the existence of the Son of God when he was not *ensarkos*. This underlines the fact that Christ was *asarkos* only in being logically prior to his state of *ensarkos*. Even so, the Logos is freely *ensarkos*. His assuming of human nature is therefore not something essential to him as being immeasurable is essential to him. McCormack rightly says that, for Calvin and for the Reformed tradition, "there is a distinction between the Logos as he appears in the eternal plan of God (predestination) and the Logos as he appears in the actual execution of that plan in time" (94). But there is also a more basic distinction, between the Logos prior to the eternal plan of God and the Logos in that plan. What these distinctions imply is that it is not necessary, for Calvin, that there should be grace and mercy for sinners. The gracious plan of redemption is the result of God's free choice, which results in a "freely given promise,"[8] a choice in which (necessarily and naturally) the Logos participates and

---

7. Karl Barth, *Church Dogmatics* (Edinburgh: T&T Clark, 1956), IV/1:181.

8. Calvin, *Institutes of the Christian Religion*, III.2.30. Cf. Calvin's celebrated definition of faith (III.2.7). "Freely" here may connote not only choice but also liberality.

in accordance with which he freely undertakes to be the Mediator and to participate in executing the plan of God, his plan, in time.

This position is the result of a complex of ideas in Calvin. He is not committed to the unconditional necessity of the incarnation, and not always to its conditional necessity either.[9] God freely chose to redeem. So, with Catholic orthodoxy, Calvin affirms that the incarnation is contingent. So the *logos asarkos* was free not to become incarnate. Any additional choice that the Logos was free to make—for example, the choice to become incarnate through some other virgin than the Virgin Mary—is of secondary importance.

For Calvin to deny divine freedom in incarnation would be at odds with the freedom of God's grace—so central to his evangelical theology— which is freedom not only in the sense that there was nothing in fallen creation that necessitated that God act graciously but also in the sense that such grace is (according to God's unfathomable election) freely bestowed on some human beings and not on others. God could have justly withheld his mercy, and he could justly be merciful to Smith rather than to Jones. And he could justly have redeemed everyone.[10] The assertion "I will have mercy on whom I will have mercy" (Rom. 9:15) is foundational for Calvin, even if the mention of Jacob as the object of such mercy is thought to refer only to that person's role in the historic covenant with Israel and not to his eternal election as an individual (and Calvin quite naturally took it to refer to both).

> Who then, I pray, will say it is not meet that God should have in his own hand and will the free disposing of his graces, and should illuminate such nations as he wills? To evoke the preaching of his Word at such places as he wills? To give progress and success to his doctrine in such way and measure as he wills? To deprive the world, because of its ungratefulness, of the knowledge of his name for such ages as he wills, and according to his mercy to restore it when he again wills?[11]

Like Calvin, Barth has a central place for divine freedom, but in a rather stronger sense than that of Calvin. According to McCormack, as we may note from the title of his essay, with its reference to "theological

---

9. That the incarnation is conditionally necessary may be said to be Calvin's overall position in the *Institutes* and elsewhere. But in several places, such as his sermons on Galatians and on Isa. 53 and his commentary on John's Gospel (15:13), Calvin expresses the view that Christ's atonement was not even conditionally necessary. I am grateful to Jon Balserak for the first two of these references, to Carl Trueman for the third. In Helm, *John Calvin's Ideas*, I suggest that Augustine is the likely source for this view.

10. For discussion of this issue, see Oliver D. Crisp, "Augustinian Universalism," *International Journal for Philosophy of Religion* 53 (2003): 127–45.

11. Calvin, *Institutes of the Christian Religion*, II.11.14.

ontology," Barth's idea of election, and especially the election of Christ, has important implications not only for the freedom of God but for the very doctrine of God. For instance: "What Barth is suggesting is that election is an event in God's life in which he assigns to himself the being he will have for all eternity" (98), "the primal decision in which God assigned to himself the being he would have throughout eternity (a being-for the human race)" (100). We will return to consider these expressions.

But does this affirmation, by Calvin and the tradition, of the *logos asarkos* and his freedom in establishing a covenant of grace lead to speculation, as Barth suggests? Did it lead Calvin to speculate? Initially it may seem so. In remarks on the righteousness of God's will, Calvin claims that in the matter of election and reprobation, God's will is the rule of all righteousness, and this may seem to sanction speculation. For it may lead us to ask, What might God will or have willed?

> For his will is, and rightly ought to be, the cause of all things that are. For if it has any cause, something must precede it, to which it is, as it were, bound; this is unlawful to imagine. For God's will is so much the highest rule of righteousness that whatever he wills, by the very fact that he wills it, must be considered righteous. When, therefore, one asks why God has so done, we must reply: because he has willed it. But if you proceed further to ask why he so willed, you are asking for something greater and higher than God's will, which cannot be found.[12]

But note the bold qualification:

> And we do not advocate the fiction of "absolute might"; because this is profane, it ought rightly to be hateful to us. We fancy no lawless god who is a law unto himself. For, as Plato says, men who are troubled with lusts are in need of law; but the will of God is not only free of all fault but is the highest rule of perfection, and even the law of all laws. But we deny that he is liable to render an account; we also deny that we are competent judges to pronounce judgment in this cause according to our own understanding.[13]

So whatever the *logos asarkos* doctrine may sanction in respect of a God "elsewhere," Calvin is clear that we cannot speculate about such a God as if he were a "lawless" God. Calvin's attitude to such speculation is borne out by his remarks on the ill-advisedness of pitting God's might against his truth[14] and of not separating justice from power[15] and

12. Ibid., III.23.2.
13. Ibid.
14. Ibid., II.7.5.
15. Ibid., I.17.2.

by his insistence that the divine ordinances are just, even though this justice may be presently hidden from us.[16] And it is underscored by his principled avoidance of theological "What if?" questions.

Yet for Calvin, though God is not "elsewhere" in being lawless, he is hidden in other senses. God's essence is incomprehensible, yet he reveals himself to us.[17] Our minds cannot encompass his mind. And God's will, what he decrees, is usually secret, not disclosed to us in advance.[18] But surely Barth could not deny that, in any theological account of God, the finite cannot encompass the infinite, knowing God as he knows himself. Yet from Barth's alternative view—centered on Jesus Christ as the Subject of election—the reader gets very little sense, if any at all, that who God is and what he does are in any respect mysterious.[19] In Jesus Christ, God reveals *himself*. Presumably, Barth fears that any degree of mystery would offer an entry point into a God "elsewhere," opening the door to speculation. What really worries him, I fancy, however, is the fact that Calvin's doctrine of God's secret will embraces particularism—his doctrine of election and reprobation. As McCormack notes, Barth replaced Calvin's version of double predestination with a universal election (93). Although McCormack alleges that the question "To whom does election apply?" is, from Barth's point of view, a secondary question (93), I think that we can see here that this and the question "Who is the God who elects?" are in fact closely intertwined in Barth's thinking.

Calvin's overall position, then, is that we are not to attempt to go behind God's decree, using the doctrine of the *logos asarkos* or anything else, in order to speculate on what God in his power—either the power of God's will in abstraction from his nature or of the entire divine nature—might have decreed. It is for this reason also that Calvin condemns as "madness" the speculation of some, such as Ockham, over whether the Son of God could have taken upon himself the nature of an ass.[20] Here is one clear sense in which Calvin will not contemplate an "other" God, a God "elsewhere," namely, where this God is a God of pure will, of absolute power divorced from his essence, divorced particularly from the so-called moral attributes. But does he contemplate an "other" God

---

16. Ibid., III.23.9.

17. For further discussion, see Helm, *John Calvin's Ideas*, ch. 1.

18. For further discussion, see ibid., ch. 4.

19. Yet against this must be set Barth's view that the speech of God is part of the mystery of God (*Church Dogmatics*, I/1:162–86). "God loves us. . . . He is in Himself the One who loves. As such He is completely knowable to us. He is in Himself sovereignly free. He is therefore completely unknowable to us" (II/1:343). I have no idea how these two strands in Barth can be reconciled.

20. Calvin, *Institutes of the Christian Religion*, II.12.5. This reminds us that Barth's fear of speculation is matched by Calvin's own fear. For further discussion, see Helm, *John Calvin's Ideas*, ch. 1.

in some weaker sense and so fail to avoid Barth's strictures? This leads us to our second question.

> 2. According to Calvin, is the Logos of the *decretum absolutum* "hidden" or "undetermined"?

Here we arrive at the heart of the difference between Barth and Calvin. What is Barth's view of Calvin's alleged "hidden God"? It is not altogether clear, though fairly clear. Barth, in the final section from the passage already quoted, remarks,

> It was his [Calvin's] aim in that theory to hold to the fact that the Son of God who is wholly this man . . . is also wholly God and therefore omnipotent and omnipresent (and to that extent *extra carnem*, not bound or altered by its limitation). He is the Lord and Creator who because He becomes a creature and exists in that *forma servi* does not cease to be Lord and Creator and therefore to exist in the *forma Dei*.[21]

We may conclude from such a remark that Barth recognizes that, for Calvin, the *logos asarkos* is at least omnipotent and omnipresent, Lord and Creator. If so, he cannot be entirely hidden in his character. But this is not sufficient to alleviate his worries. In another discussion, Barth also comments,

> Is it the case that . . . while Christ is indeed the medium and instrument of the divine activity at the basis of the election, and to that extent He is the revelation of the election by which factually we must hold fast, yet the electing God Himself is not Christ but God the Father, or the triune God, in a decision which precedes the being and will and word of Christ, a hidden God, who as such made, as it were, the actual resolve and decrees to save such and such men and to bring them to blessedness, and then later made, as it were, the formal or technical decree and resolve to call the elect and to bring them to that end by means of His Son, by means of His Word and Spirit? . . . The thought of the election becomes necessarily the thought of the will and decision of God which are hidden somewhere in the heights or depths behind Jesus Christ and behind God's revelation.[22]

Here matters become somewhat murkier. The term "hidden God" is frequently used in connection with discussions of both Luther and Calvin, though McCormack does not use it in his exposition of Barth and Calvin. Its meaning is not very clear. There is an obvious sense in which God is hidden. He is invisible. And as we have seen, for Calvin and the tradition,

21. Barth, *Church Dogmatics*, IV/1:181.
22. Ibid., II/2:64.

God is "incomprehensible," not fully fathomable by the human mind. Further, as we have also noted, for Calvin, God has "secret" purposes that God has been pleased not to disclose to us. God has, so to speak, a private life. So we have two or three possible meanings for "hidden," and a good deal of further clarification is needed, clarification which, alas, Barth does not supply. So I prefer McCormack's term, "undetermined." Here is how he uses it and related expressions. Writing of seventeenth-century Reformed theologians' use of *incarnandus* ("to be incarnate") of the Logos, McCormack notes,

> In this view, the Logos is determined to be *incarnandus* in the eternal plan of God as a consequence of a *prior* decision made by the triune God. To be sure, any decision made by the Trinity is also made by the Logos. So there is a sense in which the Logos is also the Subject of this prior decision. But the Logos appears in this prior decision as One whose identity is *not yet* determined by the decision for incarnation. He is *incarnandus* only as a result of the subsequent decision; prior to making it, His being and existence are *undetermined.* (94, emphases in the original)

By "undetermined" in character, McCormack means something like "not decided or settled or fixed in respect of character." The fact that the Logos—and the entire Godhead—is logically prior to the decision to elect and reprobate and that God freely chooses to elect and to reprobate may seem to give McCormack even more reason to write that, in this view, for the Logos to be the Redeemer is "merely a role that he plays, something he does" (97). As McCormack points out, if this is true, it is so not only for the Logos but for each other member of the Trinity. If the Logos is indeterminate, then the Triune God is indeterminate, for the Logos is God. And if the Logos merely plays a "role" in redemption, then so do Father and Spirit.

Barth's idea is this: as the Subject of election, the Logos must already have the filled-out character of Jesus Christ. There is no logical "space" for him not to become incarnate as Jesus Christ. But Calvin's view was, Barth thinks, different. According to that view, the character of Jesus Christ is something that the Logos wills to assume at the behest of a covenantal arrangement involving the persons of the Trinity, including, of course, the Logos. If this is so, Barth thinks, then the Logos merely "plays a role" in willing to become incarnate in Jesus Christ. This is the significance of Barth's saying that Jesus Christ is not the object of election, even though, as the Logos of the undivided Trinity, he would participate in his own election, but is the Subject of election (95).

This claim seems to be (or to imply) this: that unless X is essentially a Y or is "defined" as a Y (as we saw Barth put it),[23] then becoming Y in

23. Ibid., IV/I:181.

time must merely be a "role" that the person assumes. The idea is that X could just as easily have assumed a different role.

But this is a fairly extreme claim. If you ask John Cleese to impersonate Winston Churchill as a war leader, then for a while he "assumes the role" of the great man, though being totally unfitted for the task. But what of Churchill himself? Churchill was not essentially a war leader, but he became one. Did he for this reason merely "play the role" of a war leader, as John Cleese may play the role of Churchill when he attempts to impersonate him? Clearly not. When war was declared, events proved that he was eminently fitted to be a war leader. There was a naturalness, a fittingness, between Churchill's character and temperament, together with his past political record before he became prime minister, and his decision to become prime minister in a time of war.

In similar fashion, may not what is naturally implied by the pre-Barthian Reformed (and Catholic) doctrine of the incarnation be that in freely willing to become incarnate in Jesus Christ, the *logos asarkos* did something which was a fit, consistent, or appropriate expression of his character, not only of his omnipotence and omnipresence and his being Lord and Creator but of what we may call his moral character? Interestingly, McCormack himself suggests the actual Calvinian response to the hiddenness charge when he asks of Barth, "Does he merely wish to say that the activity of God the Reconciler is the perfect expression of the divine essence (so that essence precedes act as the ground of the latter)?" (96). He goes on to show that Barth does not wish to say this. But Calvin most certainly did, as becomes clear in his remarks on *electio in Christo*:

> Accordingly, those whom God has adopted as his sons are said to have been chosen not in themselves but in his Christ [Eph. 1:4]; for unless he could love them in him, he could not honor them with the inheritance of his Kingdom if they had not previously become partakers of him. But if we have been chosen in him, we shall not find assurance of our election in ourselves; and not even in God the Father, if we conceive him as severed from his Son. Christ, then, is the mirror wherein we must, and without self-deception may, contemplate our own election. . . . Moreover, since he is the eternal wisdom of the Father, his unchangeable truth, his firm counsel, we ought not to be afraid of what he tells us in his Word varying in the slightest from that will of the Father which we seek. Rather, he faithfully reveals to us that will as it was from the beginning and ever shall be.[24]

What is Calvin saying here? That God (the Father) loves his sons (and daughters) in Christ but that God the Father must not be considered as

---

24. Calvin, *Institutes of the Christian Religion*, III.24.5. For further discussion, see Helm, *John Calvin's Ideas*, ch. 13.

being severed from his Son, who is the Father's eternal wisdom, whose will cannot deviate one scintilla from the Father's but reveals it. Not only cannot God the Father be hidden behind Christ the Subject of election; Christ is the full expression of the character of his Father. Not only (as we have already seen Barth recognize) do we know the Father in respect of omnipotence and omnipresence, and Lordship and Creatorhood, but also now in respect of wisdom and truth. How could it be otherwise if, for Calvin, the Son is himself *autotheos*?

But there is more. In the course of discussing the atonement, Calvin states,

> Thus he [God] is moved by pure and freely given love of us to receive us into grace. Since there is a perpetual and irreconcilable disagreement between righteousness and unrighteousness, so long as we remain sinners he cannot receive us completely. Therefore, to take away all cause for enmity and to reconcile us utterly to himself, he wipes out all evil in us by the expiation set forth in the death of Christ; that we, who were previously unclean and impure, may show ourselves righteous and holy in his sight. Therefore, by his love God the Father goes before and anticipates our reconciliation in Christ. Indeed, "because he first loved us" [1 John 4:19] he afterward reconciles us to himself.[25]

So, the Father, or the entire Godhead, expresses not only omnipotence and omnipresence, not only Lordship and Creatorhood (which Barth concedes that the *logos asarkos* implies), not only wisdom and truth, but also love. God the Father is moved by a pure and freely given love to redeem us in Christ. Thus Barth's claim, that Calvin's view implies that God is "hidden" or undetermined, seems excessive if not straight-forwardly false.

But there is even more. In places Calvin asserts the closest possible concurrence between the Father and the Son in the work of our redemption, as when he asserts,

> As many as were at last incorporated into the body of Christ were God's sheep. As Christ Himself testifies (John 10:16), though formerly wandering sheep and outside the fold. Meantime, though they did not know it, the shepherd knew them, according to that eternal predestination by which He chose His own before the foundation of the world, as Augustine rightly declares.[26]

25. Calvin, *Institutes of the Christian Religion*, II.16.3. If it is said that this is the language of the economic Trinity, the proper response is that Calvin saw no possibility of dislocation between the character of the immanent Trinity and that of the economic Trinity.

26. John Calvin, *Concerning the Eternal Predestination of God* (1552), trans. with an introduction by J. K. S. Reid (London: James Clarke, 1961), 150, cf. 127.

Who is the agent or, to use Barth's term, the "Subject" of predestination, according to Calvin here? Not the Father, or at least not the Father in distinction from the Son, a God "elsewhere." The Son himself, the shepherd, chose his own before the foundation of the world. He is the Subject of election, he eternally chose his own and as a good shepherd laid down his life for the sheep. But not in a way which separates him one smidgen from the Father. So, although God is in certain important respects "hidden," in these equally important respects he is most clearly visible.

Although Barth, though without justification, claims that Calvin's doctrine of election lands him with a "hidden God," Barth's own doctrine is certainly no improvement. As noted earlier, in emphasizing the freedom of God, Barth says—to use McCormack's words—that "God assigns to himself the being he will have for all eternity" (100), and "election is an event in God's life in which he assigns to himself the being he will have for all eternity" (98). And so election has implications for God's very being. We have already noted that, according to McCormack, Barth's is a universal election (93). John Webster likewise thinks that, for Barth, election "forms the centrepiece of the doctrine of God."[27] It would be ironic if we are witnessing the emergence of a Barthian "central dogma"!

Let us briefly consider McCormack's words. The pressing question is, *Who* is this God who assigns himself a being (presumably a being of a certain character) that he will have to all eternity? Despite Barth's pains to eliminate every vestige of a hidden God, the idea here returns with a vengeance, at least by McCormack's understanding. Barth is positing a God who assigns himself a being, or a character (but not, apparently, a "role"!). Barth's God freely gives himself the character of Redeemer together with all that is necessary for having such a character. But who is this God who so acts? It is no good saying, with McCormack, that "'essence' is given in the act of electing, and is, in fact, constituted by that eternal act" (99). Actions necessarily have agents. The act of electing is the act of someone; it cannot be an act of no one which, upon its occurrence, constitutes a someone. That is incoherent.

So Barth is hoisted by his own petard. The God of Karl Barth, who wills his essence in the act of electing, is by definition a hidden, undetermined God. Paradoxically—although, as we have seen, despite Barth's fears—Calvin's God is far from hidden, Barth's God is truly buried away. We are left with a much more radical sense of divine hiddenness surrounding this "primal decision" than Calvin's *electio in Christo*, for Calvin's view is that there is nothing more basic than the trinitarian character of God with the power and love to redeem. What could be more visible than such a Triune God?

27. John Webster, *Karl Barth*, 2nd ed. (London: Continuum, 2004), 88.

Besides being more radical, Barth's proposal carries with it all the problems beset by the alleged indeterminateness of God in Calvin. Any efforts to rid the proposal of such hiddenness by appealing to a "primal" character simply begs the question. Given Barth's radical view of divine freedom, this primal character must itself be constituted by a yet more hidden God, and so on ad infinitum. In any case, from the point of view of Barth's earlier remarks against Calvin's view, how can we escape the conclusion that for God to become the Trinity is for him to "play a role"? How could God *become trinitarian* in an action of election? It is clear what John Calvin, with his sharp eye for the presence of self-contradiction in theology, would have made of this suggestion. And what of the pastoral consequences of this? In Calvin's view, surely Barth's alleged cure for his doctrine of the hidden God would be far worse than the alleged disease.

Furthermore, Barth's own version of the claim that Jesus Christ is the Subject of election looks strongly deterministic; in fact, it amounts to a form of *logical* determinism, "being in the mode of anticipation" as McCormack puts it (100). Who is the Jesus who is the Subject of election? One would expect that he is the Christ we find unfolded in the pages of the New Testament. There is, after all, no other Jesus Christ knowable to us. Is it this Jesus? If it is, then this historical Jesus is logically determined to be as he is by the character of the preincarnate Logos as the character of the photograph is logically determined to be what it is by what it is a photograph of. If not, then to that extent the Subject of election remains, by Barth's own standards, a *Deus absconditus*. But perhaps not. Hiddenness is, after all, a matter of degree. Perhaps the Jesus Christ who is the Subject of election is somewhat like the historical Jesus Christ, like him in some of his main features. And perhaps this is an accurate understanding of Barth's own view, for the figure that is Barth's Subject of election has universalistic purposes. As McCormack puts it, he is "the Representative of all men and women" (105). I know that some people say Barth is not a universalist. But this doctrine looks to be universalist; in it universalism seems to be the default position, does it not?[28]

One reason for thinking that this is Barth's view is his pastoral concern. For him, only a universalistic Christ can have the sort of pastoral consequences which are desirable and which, according to Barth, Calvin's doctrine of predestination and election does not deliver on account of the alleged hiddenness of his God. But Barth's version of election in Christ can have these benign pastoral consequences only if, as he says, God's hiddenness is fully eliminated (66).

28. For the claim that Barth's theology entails universalism, see Oliver D. Crisp, "On Barth's Denial of Universalism," *Themelios* 29 (2003): 18–29.

Is it the case, then, that in the divine election as such we have to do ultimately, not with a divine decision made in Jesus Christ, but with one
which is independent of Jesus Christ and only executed by Him? Is it
the case that that decision made in Jesus Christ by which we must hold
fast is, in fact, only another and a later and subordinate decision, while
the first and true decision of election is to be sought—or if we follow the
pastoral direction had better not be sought—in the mystery of the self-
existent being of God, and of a decree made in the absolute freedom of
the divine being?

   If in any sense we are forced to accept this second interpretation, it
is inevitable that there should be tension between the theological truth
and the pastoral direction which would have us hold fast by Christ. And
in this tension it is the latter which will feel the strain the more seriously.
It is only those who accidentally have not experienced or suspected the
existence of the hidden truth who can really be satisfied with the advice
simply to hold fast by the incarnate Son of God and the Word and Spirit
of God and not enquire concerning the hidden will of the Father and of
the eternal Godhead.[29]

But if the Christ who is the Subject of election is a universalistic Christ,
then what has happened to the sharply particularistic Christ of the Gospels? And this raises another question in the area of assurance: how can
we be assured that the Jesus Christ who is the Subject of election—Barth's
Jesus Christ—is the true Jesus Christ and that the particularistic Jesus
of the Gospels is a false or deviant Christ? May not our uncertainty at
this point have adverse pastoral consequences? And how does Barth's
doctrine of universal election safeguard assurance, given God's hidden,
primal decision to be a Savior God? How do we know that God will not
change his mind?

   Calvin explicitly guards himself against the charge that the particularism of eternal election needs to lead to speculation and uncertainty
as to whether we are among the elect. We must not endeavor to reason
a priori from the doctrine of election. That way we shall find "no end,
in wand'ring mazes lost." Rather we must reason a posteriori from our
communion with Christ.

> If we have been chosen in him we shall not find assurance of our elec-
> tion in ourselves; and not even in God the Father, if we conceive him as
> severed from his Son. Christ, then, is the mirror wherein we must, and
> without self-deception may, contemplate our own election. For since it is
> unto his body the Father has destined those to be engrafted whom he has
> willed from eternity to be his own, that he may hold as sons all whom he
> acknowledges to be among his members, we have a sufficiently clear and

29. Barth, *Church Dogmatics*, II/2:64.

firm testimony that we have been inscribed in the book of life [cf. Rev. 21:27] if we are in communion with Christ.[30]

So I say, first, that Barth's supposition of a "hidden God" in Calvin is greatly exaggerated. God is not pure will for Calvin; he is a God who is revealed to us in a character fitted, perfectly fitted, to be for us incarnate in Jesus Christ in his Second Person. And Barth is saddled with a hidden God of his own. Second, for Barth, unless the Jesus Christ who is the Subject of election is the Jesus Christ of the New Testament, he is an a priori theological construct at variance with the Christ of the Gospels. And we may find ourselves having less confidence in such a Christ than Barth thinks we ought to have in the allegedly hidden God of Calvin.

Thinking Aloud

With immense erudition Barth noted some of the doctrinal specifics of Calvin's theology, on the *extra Calvinisticum* and on the *logos asarkos*. But we have also seen serious misunderstanding and exaggeration of Calvin's view. What took Barth in this direction? Could it be that in some of his historical evaluations, Barth is less driven by the need for historical accuracy than by a desire to present a revisionist doctrine of God, that he is driven by ideology? There also seems to be a strong fear of skepticism about God in Barth. He seems to have believed that unless God is "defined" (that is Barth's word) as the *logos ensarkos*, as Jesus Christ, then we necessarily confront a fearful, hidden God. But why does this follow? Less alarmingly, perhaps Barth simply believed he needed a foil, a point of contrast in order to set off his own view from that of Calvin's. In particular, he may have thought of his own developments as countering the dangers that he believed to be inherent in Calvin's views, even though, when looked at squarely, these dangers appear to be more imaginary than real and his own revisionist proposals no improvement.[31]

30. Calvin, *Institutes of the Christian Religion*, III.24.5.

31. Thanks are due to David Hoffner and Oliver Crisp, who helped me in various ways in the preparation of this paper, which has been revised in the light of comments made at the conference.

5

Jonathan Edwards's God

Trinity, Individuation,
and Divine Simplicity

Oliver D. Crisp

And if they had been taught aright,
Small children carried bedwards,
Would shudder lest they meet that night,
The God of Mr. Edwards.

Abraham's God, the Wrathful One,
Intolerant of error.
Not God the Father, or the Son,
But God, the Holy Terror.

Phyllis McGinley

Thankfully, the caricature of Jonathan Edwards's doctrine of God captured by Phyllis McGinley's poem is now receding into the past. Gone are the days when a passing familiarity with an anthologized version of the dreaded Enfield Sermon, "Sinners in the Hands of an Angry God," was thought sufficient to inform a person about the nature of Edwards's theology or even—perish the thought!—Edwards's understanding of God. This essay is an attempt to make sense of one important aspect of what is perhaps the center of his doctrine of God, the Holy Trinity. In the recent literature, several essays have touched upon the way in which Edwards individuates the persons of the Trinity, although much of this discussion has been concerned to establish the extent to which Edwards's doctrine reflects social and/or psychological analogies of the Trinity.[1] I shall not address this question directly. Instead this essay contributes to the discussion of Edwards's doctrine of the Trinity by considering his understanding of the individuation of the divine persons of the Trinity. There are several different *strategies* that can be discerned in Edwards's writings on this matter.[2] One of these is an a priori argument for the Trinity, which attempts, unsuccessfully, to make sense of the Augustinian (and biblical) argument that the Son is the very image of the Father. Another involves a novel way of conceiving the individuation of the divine persons via their divine attributes, a way that is illuminating but, in several important respects, problematic. Where Edwards's

1. See, e.g., William J. Danaher Jr., *The Trinitarian Ethics of Jonathan Edwards* (Louisville: Westminster John Knox, 2004), chs. 1–2; Paul Helm, "Editor's Introduction to Jonathan Edwards," in Jonathan Edwards, *Treatise on Grace and Other Posthumously Published Writings* (London: James Clarke, 1971); Stephen R. Holmes, *God of Grace and God of Glory: An Account of the Theology of Jonathan Edwards* (Edinburgh: T&T Clark, 2000), ch. 2; Sang Lee, "Editor's Introduction to Jonathan Edwards," in Jonathan Edwards, *Writings on the Trinity, Grace, and Faith*, Works of Jonathan Edwards 21 (New Haven: Yale University Press, 2003), 1–34; Amy Plantinga Pauw, *"The Supreme Harmony of All": The Trinitarian Theology of Jonathan Edwards* (Grand Rapids: Eerdmans, 2002), and "Response," *Scottish Journal of Theology* 57 (2004): 486–89 (her response to Steven Studebaker's review article of *"The Supreme Harmony of All"*); Steven M. Studebaker, "Jonathan Edwards's Social Augustinian Trinitarianism: An Alternative to a Recent Trend," *Scottish Journal of Theology* 56 (2003): 268–85, and "Supreme Harmony or Disharmony?" review of *"The Supreme Harmony of All"* by Pauw, *Scottish Journal of Theology* 57 (2004): 479–84; there is also relevant material in Robert W. Jenson, *America's Theologian: A Recommendation of Jonathan Edwards* (New York: Oxford University Press, 1988); and Michael J. McClymond, *Encounters with God: An Approach to the Theology of Jonathan Edwards* (Oxford: Oxford University Press, 1998). There are other places where this is discussed, but these are some of the most important treatments in the recent literature.

2. The two strategies I consider are not meant to be exhaustive, merely representative. There is, arguably, another strategy in Edwards's early idealist thought about the necessity of plurality in the divine nature in order for God to exemplify "excellency." This Edwardsianism has to do with God being a perfect and hence excellent being, which reflects something of the medieval perfect-being theological tradition with an aesthetic twist (excellency having to do with beauty and proportion as well). But this early philosophical foray by Edwards is neither systematic nor fully trinitarian (a plurality in God is necessary but not sufficient to the purpose). Nor is the extent to which Edwards remained committed to the idealism of his youth in his more mature thinking entirely clear (to me at least). For these reasons, we will not consider what we might dub his "argument from excellency to plurality (in the divine nature)" here. This view of Edwards's idealist argument is not, however, shared by all. Danaher refers to it as part of Edwards's use of a social analogy in his doctrine of the Trinity! See Danaher, *The Trinitarian Ethics of Jonathan Edwards*, 69–71.

thinking comes to grief, it poses important questions about the extent to which Edwards was able to reconcile his trinitarian theology with his commitment to divine simplicity. It also raises a similar question for contemporary theological reflection on the relationship between the Trinity and the classical doctrine of divine simplicity. This is, I suggest, a problem which contemporary theologians committed to a classical doctrine of God need to address.

Edwards does not formulate his views on this topic in a systematic fashion. Despite his logical bent of mind, Edwards, like Augustine, did not leave a systematic body of divinity. But this is not to say he was not someone who thought systematically; he did, and one of his great, un-finished projects was a systematic theology, *The History of the Work of Redemption*. His circumstances dictated that the work he did complete during his lifetime was occasional in nature, directed to the goal of representing classical theology by using the tools of the early Enlightenment.[3] What is more, Edwards's thinking on the Trinity was never in the final form he wished it to be. During his lifetime he did not publish a sustained treatment of the doctrine. The literary remains we have of Edwards's doctrine of the Trinity are piecemeal, and there is no clear indication that he intended to publish them, as there is with other work that remained unpublished at his death (such as his "Two Dissertations").[4] The fragmentary nature of Edwards's work on the Trinity and the fact that this work was not in the public domain for some time have generated a number of false trails in the literature on Edwards, with some early interpreters even whispering that Edwards did not hold to an orthodox doctrine of the Trinity.[5] There are several places in which his doctrine of the Trinity is developed, including his *Observations concerning the Trinity and the Covenant of Redemption*, the *Essay on the Trinity* (now often referred to as the *Discourse on the Trinity*), *The End of Creation*, as well as some of his *Miscellanies*, particularly no. 94. (His *Miscellanies* were a semipublic set of notebooks in which Edwards kept a careful record

3. Douglas A. Sweeney makes a similar point: "Edwards was an occasional rather than a systematic thinker. He did not present his theology in a well-wrapped package, with all its loose ends neatly tied up. His thought emerged from his pastoral labours, from his love affair with the Bible, and from the heat of controversy" in *Nathaniel Taylor, New Haven Theology, and the Legacy of Jonathan Edwards* (Oxford: Oxford University Press, 2003), 11. Cf. the final chapter of Pauw, *"The Supreme Harmony of All."*

4. At his death, the "Two Dissertations," consisting of *The End of Creation* and *True Virtue*, were found among Edwards's papers bound with a blue ribbon, in a fair hand, apparently set aside ready for publication. See Paul Ramsey, "Editor's Introduction to Jonathan Edwards," in Jonathan Edwards, *Ethical Writings*, Works of Jonathan Edwards 8 (New Haven: Yale University Press, 1989).

5. Such an assertion was made in the late nineteenth century by Oliver Wendell Holmes Sr. See Helm, "Editor's Introduction to Jonathan Edwards," 1–5.

of his intellectual development, jotting down ideas, arguments, and ruminations that he later plundered for his published treatises. They were semipublic because he apparently used them in the instruction of ministerial students who stayed with him while he was minister at Northampton.)[6] These works—in particular, the *Essay on the Trinity*—are at the heart of what follows.[7]

Edwards's A Priori Argument for the Trinity

We begin with the first strategy in Edwards's writings, his a priori argument for the Trinity.[8] What we will see is that Edwards's attempt at an a priori Trinity, although motivated by a pious desire to understand something of the biblical doctrine, is extremely problematic.[9] Indeed, given Edwards's reasoning, it is not difficult to see why some nineteenth-century interpreters of Edwards thought he had abandoned orthodox trinitarianism. Yet like Anselm's ontological argument, Edwards's a priori argument has retained a fascination for Edwardsian scholars.

Edwards had a high view of the capacity of human reason to comprehend what can be known of the doctrine of the Trinity, while maintaining, it must be said, that the Trinity was a profound mystery.[10]

> I think it really evident from the light of reason that there are these three distinct in God. If God has an idea of himself, there is really a duplicity; because [if] there is no duplicity, it will follow that Jehovah thinks of

6. For discussion of this point, see Ava Chamberlain, ed., introduction to *The "Miscellanies" 501–832*, Works of Jonathan Edwards 18 (New Haven: Yale University Press, 2000).

7. All references to, and pagination for, *Observations Concerning the Trinity* and *Essay on the Trinity* are taken from Edwards, *Treatise on Grace and Other Posthumously Published Writings*. All other references to Edwards's works are from the Works of Jonathan Edwards series (1957–).

8. Edwards is not alone in trying to demonstrate the reasonableness of the Trinity a priori. Anselm, for example, does just this in *Proslogion* XXIII, where he says that God is triune and simple. And in recent times Richard Swinburne has presented an a priori argument for the Trinity in *The Christian God* (Oxford: Oxford University Press, 1994), ch. 8, in the tradition of Bonaventure and Richard of Saint-Victor.

9. For a treatment of Edwards's a priori argument in the wider context of his idealist take on the psychological analogy for the Trinity, see Helm, "Editor's Introduction to Jonathan Edwards"; Danaher, *The Trinitarian Ethics of Jonathan Edwards*, ch. 1. For reasons of space, I shall be concerned only with the a priori argument here.

10. "I am far from pretending to explain the Trinity so as to render it no longer a mystery. I think it to be the highest and deepest of all divine mysteries still, notwithstanding anything I have said or conceived about it. I don't intend to explain the Trinity" (Jonathan Edwards, *Essay on the Trinity* [pp. 121–22]).

himself no more than a stone. And if God loves himself and delights in himself, there is really a triplicity, three that cannot be confounded, each of which are the Deity substantially. And this is the only distinction that can be found or thought in God.[11]

The cogency of his claim to be able to demonstrate the coherence of the doctrine of the Trinity a priori is not the concern of the present discussion. But how Edwards uses this opportunity to delineate the persons of the Trinity is. Edwards is careful to point out, in distinguishing the divine persons, that the divine essence truly and distinctly subsists in both the divine idea (the Son), and the divine love (the Spirit) and that each is a distinct person (alongside the Father). This is a way of thinking about the divine persons that goes back to Augustine at least (although Edwards does not acknowledge this).[12] In order to understand why Edwards believed that naked reason alone was able to formulate the outline of a doctrine of the Trinity, we need to consider his argument in places such as "Miscellany 94" and *Essay on the Trinity*. There Edwards's main contention is that reason serves to justify the notion that the three persons of the Trinity are all distinct and all participate in the divine essence. Moreover, in keeping with orthodoxy, the divine persons can be individuated in a way that ensures they all share in the one divine essence, while retaining those properties particular to the function of each divine person.

Of the Father, Edwards says little. He is "the deity subsisting in a prime, unoriginated and absolute manner," in "direct existence."[13] He is not begotten and is not proceeding.[14] Edwards has much more to say on the Son and the Spirit.

---

11. Jonathan Edwards, "Miscellany 94," in *The "Miscellanies" (Entry Nos. a–z, aa–zz, 1–500)*, ed. Thomas A. Schafer, Works of Jonathan Edwards 13 (New Haven: Yale University Press, 1994), 262. Taken in isolation, this is a somewhat puzzling statement. Edwards does not explain in this miscellany why only these things are distinctions in God. Why not include "God revealing himself," or "God expressing himself," or "God glorifying himself" as distinctions in God, since they seem, prima facie, to be distinct acts? The obvious answer lies in Edwards's commitment to a classical "pure act" (*actus purus*) account of the divine nature, which denies any distinction between the being and acts of God. But then, as we shall see, one has to give some account of how there can be any distinctions in the divine nature whatsoever. I have argued this point in Oliver D. Crisp, "Jonathan Edwards on Divine Simplicity," *Religious Studies* 39 (2003): 23–41. See also Stephen Holmes, "Does Jonathan Edwards Use a Dispositional Ontology? A Response to Sang Hyun Lee," in *Jonathan Edwards: Philosophical Theologian*, ed. Paul Helm and Oliver D. Crisp (Aldershot, UK: Ashgate, 2003).

12. Robert W. Jenson notes that it can be found in Origen also. See Jenson, *Systematic Theology*, vol. 1, *The Triune God* (New York: Oxford University Press, 1997), 99.

13. Edwards, *Essay on the Trinity* (p. 118).

14. Edwards, "Miscellany 94," 257.

With respect to the Second Person of the Trinity, Edwards, like Augustine, takes up the biblical picture of the Son as the perfect idea of the Father (cf. Col. 1:15 and Heb. 1:3). One presentation of this argument that has attracted attention in the literature is derived from Edwards's mantra that God delights in himself as the one truly excellent being who does all things for his own glory. This argument can be found in "Miscellany 94" and in *Essay on the Trinity* in particular.[15] I shall present here a synthetic account of Edwards's central argument for the individuation of the Word, drawing upon these sources in Edwards's corpus.

He reasons as follows: God's perfect, infinite delight is in himself, not in any other created thing. This divine self-delight is equivalent to God's infinite delight in his Son, the reason being that his infinite delight is in himself, and God, unlike human beings, has a perfect *idea* of the object of his delight. (The Son is, of course, the perfect idea of himself that Edwards has in mind.) So God has a perfect idea that is the object of God's delight, and this idea is a perfect idea of *himself* (i.e., this idea is the Son).

This presumes that the idea of himself that God has must be a *perfect* idea, as befits a perfect being. It also presumes that the perfect idea that God takes such delight in must be a perfect idea of *himself* for God to be able to truly and completely delight in this idea. For—to reason in an Edwardsian fashion for a moment—if God is a perfect being, it could be argued that it is a virtue, rather than a vice or the result of vanity, for God to take infinite delight in the idea he has of himself. After all, a perfect being must delight in what is perfect. And the perfect idea God has of himself is, presumably, a perfect idea of a perfect being. So God must delight in the perfect idea of himself. As Edwards says, "'Tis often said that God is infinitely happy from all eternity in the view and enjoyment of himself, in the reflection and converse love of his own essence, that is, in the perfect idea he has of himself, infinitely perfect."[16]

Problems with Edwards's A Priori Argument for the Trinity

But there is a crucial sleight of hand in this reasoning. What Edwards says is that God takes infinite delight in himself *and* God takes infinite delight *in his perfect idea of himself*. This seems contradictory: how can God have an infinite delight in himself and also have an infinite delight in something other than himself, namely, his perfect idea of himself? Edwards tries to solve this problem by asserting that a perfect idea of a thing is the very thing itself, "for it wants nothing that is in the thing,

15. Ibid., 256–63; and Edwards, *Essay on the Trinity* (pp. 99–108).
16. Edwards, "Miscellany 94," 257.

substance or nothing else."[17] So God's idea of himself (God's idea of
the object of his infinite delight, which, as Edwards has already said,
is himself) is itself God, for "whatsoever is perfectly and absolutely like
a thing, is that thing."[18] As Edwards is well aware, however, Scripture
teaches that God's infinite delight is in his Son (Matt. 12:18; John 3:3;
Eph. 1:6).

Edwards acknowledges that it is not reasonable to assume that God's
infinite delight is in his idea of himself (which is itself God) *and* that
his infinite delight is also, additionally, in his Son as a separate entity.[19]
Thus Edwards seems to have reasoned himself to a standstill. On the
one hand, he asserts that God's infinite self-delight and the idea God
has of this infinite self-delight are, contrary to what we would normally
think, one and the same thing. Both are divine. On the other, he says
that, despite this, Scripture teaches that God's infinite delight is in his
Son, who is a distinct person in the Godhead. But he cannot have it both
ways. Either the Son is the object of the Father's infinite self-delight, in
which case we have an intratrinitarian relation between the Father and
Son that distinguishes the First from the Second Person of the Trinity.
Or alternatively, the Father's infinite self-delight is in himself or in his
idea of himself. But Edwards has not shown how the Father's infinite
self-delight can, at one and the same time, encompass all of (a) his infinite
self-delight, (b) the idea God has of his infinite self-delight, and (c) the
fact that the Father's infinite delight is in his Son, a distinct person of the
Trinity. His assertion that God's "infinite delight in the idea of himself
is the same with the infinite delight he has in his Son; and if so, his Son
and the idea he has of himself are the same,"[20] coupled with the previous comments, simply does not make sense. Taken together with his
earlier claim that God's idea of his infinite self-delight is itself God, this
means that there is no distinction whatsoever between the Father and
the Son. They are one and the same entity. In one sense, it is orthodox
to say that the Father and the Son are both God. But the mystery of the
Trinity is that, despite this fact, there are attributes that distinguish these
two divine persons. Taken in one direction, Edwards's position entails
that there are no such attributes. In which case, there can be no such
distinctions in the Godhead, and we have a version of modalism (the
heresy that the different persons of the Godhead are merely "masks"
worn by one divine entity). But Edwards's thinking can be taken in a
very different direction. He maintains that God's infinite delight is in
his perfect idea of himself, which is another divine person. That is, the

17. Ibid., 258.
18. Ibid.
19. Ibid., 259.
20. Ibid.

divine idea of infinite self-glorification *just is* another divine person, the person of the Son. But then we no longer have an a priori argument for the individuation of the Second from the First Person of the Trinity. Instead, as both Paul Helm in the twentieth and Benjamin Warfield in the nineteenth century have shown, we have an a priori argument that yields two Gods.[21] The problem that Helm and Warfield detect can be stated thus: If X has a perfect idea of Y and X's perfect idea of Y somehow entails that Y exists, then Edwards has demonstrated too much. Instead of another person in the Trinity, he is left with a second divine essence, a second God. Moreover, as Helm points out, the assumption upon which this rests, that an idea of X (X being immaterial) is equivalent to an instance of X, appears fallacious. I can have an idea of happiness without being happy.

As if the situation were not serious enough for this particular Edwardsian strategy for individuating the Father and the Son (no mention of the Holy Spirit as yet), there is another serious problem in the neighborhood. Edwards's argument entails the infinite iterability of ideas in the divine mind. Assume, with Edwards, that a perfect idea of a thing is that thing itself, "for," as Edwards says, "it wants nothing that is in the thing, substance or nothing else" and that "whatsoever is perfectly and absolutely like a thing, is that thing."[22] If these are taken at face value, then the following are all true:

a. God infinitely and perfectly delights in himself (which is itself an infinite and perfect idea in the divine mind).
b. God infinitely and perfectly delights in the infinitely perfect idea of himself.
c. God infinitely and perfectly delights in the infinitely perfect idea of his infinite and perfect delight in himself . . . etc.

This arises because there are no unrealized possibilities in the divine mind, according to Edwards. He held the classical *actus purus* (pure act) account of the divine nature, according to which there is no dis-

21. See Helm, "Editor's Introduction to Jonathan Edwards," 20–21, following Benjamin B. Warfield's comments in "The Biblical Doctrine of The Trinity," in *Works*, vol. 2, *Biblical Doctrines* (Oxford: Oxford University Press, 1929), 137–38. It seems to me that the Helm-Warfield attack on Edwards is slightly wide of the mark, since they set the problem up in terms of an idea of a particular thing and a physical instance of a particular thing. But Edwards is not concerned with physical things. Still, it is the case that Edwards's argument falls foul of a modified Helm-Warfield attack. He is still guilty of "reasoning into existence" a second divine *being*, not merely a second divine person of the Trinity.

22. Edwards, "Miscellany 94," 258.

tinction between God's being and act.[23] Thus the infinite delight God
has in himself seems infinitely iterable. Edwards may not consider this
to be a serious problem for his view. If the divine mind is infinite, then
why cannot God have an infinite regress of infinite and perfect ideas
of himself? But assume that God has an infinite number of infinitely
perfect ideas of ideas . . . and so on, in an infinite regress of infinite and
perfect ideas of himself in his divine mind. Then, it seems, given the
logic of Edwards's position, there are an infinite number of persons in
the Godhead by an application of Aristotle's third-man argument. God
has an infinite and perfect idea of himself. This idea is an infinite and
perfect idea of an infinite and perfect idea . . . and so on. Then we are left
with an infinite number of divine ideas and a correspondingly infinite
number of persons in the Godhead.

But we have already hinted that there is more than one direction in
which Edwards's argument could be taken. Edwards could be understood
as saying that we do not have an infinite regress of divine persons but
something more like an infinite number of "descriptions" of just one
divine person. Recall that, according to Edwards, God's "infinite delight
in the idea of himself is the same with the infinite delight he has in his
Son; and if so, his Son and the idea he has of himself are the same."[24] If
we follow this line of thought in Edwards's argument, then we are left
with something like this:

> God = his idea of himself = his idea of his idea of himself = his
> idea of his idea of his idea of himself . . . etc.

So, even if Edwards is successful in his bid to individuate the Son a priori,
he actually ends up proving too much; the third-man argument applies,
and we have an infinite regress of divine persons. But if Edwards is not
successful and his argument turns out to be modalist, the third-man
argument applies once more, and we have a reductio ad absurdum.

We come, more briefly, to Edwards's individuation of the Holy Spirit.
He explains that the Holy Spirit is required as the perfect act of love
and delight subsisting between the Father and the Son. This act of delighting in and loving each other is distinct from both the Father and
the Son, since

23. See text above and *Essay on the Trinity* (pp. 108–9), where Edwards says that
the Holy Spirit is "the eternal and most perfect and essential act of the divine nature,
wherein the Godhead acts to an infinite degree and in the most perfect manner possible.
The Deity becomes all act, the Divine essence itself flows out and is as it were breathed
forth in love and joy. . . . The name of the third person of the Trinity, viz. the Holy Spirit
. . . naturally expresses *the Divine nature as subsisting in pure act* and perfect energy"
(emphasis added).

24. Edwards, "Miscellany 94," 259.

the delight and energy that is begotten in us by an idea is distinct from the idea. So it cannot be confounded in God, either with God begetting or [with] his idea and image, or Son. It is distinct from the other two, and yet it is God. For the pure and perfect act of God is God, because God is a pure act. It appears that this is God, because that which acts perfectly is all act, and nothing but act.[25]

So the Holy Spirit is required as a distinct person in the Trinity, who acts as the *vinculum caritatis* (bond of love) between the Father and the Son.

Edwards maintains that these three are all the distinctions that can be found in God and that no other distinctions can be reasonably demonstrated. If God is perfect and thinking, then God must have an idea of himself. And if God is perfect, this idea must itself be a perfect representation of God in whom he delights. And since God does not change in his thoughts about himself, this idea must be eternal and eternally begotten by the Father. Thus the Son is the eternally begotten idea of the Father. And since the Father and the Son subsist in a relationship of infinite love and delight in each other, there must be an act that is distinct from either, namely, this act of loving and delighting between Father and Son. And this love and delight are eternal as well as distinct from the Father and the Son; hence the Holy Spirit is spirated (by the Father) and proceeds from both the Father and the Son.[26]

Unfortunately, this argument for the individuation of the Holy Spirit seems susceptible to the same sort of problem that the Helm-Warfield attack raised for the individuation of the Son. If the Father and the Son infinitely and perfectly delight in the Holy Spirit, then there are four persons in the Godhead. On the basis of Edwards's own reasoning, if the love and delight of the Father and the Son are a love and delight in something other than the Father and the Son, then the Father and the Son love and delight in some other person of the Godhead. (Or some thing other than the Godhead that gives rise to this relation of love and delight—but let us ignore this possibility.) But here is a question: Does this other divine person love and delight in himself? If he does, then we seem to have the same problem of the third-man argument as before. That is, if the Holy Spirit delights in himself and the infinite and perfect idea of his delight in himself is himself, then, presumably, the Holy Spirit

25. Ibid., 260.
26. Ibid., 262. Compare the following: "God is glorified within himself these two ways: (1) by appearing or being manifested to himself in his own perfect idea, or, in his Son, who is the brightness of his glory; (2) by enjoying and delighting in himself, by flowing forth in infinite love and delight towards himself, or, in his Holy Spirit" (Edwards, "Miscellany 448," in *The "Miscellanies" (Entry Nos. a–z, aa–zz, 1–500)*, 495). It is clear from the context that these two ways are to be taken exhaustively.

also infinitely and perfectly delights in the infinite and perfect idea of his delight in himself and so on ad infinitum. In which case, we have much more than a Trinity.

Taken together with what has already been said regarding the individuation of the Son from the Father in Edwards's a priori argument, this problem with the individuation of the Holy Spirit means that this first Edwardsian strategy is subject to serious and debilitating objections.[27]

Edwards on "Real" Distinctions and "Relations of Existence" in the Godhead

We come to the second strategy in Edwards's writings. Unlike the first, this is more promising, although it too is not without difficulties. This second strategy relies upon a distinction between different divine attributes and an idiosyncratic apportioning of divine attributes to the divine persons.[28]

First, Edwards speaks of *"real"* attributes that can be predicated of *one and only one person of the Trinity*. In the *Essay on the Trinity* in particular, but also in *The End of Creation* and "Miscellany 94," Edwards clearly identifies many of the divine attributes traditionally thought to belong to the divine essence with one or other (but not more than one) of the persons of the Trinity. Wisdom is seen as the preserve of the Son, along with related attributes such as omniscience (since, as the idea of God, the Son is the perfect representation of the knowledge of God in its entirety). The attributes of holiness, justice, goodness, mercy and grace, love, happiness, and will are all attributed to the Holy Spirit. In the *Essay on the Trinity* in particular, Edwards maintains that it is a theological principle that all predicates pertaining to God must pick out some real

27. Stephen Holmes has suggested to me that Edwards's a priori argument might be taken as a way of thinking about the so-called relations of origin in the Trinity. One traditional way of individuating the divine persons relies on relational properties that denote the "origin" of each divine person in the ontological Trinity, e.g., the Son as "eternally begotten," the Spirit as "proceeding from Father and Son," etc. But even if this observation is right, it does not get around the fact that, *as it stands*, Edwards's argument is open to the criticisms I have enumerated.

28. For present purposes, I shall speak of divine attributes rather than divine properties. This is a deliberate maneuver. It could be argued that divine attributes are not divine properties as such but merely predicates that are applied to the divine nature. This distinction is important if properties are thought to be distinct abstract objects to which sentences may refer whereas predicates are merely linguistic conventions that do not (necessarily) refer to abstract objects. Someone who held a traditional account of divine simplicity might take this view, and Edwards defends a traditional view of divine simplicity. But to my knowledge, he does not make the distinction between predicates, attributes, and properties.

attribute ("real" in the Edwardsian sense) and not a "mere relation" or "modality" that God has.

> It is a maxim amongst divines that everything that is in God is God which must be understood of real attributes and not of meer [sic] modalities. If a man should tell me that the immutability of God is God or that the omnipresence of God and the authority of God, is God, I should not be able to think of any rational meaning of what he said. It hardly sounds to me proper to say that God's being without change is God, or that God's being everywhere is God, or that God's having a right of government over creatures is God.[29]

Attempts to speak of modalities and relations as if they were real attributes and as if they actually picked out something substantial in God are, according to Edwards, actually meaningless. Accordingly, all distinctions that can be truly predicated of God pertain to his real attributes, since with all real attributes, such as love or wisdom, deity subsists in them distinctly, since they are aspects of divine persons. Or as he puts it, "all attributes can be reduced to these, or to the degree, relation and circumstance of these."[30]

This brings us into the second group of attributes, namely, *modes and relations of existence*. Among these, Edwards lists infinity or extent, eternity or duration, and immortality, immutability, and power. They are all, he claims, modes and relations between things, which all existing things possess in some measure, since all things have some duration, extent, (im)mutability, and power. For example, Tony Blair persists through time for a particular duration and has a certain extension in space during that period. He is mutable (unlike God) and has certain powers pertaining to his humanity and strength and so on. Conversely, God has no duration (being timelessly eternal according to Edwards) or extent and is omnipotent and immutable. Clearly, there are significant differences between God and all other existing things (since all other existing things are created and therefore mutable, finite, and contingent). Yet all things share the common characteristic of having relations and modes of existence. God is not peculiar among existing things in having such relations. But according to Edwards, the relations of existence that God does have *insofar as the created order is concerned* are peculiar *to* God.

In contemporary language, we might put it like this: God alone has a relation of maximal power with respect to the creation, and no other thing has this relation because no other thing can have power in a maximal way. This seems to imply that the difference envisaged by Edwards is one of

29. Edwards, *Essay on the Trinity* (p. 119).
30. Edwards, *The End of Creation*, 528.

quantity, not quality. God shares with all existing things the fact of having relations of existence, such as power. But the relations that God has with the created order in particular are of a maximal kind (i.e., omnipotence) whereas all created relations are limited, finite, and contingent.

Divine power, however, appears to be rather equivocal in Edwards's philosophical theology. In addition to being a relation between God and the created order, it is also described by Edwards as a relation that resides ultimately in the Father. In "Miscellany 94" Edwards says that power always consists in the power *to do something*. It might be said that Tony Blair has the power to raise his right arm, or to invoke the Act of Parliament, or to perform certain feats of physical strength. But such power is not something distinct from Tony Blair; it is, according to Edwards, "only a relation of adequateness and sufficiency of the essence to everything." But when God's power is under consideration, "'tis nothing else but the essence of God."[31] This can be pushed further, however. If, says Edwards, divine power is the means by which God exerts himself, then this is a property of the Father, which he exercises to his own glory, incorporating the manifestation of that power *ad extra*, in creation.

From this it is apparent that, according to Edwards, "real" distinctions pertain to the persons of the Trinity, rather than the divine essence as traditionally understood. Furthermore, for Edwards, the Father exercises divine power in the generation of the Son, the spiration and procession of the Spirit, and the continuous creation of the world. Edwards wants this to remain distinct, however, from mere modes or relations of existence in God, which do not characterize an attribute of God beyond picking out properties that all existing things have in some measure qua existing things (such as duration, extent, mutability, and power). So power seems to be a predicate that serves as both a real and a relational attribute. It is a relation that all things share but that God has, or is, essentially in a maximal degree/way. Perhaps what Edwards means to say is that divine power is the preserve of the Father but is appropriated by the other persons of the Trinity via a doctrine of perichoresis. Unfortunately, this is not what Edwards actually does say.

Problems with "Real" Distinctions and "Relations of Existence" in the Godhead

This distinction between "real" and "relational" attributes generates several problems for Edwards's trinitarianism.[32] Stephen Holmes has

31. Edwards, "Miscellany 94," 262.
32. The importance of this distinction in Edwards's doctrine of the Trinity seems to have escaped at least one of Edwards's recent interpreters, however. Danaher cites the

pointed to one of these. Holmes says that in his discussions of the real attributes of God, Edwards is making the radical move of subsuming all the divine perfections under persons of the Trinity.[33] In other words, Edwards proposes that the perfections of the Father are all and only the Son and the Spirit. Holmes also claims that Edwards denies any meaning to the notion of a divine essence in the Trinity. The only referents for God are the persons of the Trinity and their perfections:

> The residue of a common "essence" which was so pervasive in Western theological discourse is wholly absent, and Edwards claims to be unable to think of "any rational meaning" behind the standard language that describes the essence. . . . Edwards is essentially seeking to appropriate different perfections of the divine *phusis* to particular *hypostases*. . . . This is a move unique in the tradition, a radical extension of the doctrine of appropriation (which classically refers to the external acts of the Trinity). I suspect that, provided the doctrine of perichoresis is remembered and asserted, a form of this move could be developed that would not damage Trinitarian theology in any fundamental way, but Edwards did not live to do this.[34]

Were this the case, Edwards's doctrine of the Trinity would be very peculiar indeed. If the referents for the concept "God" were all and only the Father, Son, and Spirit, without any common essence, with the divine individuals making up the Godhead sharing these properties merely in virtue of some doctrine of perichoresis (or mutual interpenetration),

---

Edwardsian distinction between "real" and "relational" attributes in *Essay on the Trinity*. But he does not seem to see the particular meaning with which Edwards invests these two "sorts" of divine attributes or the way in which Edwards uses these distinctions to individuate the divine persons. Instead Danaher says, "The attributes of God such as infiniteness, eternity, or immutability do not, as Augustine holds, apply to God substance-wise, but conform to the relations within a single personality" (*The Trinitarian Ethics of Jonathan Edwards*, 31). Later in the same passage he observes that Edwards resolves "the attributes of God into God's triune relations" (32). (I should point out that this is part of a discussion of Edwards's psychological analogy of the Trinity where Edwards's trinitarianism is viewed in a distinctly idealist light.) Danaher is right to observe that Edwards believes these relational attributes belong to the "single personality" of God if he means by this the divine essence. But for Edwards, they do not refer to particular divine persons.

33. Holmes, *God of Grace and God of Glory*, ch. 2. It has been suggested to me that the brief discussion of one short section of Holmes's book is unfair because it does not take into account the fact that Holmes's discussion of the Trinity pervades his account of Edwards's theology. It is true that Holmes's book is thoroughly trinitarian, but it is only in the section of his book with which I am concerned that he deals with the issues relevant here.

34. Ibid., 69, 71. The doctrine of appropriation refers to the way in which, in classical doctrines of the Trinity, the different divine persons are said to appropriate the divine attributes of each other in their perichoretic divine union.

then Edwards's doctrine looks tritheistic. But is this what Edwards intends to say?

First, Holmes is right to point out that Edwards is peculiar in subsuming the divine perfections under the Trinity. There are, in Edwards's theory, no other *real* distinctions in God apart from these three persons. It is also true that Edwards's doctrine, as it stands, seems incomplete, a matter to which we shall return presently.

But Holmes's claim about the "absence" of talk about a divine essence in Edwards's thinking is more contentious. He draws on the passage in *Essay on the Trinity* where Edwards says that it is a maxim among theologians that everything that is in God is God and that this must be understood of real attributes, not modalities or relations.[35] The problem is that this is ambiguous (and is not helped by a rather peculiar use of "modalities" in God). It could mean something like this:

> Everything that is in God is God, and this must be understood of real attributes (which pertain to one of the persons of the Trinity), not of modalities (such as immutability).

Let us call this the *Edwardsian Trinitarian Thesis*. Alternatively, it could also mean that

> everything that is in God is God, and this must be understood of *and exhausted by* "real" attributes ("real" in the Edwardsian sense, meaning attributes which pertain to one of the persons of the Trinity), not of modalities (meaning relational properties shared between the divine persons, such as immutability).

Let us call this the *Strong Edwardsian Trinitarian Thesis*.

It appears that Holmes thinks Edwards is committed to the Strong Edwardsian Trinitarian Thesis. But this cannot be right. If he were, this would involve the removal of a notion of the essence of God, and it is difficult to see what Edwards could mean by affirming a doctrine of the Trinity with no shared essence that does not entail tritheism. It is true that Edwards is locating in the persons of the Trinity perfections that have traditionally been thought to refer to the essence of God, and this is a radical move. But the absence of specific reference to the divine essence in this particular section of the *Essay on the Trinity* should not be taken to mean that Edwards has no place for a divine essence in his doctrine of the Trinity. Edwards's point is surely that the perfections of God refer to the real attributes of God (Father, Son, and Holy Spirit) but that the relations of existence (e.g., eternity, immutability, etc.) do not.

35. Edwards, *Essay on the Trinity* (p. 119, cited above).

Such relations are, we might say, merely relations God has. They do not "pick out" or distinguish distinct divine persons. In which case, all that Edwards means, contrary to Holmes, is something like the Edwardsian Trinitarian Thesis, the weaker of the two theses just given. And this is compatible with a doctrine of the divine essence. For the Edwardsian Trinitarian Thesis is commensurate with the belief that there are "real" attributes that "pick out," as it were, the real distinctions in God, that is, the divine persons of the Godhead, whereas other divine attributes which are "mere modes or relations" pertain to the divine essence, shared between the divine persons. That Edwards does retain a place for the divine essence is clear from a number of places in his writings. For instance, in his discussion of similar issues in "Miscellany 650," he says,

> 'Tis from the exceeding imperfect notion that we have of the nature or essence of God, and because we can't think of it but we must think of it far otherwise than it is, that arises the difficulty in our mind of conceiving of God's existing without a cause.[36]

An image that Edwards uses in several places to illustrate this distinction is that of the sun.[37] The Father is like the substance of the sun; the Son, the brightness and glory of the disk; the Spirit, the heat and light emanated to warm and enlighten the world. Nevertheless all three aspects of the sun do not belong to three distinct things; they all share in the essence of what it is to be a sun. The analogy is flawed, as the sun, its brightness, and the heat and light generated by the sun do not all share in the same essence of "sun-ness." But this does show that Edwards is committed to the notion of a divine essence as per orthodox trinitarianism.

But Edwards's concept of God requires that there be more than a unity of essence in the Godhead, as we have already seen from his a priori argument. In "Miscellany 96," he deploys an argument from divine goodness that develops this dynamic constituent of his concept of God:

> It appears that there must be more than a unity in infinite and eternal essence, otherwise the goodness of God can have no perfect exercise. To be perfectly good is to incline to and delight in making another happy in the same proportion as it is happy itself, that is, to delight as much in communicating happiness to another as in enjoying of it himself, and an inclination to communicate all his happiness; it appears that this is perfect goodness, because goodness is delight in communicating happiness.[38]

36. Edwards, "Miscellany 650," in The "Miscellanies" 501–832, 190.

37. See, e.g., Edwards, "Miscellany 362," in The "Miscellanies" (Entry Nos. a–z, aa–zz, 1–500), 434.

38. Edwards, "Miscellany 96," in The "Miscellanies" (Entry Nos. a–z, aa–zz, 1–500), 263.

For Edwards, the perfect exercise of this goodness must have a perfect object upon which it can lavish this perfection. And this must be in God himself, since no other (created) thing is perfect enough in every respect to warrant the exercise of perfect goodness in all its fullness. So God exercises his goodness supremely toward himself in the perichoretic union of the persons of the Trinity and toward his creatures only in a derivative way (Holmes also picks up on this).

In short, and contrary to what Holmes suggests, Edwards did maintain a place for the essence of God despite idiosyncratically subsuming the perfections of God under the persons of the Godhead. Nevertheless, Holmes is right to point out that, as it stands, Edwards's discussion of the Trinity in places such as the *Essay on the Trinity* is underdeveloped in important respects.

This brings us to the relationship between "real" and "relational" properties in Edwards's thinking (which is precisely the place where his thinking is underdeveloped). At one point in the *Essay on the Trinity*, Edwards writes,

> Reason is sufficient to tell us that there must be these distinctions in the deity, viz., of God (absolutely considered), and the idea of God, and love and delight, and there are no other real distinctions in God that can be thought. There are but these three distinctions in God that can be thought. Whatever else can be mentioned in God are nothing but meer [*sic*] modes or relations of existence. . . . It is a maxim amongst divines that everything that is in God is God which must be understood of real attributes and not of meer modalities.[39]

According to Edwards, there are relational properties that are not "real" because they do not pick out one of the distinct persons of the Trinity. This is why they cannot be "real attributes." The traditional attributes that do "pick out" some property that pertains to one of the divine persons (power, wisdom, holiness, etc.) are referred to the particular divine person that they apply to instead of being retained in the divine essence as per the tradition. Those that do not refer to one of the divine persons in particular, having to do with the modes or relations of God's existence in all three persons sharing the one divine essence, are retained as part of the divine essence. It seems that in this Edwardsian account, there are no attributes that are not particular to one or other divine person or that are not "modes or relations" in God. Edwards is pointing out that these "relations" are just that: they do not pick out that which is particular to one or another person of the Trinity, and so they cannot be said to refer to one or another of the only real distinctions in God,

39. Edwards, *Essay on the Trinity* (pp. 118–19).

namely, the Father, Son, or the Spirit. But as it stands, Edwards's distinction between "real" and "relational" divine attributes fails to differentiate those "relational" predicates in the Edwardsian sense of attributes shared in the divine essence between the three divine persons from relational predicates that do refer to one, and only one, person of the Trinity or two, and only two, divine persons. These sorts of relational attributes are well known in Scholastic theology, in which Edwards was steeped.[40] It is strange that he does not utilize this distinction in his own discussion of the Trinity. For, as it stands, Edwards's account is not able to make sense of predicates such as "eternal begottenness," or "begetter of the Son," or "one of those from whom the Holy Spirit proceeds." For such "relational" attributes clearly do belong to one, and only one, or two, and only two, divine persons. They are not shared in the divine essence. And yet these are relational attributes that have traditionally been used to distinguish the different divine persons as they relate to one another in their perichoretic divine life.

Thus, if we take him at his word, Edwards's novel recasting of the divine attributes on this second Edwardsian strategy cannot provide an adequate basis on which to individuate the divine persons of the Trinity, even if we factor in a doctrine of trinitarian perichoresis. It overlooks the fact that in the Trinity there are attributes that are relational and pertain to only one or only two divine persons. This is a peculiar oversight on Edwards's part. His theological education should have prevented him from making this mistake. I suppose it would be possible to rectify this problem by factoring this distinction into a broadly Edwardsian account of the Trinity. If we were to do so, we would be left with "real" attributes that distinguish divine persons, relational attributes that also pertain to only one or only two divine persons, and relations of existence (in the Edwardsian sense) that pertain to all three divine persons and may be retained in the divine essence.

But if Edwards's doctrine were to be tidied up in this fashion, what we have is something like the following account: God has relational attributes held in common in a divine essence, including such predicates as eternity, immutability, infinity. Then there are "real" attributes of an Edwardsian variety that refer to only one divine person, such as wisdom (the Son) or love (the Spirit). But there are also relational attributes of a more conventional variety that refer to only one or to only two divine persons, such as "being eternally begotten" (of the Son) or "being one from whom the Holy Spirit proceeds" (the Father and the Son). But this

40. Relational attributes that refer to only one divine person or only two divine persons are called *proprietates* in Scholastic theology. See Ludwig Ott, *Fundamentals of Catholic Dogma*, trans. Patrick Lynch, 4th ed. (Rockford, IL: Tan Books, 1960), 70.

still seems eccentric. It means that there are certain attributes usually thought to be shared in the divine life, such as love or wisdom, that are, according to Edwards, peculiar to only one divine person.

Even if we were, with Edwards, to invoke trinitarian perichoresis to make sense of this,[41] it still seems that Edwards's doctrine threatens to divide the works of God between the persons of the divine Trinity. Edwards's concern is to ensure that the attributes that belong to the Father, Son, or Spirit are applied to those persons, not to the divine essence, and that the attributes that simply speak of God's existence should be retained in the divine essence. The rationale behind this move was a commendable desire to keep in step with the biblical tradition: "We find no other attributes of which it is said that they are God in Scripture or that God is they, but *logos* and *agapē*, the reason and the love of God. John i. 1, and 1 John iv. 8, 16."[42] Thus attributes are predicated on the basis of whether they apply to one of the persons of the Trinity in Scripture and are therefore "real" or whether they are modes or relations in God, not particular to any one person of the Godhead, and are therefore retained in the essence of the Deity. If we add in the missing piece to Edwards's account—the relational predicates belonging to only one or only two divine persons—and take seriously Edwards's commitment to trinitarian perichoresis, we are left with a way of thinking about individuating the triune persons which, although not entirely satisfactory, is less radical than Edwards's proposal seems at first glance.

Coda

I have argued that Edwards's first strategy for individuating the divine persons, which can be found in his a priori argument for the Trinity, is so seriously mired in difficulties that it appears irredeemable. His second strategy is more promising although incomplete. Yet even here there are problems that are worrisome. Most seriously, partitioning the divine attributes into those that are "real" and those that are "relational" (in the Edwardsian sense) means that the *opera trinitatis ad extra sunt indivisa* principle, which is a crucial constituent of a doctrine of divine simplicity, is in danger of being compromised. Edwards seems unable to avoid the impression that certain divine attributes conventionally thought

41. "The whole Divine office is supposed truly and properly to subsist in each of these three, viz., God and His understanding and love, and that there is such a wonderfull [*sic*] union between them that they are, after an ineffable and inconceivable manner, one in another, so that one hath another and they have communion in one another and are as it were predicable of one another" (Edwards, *Essay on the Trinity* [p. 120]).

42. Ibid. (p. 119).

to belong to the divine essence, such as wisdom or knowledge, are the peculiar preserve of one or another divine person rather than shared together in the divine life. Thus, in individuating the divine persons, he seems to have threatened a vital aspect of the unity of God's being.[43] For how can God be simple in a traditional sense if there are "real" distinctions in God, that is, real in the Edwardsian sense?[44]

It is this ambiguity in Edwards's trinitarian theology that has led one of Edwards's recent interpreters, Amy Plantinga Pauw, to the conclusion that there is an unresolved tension in Edwards's thought between his commitment to divine simplicity—which, she claims, does not play a major role in his trinitarian theology—and his doctrine of the Trinity.[45] Steven Studebaker has objected to this.[46] He claims, contrary to Plantinga Pauw, that divine simplicity is integral to Edwards's trinitarianism because Edwards "assumes the inseparability of act and existence in God, which is a constitutive aspect of the scholastic doctrine of divine simplicity." Divine simplicity is also the ground, says Studebaker, "for Edwards's identification of the divine persons with the divine essence." He even says that, according to Edwards, each divine person "understands because each is identical with the one understanding essence."[47] I think Studebaker has the better of this argument, although his ringing endorsement of Edwards may be overhasty. Edwards does believe that there are divine attributes shared in the divine essence that each divine person has. He also endorses the idea found in the doctrine of divine simplicity, that the act and existence of God are inseparable (which is why he thinks his a priori argument works: God thinks of himself—a divine act, or one aspect of the divine act that is God—and this divine act exists because his being and acting are somehow inseparable). But it remains true that Edwards believes there are "real" attributes that belong to particular divine persons and that are not part of the divine essence. This appears to be rather at odds with his endorsement of divine simplicity. If God is truly simple, then there can be no *real* distinctions in the divine nature. Divine attributes are predicates, not properties.

43. It is ironic that the conclusions reached here are not so far from the nineteenth-century whispering about Edwards's orthodoxy on the Trinity, although, as I hope is clear, I think Edwards was an orthodox trinitarian. It is just that two strategies he uses to make sense of the Trinity are far from satisfactory.

44. It seems to me that Edwards does defend a robustly traditional account of divine simplicity, although, as I have pointed out elsewhere, this does seem to generate problems for his doctrine of the Trinity. See Crisp, "Jonathan Edwards on Divine Simplicity."

45. Plantinga Pauw, *"The Supreme Harmony of All,"* 69–75, and "Response."

46. Studebaker, "Supreme Harmony or Disharmony?" 482–84.

47. Ibid., 483, citing "Miscellany 308." He concludes, "Divine simplicity was not a marginalized or anomalous doctrine in Edwards's thought but a central component of his understanding of the Trinitarian God" (484).

They are a means by which we distinguish things about God for our own understanding of him but which are not distinct in God himself. Yet God is triune. This is the paradox Edwards struggled with and which he was, in the final analysis, unable to resolve.

All of this raises a problem that has been the subject of considerable attention in recent philosophical theology, that is, the doctrine of divine simplicity and its relationship to a robustly trinitarian theology. A number of contemporary philosophical theologians, taking their lead from Alvin Plantinga's Aquinas Lecture, *Does God Have a Nature?*[48] deny that the traditional doctrine of divine simplicity makes sense. Alternatives to the traditional doctrine that emphasize the unity of the divine nature without commitment to the most controversial aspects of the traditional account of divine simplicity, such as the idea that there are no distinct properties in God or the idea that there is no distinction between the essence and the existence of God, have been proposed to replace this traditional view.[49] There has also been work done in the theology of Thomas Aquinas that argues that he, like Edwards, does not seem to be able, in the final analysis, to hold together both a robust doctrine of the Trinity and a traditional doctrine of divine simplicity.[50] (This is troublesome not least because Thomas's doctrine is often invoked as the paradigmatic classical conception of the divine nature.) From a different direction, systematic theologians such as Colin Gunton and Robert Jenson have claimed that the classical theological doctrine of God is subject to serious objections quite apart from the doctrine of divine simplicity.[51] All this raises important questions for Edwards's theology and for those committed to a classical doctrine of God as Edwards was. The most pressing of these, it seems to me, is this: can we hold to a traditional doctrine of divine simplicity *and* have a thoroughly orthodox trinitarian theology?[52]

48. Alvin Plantinga, *Does God Have a Nature?* (Milwaukee: Marquette University Press, 1980). Cf. Joshua Hoffman and Gary S. Rosenkrantz, *The Divine Attributes* (Oxford: Blackwell, 2002), 59–68. Recent defenses of divine simplicity include John Lamont, "Divine Simplicity," *Monist* 80 (1997): 521–38; Katherin Rogers, *Perfect Being Theology* (Edinburgh: Edinburgh University Press, 2000), ch. 3; and Stephen R. Holmes, "'Something Much Too Plain to Say': Towards a Defence of the Doctrine of Divine Simplicity" *Neue Zeitschrift für systematische Theologie und Religionsphilosophie* 43 (2001): 137–54.

49. See, e.g., Jay Wesley Richards, *The Untamed God: A Philosophical Exploration of Divine Perfection, Simplicity and Immutability* (Downers Grove, IL: InterVarsity, 2003); and Richard Swinburne, *The Existence of God*, rev. ed. (Oxford: Oxford University Press, 1991).

50. Christopher Hughes, *On a Complex Theory of a Simple God: An Investigation into Aquinas' Philosophical Theology* (Ithaca, NY: Cornell University Press, 1989).

51. See Colin E. Gunton, *Act and Being: Towards a Theology of the Divine Attributes* (Grand Rapids: Eerdmans, 2002); and Jenson, *The Triune God*.

52. Thanks are due Paul Helm, Stephen Holmes, and Michael Rea for comments on previous drafts of this contribution.

PART 3

Theological Perspectives

6

Life in and of Himself

Reflections on God's Aseity

JOHN WEBSTER

I

What Christian doctrine has to say about the attributes of God is shaped by the church's confession of the Holy Trinity. When it inquires into divine aseity, therefore, theology is not asking, "What must be true of a god?" but a rather more unwieldy question: "Who is the God the enactment of whose utter sufficiency as Father, Son, and Holy Spirit includes his creative, reconciling, and perfecting works toward his creatures?" A Christian theology of the divine attributes is a conceptual schema for indicating the identity of the God of the Christian confession. God's identity is, further, to be considered both with respect to its unfathomable depth in itself and with respect to God's enactment of a wholly gracious turn to creatures. That is, a theology of God's attributes attempts to describe his immanent and his relative perfection. Within such an account, the concept of aseity, I suggest, has two dimensions. First, it indicates the glory and plenitude of the life of the Holy Trinity in its self-existent and

A previous version of this chapter appeared in John Webster, "The Aseity of God," in *Realism and Religion: Philosophical and Theological Perspectives*, ed. A. Moore and M. Scott (Aldershot, UK: Ashgate), 2007.

self-moving originality, its underived fullness. In every respect, God is of himself God. Second, it indicates that God's originality and fullness constitute the ground of his self-communication. He is one who, out of nothing other than his own self-sufficiency, brings creatures into being, sustains and reconciles them, and brings them perfection in fellowship with himself. A theology of God's aseity is an indication of the one who is and acts *thus*, who is the object of the church's knowledge, love, and fear, and whose praise is the church's chief employment.

The concept of aseity tries to indicate God's identity; it is not so much a comprehensive definition of God as a gesture toward God's objective and self-expressive form. The task of the concept is not to establish conditions for conceivability but rather to have rational dealings with the God who is and who is self-communicative, anterior to rational work on our part. God is objective and expressive form, enacting a particular identity, presenting himself to us as a specific gestalt, and so making himself perceptible, intelligible, and nameable (this is part of the meaning of "revelation"). Consequently, in theology aseity is a positive or material concept, determined by the particular form of God's self-expressive perfection. Its content is governed by the acts in which God enacts his being before us and so gives himself to be known. Because of this, theology will not overinvest in whatever generic sense may be attached to the concept of aseity (or of any of the other divine attributes). This is not because of intellectual sectarianism, a desire to segregate theological use in an absolute way from all other speech about deity; after all, aseity, like nearly all Christian theological concepts, is a borrowed term with a wider currency. Rather, theology is simply concerned to ensure that its talk of aseity concentrates on that which is proper to *this one*.

All this is simply an application of the rule which is basic to the Christian doctrine of the Trinity: *Deus non est in genere*. Concepts developed in articulating the Christian doctrine of God, including the concept of aseity, are fitting insofar as they correspond to the particular being of the Triune God in his self-moved self-presentation. A further extension of this rule is that in theological usage aseity is not primarily a comparative or contrastive concept. That is, the content of the term cannot be determined simply by analysis of the difference between God and contingent creatures. Although the contrast between divine self-existence and creaturely contingency is a corollary of the concept of God's aseity, disorder threatens when this contrast is allowed to expand and fill the concept completely. The point is worth pausing over, especially because the modern career of notions of aseity and self-existence has been quite deeply marked by comparative interpretations, particularly by theologians and philosophers with heavy investments in natural religion and its theological derivatives.

That there can be a relatively uncontroversial appeal to the "contrastive" aspects of divine aseity and that such appeal has a long history in Christian theology are beyond dispute. This way of filling out the content of aseity is used to best effect when deployed in an informal, nonfundamental way, simply for the purposes of explication and elucidation and not as a guide to the entire scope of the concept. Consider two passages from Augustine:

> See, heaven and earth exist, they cry aloud that they are made, for they suffer change and variation. But in anything which is not made and yet is, there is nothing which previously was not present. To be what was once not the case is to be subject to change and variation. They also cry aloud that they have not made themselves: "The manner of our existence shows that we are made. For before we came to be, we did not exist to be able to make ourselves." And the voice with which they speak is self-evidence. You, Lord, who are beautiful, made them for they are beautiful. You are good, for they are good. You are, for they are. Yet they are not beautiful or good or possessed of being in the sense that you their Maker are. In comparison with you they are deficient in beauty and goodness and being.[1]

> God exists in the supreme sense, and the original sense, of the word. He is altogether unchangeable, and it is he who could say with full authority "I am who I am."[2]

The changeless dignity and beauty of God's uncreated being, because it "exists in the supreme sense," are ultimately beyond comparison. They can also be glimpsed by contrast with what is "made": "you are, for they are." Yet there is no sense that God's supreme, self-existent being somehow requires this contrast with the creaturely, as a kind of backcloth without which its splendor could not be seen. God simply *is*, originally, authoritatively, and incomparably, and no creature can say, as does God, "I am who I am."

Something of the same pattern of thought can be found in Anselm:

> You alone then, Lord, are what you are and you are who you are. . . . And what began [to exist] from non-existence, and can be thought not to exist, and returns to non-existence unless it subsists through some other; and what has had a past existence but does not now exist, and a future existence but does not yet exist—such a thing does not exist in a strict and absolute

1. Augustine, *Confessions* XI.iv, ed. and trans. Henry Chadwick (Oxford: Oxford University Press, 1991), 224.
2. Augustine, *On Christian Teaching* I.xxxii, ed. and trans. R. P. H. Green (Oxford: Oxford University Press, 1997), 24.

sense. But you are what you are, for whatever you are at any time or in any way this you are wholly and forever.[3]

He alone has of himself all that he has, while other things have nothing of themselves. And other things, having nothing of themselves, have their only reality from him.[4]

Once again, the contrast of divine self-existence and creaturely contingency is informal, simply a corollary of the fundamental affirmation about the being of God: "You alone . . . , Lord, are what you are and you are who you are" (the echo of Exod. 3:14 is not to be missed). God's aseity is not a mirror image of contingency; rather, in both Augustine and Anselm, it is an aspect of the divine *solus*, the irreducible uniqueness and incommensurability of God.

A compromise of this proper attention to the divine identity occurs whenever an abstract contrast between self-existent and created being is allowed too large a role in determining the notion of aseity. When this takes place, aseity transmutes into a reverse concept of contingency. This is, in large part, because the derivation of the concept of aseity shifts. No longer arising in the context of explicating the enacted, self-expressive being of God, it emerges instead out of a consideration of the nature of contingent reality. Moreover, the content of the notion of aseity begins to be altered accordingly. It is no longer a (doxological) affirmation of God's matchless and utterly replete being in and from himself but simply that which must be said of *deitas* if contingent reality is to be secured by a ground of existence beyond itself. This takes place as the concept of aseity migrates away from the doctrine of the immanent Trinity and of the Triune God's economy of grace and instead finds its place in a metaphysics of created being. With this migration, aseity becomes a "paired" concept, inseparably attached to, and expounded in terms of, the contingency of the world. In a curious irony, divine self-existence becomes a derivative concept.

Tracing the history of this deformation is an important and instructive task, not the least because lack of historical perspective has meant that more modern philosophical and theological construals of aseity have often been read back into patristic and medieval texts. There is no substantial recent history of the concept, and even a brief account is well beyond the scope of this essay. But attention might be drawn to one or two examples.

A deformed notion of aseity is already firmly in place very early in the eighteenth century in Samuel Clarke's *Demonstration of the Being and*

---

3. Anselm of Canterbury, *Proslogion* XXII, in *The Major Works*, ed. B. Davies and G. R. Evans (Oxford: Oxford University Press, 1998), 99–100.
    4. Anselm of Canterbury, *On the Fall of the Devil* I, in *The Major Works*, 194.

Attributes of God (1704). Clarke's account of aseity is especially interesting because within it one can still find preserved the residue of an older, non-comparative, and nonderivative conception (such as we saw in Augustine and Anselm) which fits with severe difficulty into the modern frame of his argument. *"There has existed from eternity some one unchangeable and independent Being,"* Clarke proposes.[5] This—notably abstract and anonymous—being is required; otherwise we face the absurdity of "an infinite succession of changeable and dependent beings."[6] Consequently, aseity is attributed to this being, not, as it were, doxologically, from a stance in the presence of the divine self-naming as "I am," but functionally, as a property required of this being if contingent reality is adequately to be explained. The qualities of this being, because they are determined by its function, are, we should note, largely nonagential and nonpersonal. The self-existent being is "a most simple being, absolutely eternal and infinite, original and independent."[7] God is simple cause, not, for instance, luminous and self-presenting personal goodness and beauty; still less is God the bearer of the triune name. Yet in one crucial respect, Clarke retains the older conception: the self-existent being is *in se* and not merely an element in a process of explaining the world's origin. "To be self-existent is . . . to exist by an absolute necessity originally in the nature of the thing itself."[8] That is, "this necessity must not be barely consequent upon our supposition of the existence of such a being (for then it would not be a necessity absolutely in itself, nor be the ground or foundation of the existence of anything, being on the contrary only a consequent of it) but it must antecedently force itself upon us whether we will or no."[9] Yet this conception does not break free from the use which Clarke has assigned to it; the apologetic aim traps Clarke into a comparative approach. And because his account lacks any operative sense of the immanent divine life, concentrating instead upon the cosmological functions of the concept of God, it remains apersonal and functional.

Clarke's argument found, and continues to find, theological echoes. Schleiermacher did not consider aseity "a special attribute,"[10] on the grounds that nothing more is said in it than has already been said in the notions of omnipotence and eternity. Aseity is, in fact, "a speculative formula which, in the dogmatic sphere, we can only convert into the rule that there is nothing in God for which a determining cause is to be posited

5. S. Clarke, *A Demonstration of the Being and Attributes of God*, ed. E. Vailati (Cambridge: Cambridge University Press, 1998), 10.
6. Ibid.
7. Ibid., 14.
8. Ibid., 12.
9. Ibid., 13.
10. F. D. E. Schleiermacher, *The Christian Faith* (Edinburgh: T&T Clark, 1928), 218.

outside God."[11] Thus far Schleiermacher simply repeats a traditional for-mulation; what is distinctive about his account is his reference back to the earlier discussion in *The Christian Faith*, §4.4, according to which "the *Whence* of our receptive and active existence . . . is to be designated by the word 'God.'"[12] This, for Schleiermacher, is "the really original significa-tion of that word."[13] As with Clarke, the content of aseity and its function tug in different directions. Even in his lack of external determination, God has become inseparable from "our receptive and active existence." And so "in the first instance God signifies for us simply that which is the co-determinant in this feeling [of absolute dependence] and to which we trace our being in such a state; and any further content of the idea must be evolved out of this fundamental import assigned to it."[14]

A similar derivation of aseity can be found much more recently in Tillich. Here the language of causality is particularly strong. "The ques-tion of the cause of a thing or event presupposes that it does not possess its own power of coming into being. Things and events have no aseity."[15] In effect, Tillich offers an anthropological reworking of what Clarke had expressed in cosmological terms. "Causality expresses by implication the inability of anything to rest on itself. Everything is driven beyond itself to its cause, and so on indefinitely. Causality powerfully expresses the abyss of nonbeing in everything."[16] Causality thus generates the anxiety of "not being in, of, and by oneself, of not having the 'aseity' which theology traditionally attributes to God."[17] To speak of divine aseity is therefore to indicate that God "is the power of being,"[18] beyond the bifurcation of essential and existential being which characterizes the finite.

In their various ways, Clarke, Schleiermacher, and Tillich exemplify a basic disorder introduced into the concept of aseity when expounded in close relation to cosmology or anthropology: as the function of the concept shifts, its content is adapted accordingly. Aseity becomes less an affirmation of the underived beauty and goodness of God and more a property which must be ascribed to *deitas* if it is properly to fulfill its function of supporting the contingent. The sheer originality of God's aseity, the perfection and completeness of his existence in and from himself, is in some measure eclipsed, overtaken by a kind of "finite"

11. Ibid., 219.
12. Ibid., 16.
13. Ibid.
14. Ibid., 17.
15. P. Tillich, *Systematic Theology* (Chicago: University of Chicago Press, 1951), 1:196.
16. Ibid.
17. Ibid.
18. Ibid., 1:236.

transcendence or aseity, comparatively rather than absolutely different. In the course of his extraordinarily perceptive treatment of the doctrine of God in his *System of Christian Doctrine*, the great nineteenth-century dogmatician Isaak Dorner remarks that "there belongs to the divine idea something determinate, which raises Deity above comparison or mere quantitative difference. The same is true of his absolute essence, his aseity."[19] When this is lost in a theological account of the matter, the Christian character of the relation of God and creatures is jeopardized, as it turns into the reciprocal presence of two realities, each of which is in some measure necessary for the other, so that God *a se* and the world *ab alio* together form a whole. Aseity becomes detached from the theological metaphysics of God's immanent and economic love and is reduced to the bare self-positing cause of created reality.

Such is the pathology; the corrective is trinitarian. To this we now turn.

II

If theology is to move beyond a stripped-down conception of aseity, it must do so by following the instruction offered in the actual exercise of God's self-existence; that is, it must take its lead from what is given to creatures to know of God's self-willed and determinate form as *autotheos*. "We have to be taught first, by the decision made in his actual existence, that God is free in himself. This statement has to come first as the content of a knowledge whose object cannot be an idea, but only God himself in his self-evidencing free existence."[20] Aseity as a synthetic concept, correlative to and so in some way a function of creaturely contingency, can be supplanted only by something materially rich—by a notion of aseity beyond that of a merely comparative absolute, speculatively derived. In Christian dogmatics, such a materially rich notion of aseity cannot be articulated apart from the doctrine of the Trinity, for it is this piece of teaching which offers a conceptual paraphrase of the life of God, both in his inner depth and in his gracious turn to that which is not God. It is as Father, Son, and Spirit that God is of himself, utterly free and full, in the self-originate and perfect movement of his life; grounded in himself, he gives himself, the self-existent Lord of grace. God *a se* is the perfection of paternity, filiation, and spiration in which he is indissolubly from, for, and in himself and out of which he bestows himself as the Lord, Savior, and partner of his creature. This triune character is the distinguishing feature of the Christian confession of God's aseity.

19. I. Dorner, *A System of Christian Doctrine* (Edinburgh: T&T Clark, 1880), 1:203.
20. Karl Barth, *Church Dogmatics* (Edinburgh: T&T Clark, 1957), II/1:308.

As Calvin puts it: "God . . . designates himself by another special mark to distinguish himself more precisely from idols. For he so proclaims himself the sole God as to offer himself to be contemplated clearly in three persons. Unless we grasp these, only the bare and empty name of God flits about in our brains, to the exclusion of the true God."[21]

How might trinitarian teaching fill out the notion of aseity? First, in speaking of God's aseity, we have in mind both the "immanent" and the "economic" dimensions of the divine life. *God is from himself, and from himself God gives himself*. There is a certain priority to the first statement ("God is from himself"): the "immanent" dimension of God's self-existence stands at the head of everything else that must be said. This is because only in this way can the concept of aseity be kept free of the degrading synthetic or comparative elements. First and foremost, aseity is a statement of the divine "I am"; only by derivation is it a statement that God is the groundless ground of contingency. Nevertheless, the priority of the immanent would be badly misperceived if it were not related to the necessary further statement, "from himself God gives himself." Without this further statement, the first would remain abstract from the actual exercise or form of God's life. The perfection of God's life as *autotheos* includes his works as Father, Son, and Spirit in creation, reconciliation, and redemption.

With this in mind, how might God's immanent aseity be further described? God's aseity is to be understood not formally but materially. Aseity is not to be defined merely in negative terms, as the mere absence of origination or dependence upon an external cause. If this is allowed to happen, then a subordinate characteristic of aseity (God's "not being from another") comes to eclipse its primary meaning (God's "being in and from himself"). "It was," Barth notes, "a retrogression when the idea of God's *aseitas* was interpreted, or rather supplanted, by that of *independentia* or *infinitas*, and later by that of the unconditioned or absolute."[22] It is much more fruitful to understand aseity in terms of fullness of personal relations. Aseity is *life*: God's life *from* and therefore *in* himself. This life is the relations of Father, Son, and Spirit. Crucially, therefore, aseity is not a property to be affirmed *de Deo uno* anterior to God's triune life but indicates the wholly original character of the relations which are God's life (failure to see the constitutive role of this in the conception of aseity is at the root of its modern disarray). The self-existence of the Triune God is his existence in the personal, internal activities of God. These activities are personal relations, that is, modes of subsistence in which each particular person of the Trinity is identified in terms of

21. John Calvin, *Institutes of the Christian Religion*, I.13.ii, ed. John McNeill, trans. Ford Lewis Battles (Philadelphia: Westminster; London: SCM, 1960), 122.
22. Barth, *Church Dogmatics*, II/1:303.

relations to the other two persons. To spell this out fully would require an account of, for example, the act of the Father in begetting the Son and the acts of the Father and the Son in spirating the Spirit. Expressed as relations, God's life *a se* includes the Son's relation to the Father as the one whom the Father begets (passive generation) and the relation of the Spirit to the Father and the Son (passive spiration). By these activities and relations, each of the persons of the Trinity is identified, that is, picked out as having a distinct, incommunicable personal property: paternity, filiation, spiration. Together these acts and relations *are* God's self-existence. Aseity is not merely the quality of being (in contrast to contingent reality) underived; it is the eternal lively plenitude of the Father who begets, the Son who is begotten, and the Spirit who proceeds from both. To speak of God's aseity is thus to speak of the spontaneous, eternal, and unmoved movement of his being-in-relation as Father, Son, and Spirit. This movement, without cause of condition and depending on nothing other than itself, is God's being from himself. In this perfect circle of paternity, filiation, and spiration, God is who he is.

The aseity of the Triune God thus means a good deal more than absence of derivation. Indeed, if that privative construal of aseity is accented too forcefully, it can suppress the elements of generation and spiration, which are basic to the proper Christian theological sense of the term, on the grounds that begetting and proceeding seem to introduce precisely the troublesome notion of derivation, which aseity is intended to exclude from the conception of the divine. Classical trinitarian theology takes a different tack to exclude an inappropriate notion of derivation and attendant ideas such as composition. It develops a distinction between the aseity common to all three persons by virtue of their sharing in the divine essence and the aseity which is the personal property of the Father alone: although all the persons of the Trinity are *a se* according to essence, the Father alone is *a se* according to person. Phrased in rather more technical language: all three persons are *agenētos* ("uncreated") by virtue of their common divine essence, but only the Father is *agennētos* ("unbegotten)" because he alone is the *principium* of the Son and the Spirit. The consensus on the point is neatly encapsulated by John of Damascus: "The Father alone is ingenerate, no other substance having given him being. And the Son alone is generate, for he was begotten of the Father's essence, without beginning and without time. And only the Holy Spirit proceeds from the Father's essence, not having been generated but simply proceeding."[23] The Father, accordingly, is *a se* not only according to essence (as God)

23. John of Damascus, *Exposition of the Orthodox Faith* I.8, trans. S. D. F. Salmond (Oxford: Parker, 1899), 8.

but also as a property of his own person; but neither to the Son nor to the Spirit, who are begotten and proceed from the Father respectively, can aseity be attributed as personal property.

At first glance, this set of distinctions appears to undermine a construal of divine aseity in terms of the personal relations which make up the triune life, precisely because it distinguishes between a "common" aseity and an aseity proper to the Father. This might be judged to focus too much on the relations of origin within the Trinity, with the result that the reciprocally constituting character of the immanent relations of the Godhead is threatened, resulting in some kind of subordinationism. If the Father's "unbegottenness" becomes definitive of the divine essence, then the personal properties *ad intra* of the Son and the Spirit (i.e., filiation and spiration) may easily seem secondary, derivative from and not equiprimordial with paternity. And when this happens, aseity once again is associated with a common divine essence behind the relations of the divine life.

This retreat into a monistic concept of aseity is not necessary, however, and can readily be corrected by appeal to the reciprocally determinative character of the divine persons. The Son, for example, is eternally begotten of the Father. As such, he is not, as Son, *a se*, since he does not share the Father's property of being *anarchon*. But this does not entail that the Son is in some manner subsequent to or inferior to the Father. The Son's generation is eternal: not a "coming-to-be" as the Father's creature but a relation which is constitutive of the divine essence and of the identity of the Father as well as of the Son. John of Damascus again (here stating a commonplace of the tradition in interpreting John 14:28): "If we say that the Father is the origin of the Son and greater than the Son, we do not suggest any precedence in time or superiority in nature of the Father over the Son (for through his agency he made the ages), or superiority in any other respect save causation."[24] Causation and filiation, because both are eternal, do not relate as fullness of being and absence of being. Filiation is not a lack but a mode of God's eternal perfection, intrinsic to the wholly realized self-movement of God. Begetting—and likewise spiration—are the *form* of God's aseity, not its result or term, still less its contradiction.

To make affirmations along these lines requires that we do not draw too sharp a distinction between the unity of the divine essence and its triunity; the aseity of the Son and the Spirit which they possess as sharers in the one divine essence is not wholly separate from their distinctive personal properties as the one who is eternally begotten and the one who eternally proceeds. Further, it requires that we allow that the relations

24. Ibid., 8–9.

of the Godhead are not secondary and that they are mutually constitutive and conditioning. The Father is, according to his person, *a se* only as he stands in relation to the Son; his aseity is not anterior to the act and relation of begetting. This does not mean that the relation of Father and Son is reversible (the Son does not beget the Father), but the relation is reciprocal because both "Father" and "Son" are relative terms.[25] Above all, we need to grasp that God's aseity is his self-existence *in* these relations. God is from himself as he enacts his life in the reciprocity of paternity, filiation, and spiration.

We may close this account of aseity as a characteristic of God's inner-trinitarian life with some comments on two closely associated concepts which have been used to state God's self-existence, namely, God as *causa sui* and God as *ens necessarium*. Both illustrate the need to ensure that concepts used in the course of explicating the Christian confession be kept in the closest possible proximity to substantive theological doctrine and not simply introduced already full of content derived from their deployment elsewhere.

The concept of God as *causa sui* has a long history in patristic and medieval usage; the locus classicus is a comment of Jerome's on Eph. 3:15:

> Other things receive their substance by the mediation of God, but God—who always is and does not have his beginning from another source but is himself the origin of himself and the cause of his own substance—cannot be understood to have something which has existence from another source. Warmth, indeed, is something which belongs to fire, but something which has been warmed is something else. Fire cannot be understood without heat; other things which become warm from fire borrow its heat and, if the fire should withdraw, the heat gradually decreases and they return to their own nature and are by no means referred to as warm.[26]

Toward the end of the nineteenth century, the concept was revisited by the Roman Catholic dogmatician Herman Schell, who appealed to the language of God as *causa sui* to achieve much the same as Dorner sought to achieve by speaking of God's "life," namely, to overcome what he judged to be a static conception of God as subsistent being and so to draw attention to God's eternal self-activation.[27]

When pressed, the concept soon shows itself incoherent and dogmatically precarious. At a purely formal level, it seems to suggest that God

25. See W. Pannenberg, *Systematic Theology* (Edinburgh: T&T Clark, 1991), 1:312.

26. R. E. Heine, ed., *The Commentaries of Origen and Jerome on St. Paul's Epistle to the Ephesians* (Oxford: Oxford University Press, 2002), 158.

27. See H. Schell, *Katholische Dogmatik* (Paderborn: Schöningh, 1889), 1:238–41.

in some way precedes himself as his own cause, and "it is absurd to suppose that something is *explanatorily prior* to *itself*."[28] The dogmatic difficulties are equally serious. Talk of God as his own cause cannot easily cohere with teaching about divine eternity or immutability, since it appears to introduce an actualist concept of God's "coming-to-be" as the result of some causal process. Further, it imperils divine simplicity, introducing distinctions between cause and that which is caused or between potentiality and act, which, by attributing potentiality to God, undermine the all-important identity of essence and existence in God (reasons such as these led to Schell's work being placed on the *Index* in 1898). By suggesting that God produces himself, it seems to require the possibility of God's nonexistence as a kind of background to his being. In effect, a God who is his own cause lacks an integral element of perfection. If the concept of *causa sui* is to be used, therefore, the notion of cause must first be stripped of any associations with "becoming" or "coming-into-existence"—of anything that might corrode the eternal fullness of God's being. Further, it must be used not to conceive God on the basis of a general metaphysics of causality but to indicate what Ringleben calls "the divine livingness" and "the uniqueness and incomparability of the divine being itself."[29] In the end, however, causal concepts are less than adequate to the task; what is needed is the language of person and action.

Similar difficulties attend the idea of God as necessary being. We have already noted that this way of speaking of aseity is commonly dominated by the idea of "necessity for . . ." Necessity thereby becomes a determination of God, reduced to a merely functional relation to the creatures of whom God is the necessary ground. These problems can, certainly, be eased by deployment of a more complex modality of necessity, according to which necessity is not simply "necessity for another." The necessity predicated of God when he is spoken of as *ens necessarium* is *necessitas absoluta*. It is equivalent to absolute existence, existence without ground or determination and so different from functional or contingent existence. Consequently, the necessity of God for the world is properly to be understood as *necessitas consequentiae*, that which simply follows from God's will or self-determination, and has no further reference to realities beyond that will. Strictly speaking, divine necessity is not a

---

28. J. Hoffman and G. S. Rosenkrantz, *The Divine Attributes* (Oxford: Blackwell, 2002), 91; cf. R. Swinburne, *The Coherence of Theism* (Oxford: Clarendon, 1977), 262: "Certainly given that at some time God is, his subsequent existence will indeed be due to his actions. But what has no cause, and so is inexplicable, is the non-existence of a time before which God was not."

29. J. Ringleben, "Gottes Sein, Handeln und Werden," in *Arbeit am Gottesbegriff* (Tübingen: Mohr Siebeck, 2004), 1:229–30.

matter of *necessitas coactionis*, according to which God and the world would be mutually constitutive, thus reducing God to finitude. Yet even if *ens necessarium* can be construed in this way, as equivalent to pure self-original existence, it remains a rather blank, empty concept. Like the parallel notion of "the absolute," it invites filling out from elsewhere. Accordingly, as with the notion of God as *causa sui*, it has to be judged materially inadequate as an account of God's life.

III

God is *a se* in the eternal fullness of the loving relations of Father, Son, and Spirit. From himself God has life in himself. But God is from himself not only in his inner life but also in the external works which correspond to his inner life. With this we can complete the material description of God's aseity by expanding the second statement that "from himself God gives himself."

A theology of aseity finds itself under a very specific constraint at this point: if it is diligently to follow the logic of the triune self-movement, then it cannot remain content with a definition of divine self-existence which refers exclusively to the being of God *in se* apart from God's relation to creatures. If theology were to try to do this, it would in fact fail to grasp the real content of God's aseity, even in its "internal" dimension. The movement of God's triune life has its perfection in and of itself and is utterly sufficient to itself, but this perfect movement is not self-enclosed or self-revolving. In its perfection, it is also a movement of self-gift in which the complete love of Father, Son, and Spirit communicates itself *ad extra*, creating and sustaining a further object of love. Of himself, God is *gracious*. "Since, then, God, who is good and more than good, did not find satisfaction in self-contemplation, but in his exceeding goodness wished certain things to come into existence which would enjoy his benefits and share in his goodness, he brought all things out of nothing into being and created them."[30]

God is from himself not simply in absolute independence but in his "exceeding goodness." The inclusion of the *opera exeuntia* in the description of aseity is, however, not common in the Christian doctrinal tradition, especially when the doctrine of God is expounded in terms of the metaphysics of self-existent substance or if the theology of the divine processions is isolated from that of the divine missions. But some precedents may be found in the exegetical tradition, notably in the interpretation of John 5:26: "As the Father has life in himself, so he has granted the Son

---

30. John of Damascus, *Exposition of the Orthodox Faith* II.2 (Salmond, 18).

also to have life in himself."[31] Two examples are particularly instructive in holding immanent and economic aspects of aseity.

Augustine suggests an understanding of God's "life in himself" (that is, of what will later be signified by the term "aseity") in both its intratrinitarian and its soteriological dimensions. His reflections stem from a vivid sense of the present fulfillment of the Son's promise of life, recorded in the previous verse: "the hour is coming, and now is, when the dead will hear the voice of the Son of God, and those who hear him will live" (John 5:25). "This hour is now occurring, and this is assuredly occurring and is not at all ceasing," Augustine tells his congregation. "Men who were dead are rising, they are passing to life, they live at the voice of the Son of God, from him persevering in his faith."[32] Immediately, however, Augustine traces this saving reality of new life in Christ back to its foundation in the Son's eternal relation to the Father. If there is indeed a present reality of resurrection life for believers, it can only be because "the Son has life; he has that by which the believers may live."[33] This, in turn, prompts the question which guides the rest of what Augustine has to say: "how does he have it?"[34] That is, how does the Son have life, by virtue of which he can bestow life on believers? The answer runs thus: the Son has life "as the Father has it," that is, "in himself."[35] Why is this point so significant for Augustine? Because the Son's having life *in semetipso*, as a mode of divine aseity, at one and the same time distinguishes the Son absolutely from creatures and grounds the believers' partaking of life.

Accordingly, Augustine explicates God's life *in semetipso* and so *a se* in terms of the eternal relations of Father and Son. The Father, he says, "'has given to the Son also to have life in himself.' As he has, so he has given to have. Where does he have it? 'In himself.' Where has he given to have it? 'In himself.'"[36] Here Augustine seeks to articulate an understanding of paternity and filiation in which the Father's giving does not in any way entail the Son's inferiority: what the Father gives the Son is what he, the Father, has—life in himself—and the mode of life which is the Son's by the gift of the Father is characterized not by its being "in another" but, again, by its being in himself. "The Son of God was not as if at first without life and [then] he received life. For, if he so received it, he would not have it in himself. For what does 'in himself' mean? That

31. Scripture quotations in this chapter are from the RSV.
32. Augustine, *Tractates on the Gospel of John* 22.8.2, trans. John W. Rettig (Washington, DC: Catholic University of America Press, 1988), 2:204–5.
33. Augustine, *Tractates on the Gospel of John* 22.8.2 (Rettig, 2:205).
34. Augustine, *Tractates on the Gospel of John* 22.9.1 (Rettig, 2:205).
35. Ibid.
36. Augustine, *Tractates on the Gospel of John* 22.9.2 (Rettig, 2:205).

he himself is life itself."[37] This is why the relation of Father and Son is wholly unique, consisting as it does of a giving and receiving which is devoid of any subordination, so that of the Son to whom the Father gives life it can be said, *Ipsa vita ipse esset* ("He himself is life itself").[38] "'As the Father has life in himself, so he has given the Son also to have life in himself,' so that he [the Son] does not live by participation, but lives without change and in every respect he, himself, is life."[39] Thus *I am* the logic of "life-giving" is strictly parallel to that of "begetting": "What is said, 'He has given to the Son' is such as if it were said, 'He begot a Son'; for he gave only by begetting. As [the Father] gave that he might be, so he gave that he might be life, and so he gave that he might be life in himself."[40]

This is rather distant from later notions of aseity as independence; it is aseity as the eternal and lively perfection of Father and Son. Yet to this immanent reality there corresponds the Son's mission; the life which the Son receives and has in himself is that which he in turn bestows upon creatures. Augustine is, of course, sharply aware of the gulf between God and creatures. The apostle or the believer only has life in Christ, not in himself; life *in semetipso* is entirely incommunicable, and so the identity of "Son" and "life" cannot in any way be replicated in the creaturely realm. But if aseity differentiates the divine Son from creatures, it is also at the same time the ground of his saving gift. The Son has and is life, and "as he has, so he has given."[41] Indeed, the full scope of the Son's being life in himself must be understood both immanently and economically. As the one who has life *in semetipso*, the Son "would not need life from another source, but would be fullness of life by which others, believing, might live the life they live."[42]

Augustine's exegesis, then, directs us to two primary aspects of a theological conception of aseity: (1) that aseity is materially to be understood out of the eternal relations which constitute God's inner triune life, and (2) that this aseity is, as it were, the eternal impetus of the Son's life-giving mission of salvation. Something of the same can be found in Calvin's rather more terse remarks on the same verse in his 1553 commentary on John's Gospel:

37. Augustine, *Tractates on the Gospel of John* 22.9.3 (Rettig, 2:206).
38. Augustine, *In Evangelium Johannis tractatus* 22.9 (=Rettig, 2:228).
39. Augustine, *Tractates on the Gospel of John* 22.10.3 (Rettig, 2:207).
40. Augustine, *Tractates on the Gospel of John* 22.10.4 (Rettig, 2:207). With this emphasis on "begetting," Augustine safeguards the distinction between the aseity which is the personal property of the Father alone and the common divine aseity in which both Father and Son participate: the Son's aseity is not identical with that of the personal aseity of the Father, who begets him.
41. Augustine, *Tractates on the Gospel of John* 22.10.3 (Rettig, 2:207).
42. Augustine, *Tractates on the Gospel of John* 22.10.4 (Rettig, 2:207).

[Christ] shows the source of the efficacy of his voice—that he is the fountain of life and by his voice pours it forth on men. For life would not flow to us from his mouth unless its cause and source were in himself. For God is said to have life in himself, not only because he alone lives by his own inherent power, but because he contains the fullness of life in himself and quickens all things. And this is peculiar to God; as it is said, "With thee is the fountain of life" (Ps. 36:9). But because God's majesty, which is far removed from us, would be like a secret and hidden spring, he has revealed himself in Christ. And so we have an open fountain at hand to draw from. The words mean that God did not want to have life hidden and as it were buried within himself, and therefore he transfused it into his Son that it might flow to us.[43]

If Augustine is concerned to emphasize how the immanent trinitarian dimensions of the Son's life in himself form the deep ground of his saving gift of life, Calvin appears to be concerned primarily with Christ, who is of himself Savior and life-giver. The immanent dimension is certainly rather more muted in what Calvin has to say, and he concentrates on Christ's *efficacia*, Christ as *fons vitae*. Yet Calvin does root what he says on this matter in the immanent reality of Christ's deity; only as one who *is* life can he give life. "Life would not flow to us from his mouth unless its cause and source were in himself." Having life *in se* is "peculiar to God," the one who is alone the fountain of life; for Calvin, therefore, the deity of the Son, his coequality with the Father who "contains the fullness of life in himself," is the presupposition of the Son's saving acts. Without this immanent aseity, the Son's work would be entirely lacking in the power to vivify. But Calvin is equally firm that the Son's life *in se* is superabundant, overflowing. His imagery—*fons, causa, origo*—is telling, indicating what he clearly considers to be the chief practical aspect of aseity, namely, that "God is said to have life in himself, not only because he alone lives by his own inherent power, but because he contains the fullness of life in himself and quickens all things." The sole perfection of God *a se* is unquestioned, for God is the one who "alone lives by his own inherent power." But the life with which God alone lives of himself is the fullness of life which *quickens*. The form of this life-giving overflow of God's life is the Son. "Because God's majesty, which is far removed from us, would be like a secret and hidden spring, he has revealed himself in Christ," in whom "we have an open fountain at hand to draw from." The divine will is not simply to possess life as something "hidden and as it were buried within himself" but rather to transfuse that life "into his Son that it might flow to us." Calvin is characteristically reticent

43. J. Calvin, *The Gospel according to St John 1–10*, ed. and trans. T. H. L. Parker (Edinburgh: Oliver & Boyd, 1959), 131.

about the trinitarian dimensions; he is less concerned than is Augustine to clarify that filiation ("transfusing" life into the Son) does not entail subordination. What Calvin offers is an account of the aseity of God from the economic perspective.

Taken together, Augustine and Calvin suggest a number of characteristics for an adequate theology of divine aseity. Aseity is not only the absence of external causation but the eternal life which God in and of himself *is*. It is therefore (following the Gospel's usage) *in*seity as much as *a*seity. This life cannot be conceived apart from the mutual relations of Father and Son; its perfection includes the perfect mutuality of the Father's giving of life to the Son, who in his turn has life in himself. Nor can it be conceived apart from its overflowing plenitude in giving itself to creatures. God's aseity, although it marks God's utter difference from creatures, does not entail his isolation, for what God is and has of himself is life and this life includes a self-willed movement of love.

IV

Both the pathology and the material exposition sketched here suggest that an account of aseity goes wrong when it is alienated from its proper trinitarian setting and deployed to perform different functions. When this alienation takes place, its content is reworked into something more basic (less positive); the biblical and theological texts in which its primary Christian sense is encapsulated are either pushed to the margins or reinterpreted in line with what is taken to be a more basic sense; above all, the location of the concept drifts from trinitarian to cosmological teaching. These are, it should be emphasized, not simply the errors of philosophers, for it is at least arguable that the development of a bare, nontrinitarian concept of aseity owes as much to abstract theological notions of God's *independentia* as it does to philosophical apologetics for natural religion. In this matter and others, theology has not always successfully resisted the forces that lead to the alienation of inquiry from Christian confession and praise.

If Christian dogmatics wishes to offer a corrective, it can be only by recalling itself to its proper calling, which is the praise of God by crafting concepts to turn the mind to the divine splendor. But deeply important as they are, concepts are only serviceable as the handmaids of spiritual apprehension. In an early sermon, Jonathan Edwards spoke thus:

> It may be the natural man may have a great notional knowledge concerning God's attributes—how he is the most excellent of all beings, and has infinite perfection; is the fountain of all excellency and loveliness; is immensely holy and merciful, and the like—yet he has not half so deep and

lively an apprehension of God's amiableness as he has of the beauty of some things earthly. Though he can talk as well and as rationally as most about the gloriousness of God, yet he loves him not half so well as some other things. And what is the reason? . . . It must be because there is a certain knowledge of God's excellency that he has not. . . . The knowledge of a thing is not in proportion to the extensiveness of our notions, or number of circumstances known, only; but it consists chiefly in the intensiveness of the idea.[44]

Indeed so. Like all the divine attributes, the notion of aseity remains a notion until it becomes a matter of "intensive" apprehension. Not the least sign that all is well with dogmatics (and its practitioners) is that it is aware of the need to resist the enticements of natural divinity. Such resistance is a matter of reason disciplined by attention to the instruction of the word and by prayer, and this is why the chief act of theological existence is the petition "Give me understanding according to thy word!"

44. Jonathan Edwards, "A Spiritual Understanding of Divine Things Denied to the Unregenerate," in *Sermons and Discourses, 1723–1729* (New Haven: Yale University Press, 1997), 75–76.

7

God and the Cross

HENRI A. BLOCHER

[W]e speak the wisdom of God in mystery, the hidden wisdom . . . which none of the princes of this age has known, for, had they known it, they would not have crucified the Lord of glory. . . . To us, God has revealed it through the Spirit.

1 Cor. 2:7–8, 10

God, the cross: associating Deity, the Blessed Potentate who dwells in unapproachable light (1 Tim. 6:15–16), and that horrendous mode of execution, the *mors turpissima crucis*, "the most shameful death by crucifixion"—what a monstrous combination! And yet it is the hallmark of the original gospel. God and the gallows on which Jesus was nailed are the two foci of the message, and the ancient church showed the spiritual mettle to maintain the combination despite scorn, disgust, and taunts (remember the *graffito* of the Domus Gelotiana, "Alexamenos is worshiping [*sebei*] his god," a crucified one with the head of an ass!).[1]

At once a phrase resonates in our ears: *the crucified God*. It echoes very ancient ways of speaking; Tertullian affirmed that Christians believe in

1. To be seen, we are told, in the former Kircherian Museum of the Collegio Romano; reproduced as a full-page picture in Annie Jaubert, *Les premiers chrétiens* (Paris: Seuil, 1967), 118.

a God who was crucified and died.[2] The fifth ecumenical council (Constantinople II in 553) anathemized whoever "would not confess that our Lord Jesus Christ, crucified as to the flesh [or in the flesh, *sarki*], is true God, Lord of Glory and One of the Holy Trinity" (canon 10).[3] But what is the precise thought-content of such proclamations and confessions? What do they entail for the doctrine of God, the subject of "theology proper"?

A few decades ago the phrase and the theme of the "crucified God" were raised to unprecedented prominence by several influential theologians who made it the key to a renovated doctrine of God. Best-known among them were Jürgen Moltmann,[4] probably the most "ecumenical" of all theologians in the third part of the twentieth century, and Eberhard Jüngel, whom many consider the most rigorous and profound thinker—and who claimed he had been the first to introduce the new perspective.[5] They appealed to Luther's taste for the alliance of words and, more generally, to his "theology of the cross"; apart from their indebtedness to Hegel, they showed the influence of some accents of Karl Barth (to say the least) and of the most daring thoughts in Bonhoeffer's letters from prison, *Widerstand und Ergebung* ("Resisting and Yielding").

The interval of time may facilitate a more balanced appraisal of their theses (or at least one unswayed by quick reactions and excessive passion). The present study, while prompted by the wide reception of Moltmann's and Jüngel's proposals, will, under the guidance of the normative interpretation of Holy Scripture, explore the implications of Jesus Christ's crucifixion for an evangelical theology of the divine attributes and Trinity. It will consider first the issue of method and principle (in the sense of the *principium cognoscendi*, the principle of knowledge) whereby we should draw the main propositions of our doctrine of God from the Calvary event. It will then apply what may appear as the sounder procedure to the following questions:

2. Tertullian, *Adversus Marcionem* II.16 (*mortuus*), 27 (*crucifixus*).

3. Bauckham has noticed that Jürgen Moltmann mistakenly wrote that the proposition had been rejected, whereas it was affirmed. See Richard Bauckham, "In Defence of *The Crucified God*," in *The Power and the Weakness of God*, ed. Nigel M. de S. Cameron (Edinburgh: Rutherford House Books, 1990), 109 (where n. 15 points to another inaccuracy in Paul S. Fiddes's statement of the matter).

4. Mainly in Jürgen Moltmann, *Der gekreuzigte Gott: Das Kreuz Christi als Grund und Kritik christlicher Theologie* (Munich: Kaiser, 1972); translation, *The Crucified God*, trans. John Bowden and R. A. Wilson (London: SCM, 1974).

5. Eberhard Jüngel, *God as the Mystery of the World: On the Foundations of the Theology of the Crucified One in the Dispute between Theism and Atheism*, trans. Darrell L. Guder (Grand Rapids: Eerdmans, 1983), 220n65; translation of *Gott als Geheimnis der Welt*, 3rd ed. (Tübingen: Mohr Siebeck, 1977), 298–99.

If God was capable of the cross, what does it teach us about God?
What aspects of his being (attributes) did God prominently reveal
through the cross of Christ?

Deriving Theology from the Cross?

The Crucified God

In a way, the new "crucified God" theologies were born of a renewed
sense of the violent incompatibility between the centrality of the cross
(the focal point of the Christian *kērygma*) and the classical view of God
as the "Blessed Potentate." Their champions felt that traditional interpretations had managed to tame this incompatibility by losing sight of
the horror of the cross *for God*.

How did it happen? As early as Justin Martyr, the cross had become a
symbol of victory, the *tropaion* made with the weapons of the defeated foe
on the very battlefield (a similar shape and the proclamation of the Crucified as the *Christus Victor* facilitated this glorious reinterpretation).[6] One
could lose sight of the shame so unworthy of the supreme Ruler. At the
same time, theology was able to render the divine nature immune from any
real involvement in the event. Patripassianism, the opinion that the Father
had suffered on Good Friday (*Pater passus est*), the extreme consequence
of a modalistic view of the Trinity, became the scarecrow. Among the
orthodox it would be hard to deny an important strain of subordinationism; inasmuch as the Son was assigned a lower rank than the Father, the
Son's suffering was kept at a safe distance from absolute Deity (a logic that
led to Arianism). A Nestorian-like division between Christ's two natures
was a tool used to the same end: if Jesus's humanity is only joined to the
Logos in a loose, merely "moral" manner, this humanity may appear as
the subject of an ordeal from which the Logos himself escapes. Thus the
consequences of the cross were not drawn for the Christian view of God,
who remained the Most High, immutable, impassible, the Omnipotent
One who enjoys the fullness of being in beatific aloofness.

From several angles, among "crucified God" theologians, this classical
view was considered no longer acceptable. It was typical, they charged,
of a *theologia gloriae*—Luther's phrase—the expression of a hunger for
power and dominion which was also manifest, all too manifest, in church
politics.[7] It was borrowed from Greek metaphysics—and so not really

6. A fine account is given by Flemming Fleinert-Jensen, *Das Kreuz und die Einheit der
Kirche: Skizzen zu einer Kreuzestheologie in ökumenischer Perspektive* (Leipzig: Evangelische
Verlagsanstalt, 1994), 50–51.

7. Jüngel, *God as the Mystery of the World*, 206 (*Gott als Geheimnis der Welt*, 280), dis-
cerns in it the deification of power. Moltmann's political concerns are well known indeed;

biblical—and part of the onto-theological tradition now out of date (at least for those impressed by Heidegger).[8] It was a dogma of natural theology, which made it suspect to Barthians. It was, following Bonhoeffer's most damaging critique, a god of the heathen, a resource-figure for us to exploit, the convenient counterpart of our wishes and anxieties.

The "crucified God" theologies claimed to be *radically* Christian, since the very notion of God was re-formed in accordance with the central proclamation of the gospel. But they were also more modern, not only in their assurance of having freed themselves from the fetters of older generations (nineteen centuries) but, above all, in their ability to dialogue with the contemporary world. Moltmann explained that he was moved to concentrate on the theology of the cross by the painful disappointments of the late sixties: the Prague Spring was suppressed, the civil-rights movement came to an end, the progressive momentum of Vatican II and the Uppsala World Council of Churches assembly was checked or lost.[9] Jüngel's project has been to break through the deadlock of theism and atheism, as his subtitle indicates, by going beyond them both. For the "God" to which atheists (as supremely represented by Nietzsche) object is the classical God of Greek metaphysics, not the "crucified God."[10]

Two motives have been especially conspicuous in the success of "crucified God" theologies. First, as they involve God himself in utmost suffering, they provide a new theodicy (the "theology after Auschwitz line"),[11] they exalt solidarity (one of the few values that still shine, even brighter than ever, in our common firmament), and they can point to the most striking contrast between the classical view (God impassible) and the

---

his aversion to power and hierarchy in human societies is a constant motivation of his work.

8. Jüngel, *God as the Mystery of the World*, 203 (*Gott als Geheimnis der Welt*, 275).

9. Moltmann, *The Crucified God*, 2; cf. 318 on forwarding the dialogue with socialist movements.

10. Jüngel does not word this thesis so bluntly, probably because he self-consciously eschews any appearance of apologetics (cf. *God as the Mystery of the World*, 253n15, "It is not a concern of Christian talk about God to present an apology [defense] over against atheism"). He deals *ex professo* with the "thinkability" of God in our cultural situation. But setting the theology of the cross as an answer to atheism may be discerned as a burden of *God as the Mystery of the World*; cf. 43–44, 57–63 (on Bonhoeffer, whom Jüngel venerates), 97–100, 156–57. On our relationship to the historical situation, he says that we should not yield to the tyranny of the spirit of the age but we cannot abstract ourselves from the history of thought (200–202 [*Gott als Geheimnis der Welt*, 270–71]). Moltmann also criticizes both traditional theism and atheism from the vantage point of his theology of the cross (*The Crucified God*, 249–52; cf. 223–25 on Max Horkheimer's theses).

11. On the theological import of the Shoah, see the sober and courageous study by John J. Johnson, "Should the Holocaust Force Us to Rethink Our View of God and Evil?" *Tyndale Bulletin* 52/1 (2001): 117–28.

language of Scripture (with the divine *pathos*, as A. Heschel called it). Second, they bind God's being with history, and an emphasis on history is both biblical and modern. Statements by Moltmann go so far as to suggest that the Trinity is *constituted* by the event of the cross, the Trinity understood as the "history of God";[12] and even Jüngel, despite his greater caution and reverence for tradition, appears to lean toward the same side.[13] Other statements, however, especially in the case of Moltmann in works published after *The Crucified God*, seem to revert to a more traditional preexistence of the Three.[14] Due caution advises me to say that the more extreme interpretation is not established beyond all possible ambiguity

12. A "complete reshaping" of trinitarian theology is called for in which "the nature of God would have to be the human history of Christ and not a divine 'nature' separate from man" (Moltmann, *The Crucified God*, 239); "The persons constitute themselves" in the event of Golgotha (245); "The unity of the dialectical history of Father and Son and Spirit in the cross of Golgotha, full of tension as it is, can be described, so to speak retrospectively, as 'God.' . . . In that case, 'God' is not another nature or a heavenly person or a moral authority, but in fact an 'event'" (247); "The Trinity is no self-contained group in heaven, but an eschatological process open for men on earth, which stems from the cross of Christ" (249 [cf. 255]).

13. Jüngel, *God as the Mystery of the World*, 328 (*Gott als Geheimnis der Welt*, 449): "As this *history*, he is God, and in fact, this *history of love* is 'God himself'"; "God is the one and living God *in that he* as the loving Father gives up his beloved Son and thus turns to those others, those people who are marked by death, and draws the death of these people into his eternal life"; 329 (*Gott als Geheimnis der Welt*, 450): "The identification of God with the crucified Jesus requires the differentiation of God the Father, God the Son and God the Holy Spirit!" Jüngel repeatedly rejects the disjunction between the "immanent" and the "economic" Trinity (e.g., 369–70). (All italics are Jüngel's.)

14. In the esssay "L'absolu et l'historique dans la doctrine de la Trinité," trans. F. Thévenaz and J.-P. Thévenaz, in *Hegel et la théologie contemporaine*, ed. Louis Rumpf et al. (Neuchâtel, Switz., and Paris: Delachaux & Niestlé, 1977), presented at a conference in Switzerland, Moltmann affirmed that "starting from the *Trinity in Jesus' mission* one goes back to the *Trinity of origin* in God himself, in order to grasp Jesus' history as revelation of the divine life" (193). The Trinity is no longer constituted by the cross, but being *open* from the origin, the Trinity experiences history and change—that is, something *new* happens to God (201). At this point, then, Moltmann still understands the Trinity as the "Trinitarian history of God" (191). In Jürgen Moltmann, *The Trinity and the Kingdom of God*, trans. Margaret Kohl (London: SCM, 1981), the shift is obvious to the "social Trinity," which I feel to be a different scheme (tritheistic temptations are combined with a conspicuous concern to honor tradition, with an original, eternal Trinity), though Moltmann did not recant his more Hegelian one. In Jürgen Moltmann, *History and the Triune God: Contributions to Trinitarian Theology*, trans. John Bowden (London: SCM, 1991; New York: Crossroad, 1992), 81–85, Moltmann, who again criticizes Rahner and Barth, stresses the starting point in salvation-history but does not clarify the relationship with antecedent eternity. Eberhard Jüngel, *Das Evangelium von der Rechtfertigung des Gottlosen als Zentrum des christlichen Glaubens: Eine theologische Studie in ökumenischer Absicht* (Tübingen: Mohr Siebeck, 1998), 69, speaks of God's "threefold personal existence," "not first in relationship with his creature, but already in relationship with himself," and uses orthodox formulations (he quotes from the *Fides Damasi*); other statements are, however, more problematic.

(I shall come back to the point). Perhaps the link shall be found between the "history of Jesus" and the essential Trinity in the "eternalization" of the event. One thing is clear, however: in the work of the "crucified God" theologians, history counts for God's own *definition*. *(was Jesus m)*

① *J. said - I am in you, and you are in me)*

Evaluation

The effort to align one's theology, in the stricter sense, with the implications of the message of the cross, the central message of the New Testament, is, as such, praiseworthy indeed. The biblical sense of truth rules out a real contradiction: if a view of God makes it impossible for him to be in Christ on the cross, reconciling the world unto himself, it cannot be entertained. The mystery of God is no cloak for the absurd—it is foolishness *for those who perish*! But for the redeemed, at least when they reach a sufficient degree of maturity (1 Cor. 2:6, *en tois teleiois*; cf. 14:20), it is truly wisdom with the connotations of coherence that go with that notion. Therefore the theologian rightly aims at some perceptible harmony between the doctrine of God and the _kērygma_ of the cross.

Other strong points of "crucified God" theologies include the warning about the influence of pagan Greek philosophy on Christian theology and the recognition of God's *pathos* ("passion"), that entails *sympatheia* ("compassion"); if "impassibility" is to be "saved," it will be through a concept different from the usual (mis)conception.

The distance from the language of Scripture, however, even on these points is also striking, as Adrio König and others observed.[15] Nowhere in the New Testament do we find the theopaschite overtones so typical of Moltmann and Jüngel. The latter has to admit that Paul in 2 Corinthians 13:4 "appears to be inconsistent" if one adopts the "crucified God" perspective.[16] The crude spatial metaphor (which these writers seem to take quite literally!) of God incorporating within himself death, suffering, and nothingness is utterly absent from the biblical testimony. Apart from the "magic" (*Zauberkraft*, Hegel's own word) of Hegel's negative, it gives us no assurance of any victory over adverse realities: victory is merely affirmed, in no way accounted for.[17] Karl Rahner protested that the God of Moltmann and his peers is unable

15. Adrio König, "Le Dieu crucifié?" *Hokhma* 17 (1981): 73–95, here 85. König relies, in several of his criticisms, on similar estimates by Dutch theologians Hendrik Berkhof and H. H. Miskotte (84, 88, 91, 94). He shows how Jüngel mishandles a passage such as Rom. 1:4 ("Je trouve spécieux cet usage de Rm 1,4") (86–87).

16. Jüngel, *God as the Mystery of the World*, 39 (*Gott als Geheimnis der Welt*, 50). Jüngel, however, thinks he can explain the apostle's thought otherwise.

17. König, "Le Dieu crucifié?" 93–94. The meaning of Christ's resurrection is obscured (86–88), and the *nihil* made into something (94).

to *comfort* us in our trials; the immutable and impassible God (rightly understood), *he* is able.[18]

After all, there is much *biblical* evidence testifying to the immutable "Blessed Potentate"! Apart from Malachi 3:6, which comes immediately to mind and may not be the strongest proof, James 1:16–17 is a finely, self-consciously elaborated theologoumenon that contrasts the Lord's immutability with the variations of all creatures, including the luminaries that pagans divinized. And beyond particular texts (these and others), there are the sovereign proclamations *'ǎnî hû '*, "I—HE," in Deuteronomy 32:39 and, in the Septuagint, *egō eimi*, "I AM," five times in Isaiah 41–48, and the praise throughout Scripture of stability, endurance, and firmness forever. The key metaphor is that of the rock.

Though interpreters of Luther may differ, I surmise that the Reformer's orientation in his theology of the cross (a phrase which he used only *once* after 1520, in extant writings) does not match Moltmann's and Jüngel's.[19] Luther maintained the "classic" God, as the *Deus nudus*, the "naked God" of creation and of the law. The paradoxical revelation of God *sub specie contraria* (in contrary appearance), in weakness and death, does not imply the integration of the negative in God but characterizes his action *in the world*, the other *regiment* or realm; God's action is hidden, the object of faith, but it is powerful in itself. God's power reaches its goal in *human* weakness, so that Luther's theology of the cross generates praise of God's *Alleinwirksamkeit*[20] and a call to patient suffering for Christ's disciples here below (the political consequences being quite different from those drawn by Moltmann from his theology of the cross!).[21]

A positive valuation of history and a constant stress on the doctrine of the Trinity are welcome indeed. I have expressed elsewhere my suspicion that the "classic" notion of divine eternity (the Platonic pure present, *nunc aeternum*, "eternal now") may undermine the consistency of his-

18. Paul Imhof and Hubert Biallowons, eds., *Karl Rahner in Dialogue: Conversations and Interviews, 1965–1982*, translation ed. Harvey D. Egan (New York: Crossroad, 1986), 126–27. Rahner candidly exclaims (126), "To put it crudely, it does not help me to escape from my mess and mix-up and despair if God is in the same predicament." The passage is reproduced in Moltmann, *History and the Triune God*, 122, with an answer by Moltmann (written after Rahner's death), 123–24.

19. I am indebted to Fleinert-Jensen's fine chapter on Luther's *theologia crucis* in *Das Kreuz und die Einheit der Kirche*, 19–31.

20. Interpreters debate whether Luther affirmed God's *Alleinwirksamkeit* (God alone is active, is the only Agent in an absolute sense, thus ruling out any form of synergism) or the less extreme *Allwirksamkeit* (God works in all things and is the Agent whose activity encompasses everything—i.e., the universe).

21. Moltmann is aware of the difference between Luther's and his own views. According to Moltmann, *The Crucified God*, 72, Luther, in a way, missed the mark in that he did not elaborate a philosophy of the cross or a social critique based on the cross.

torical succession that is so decisive in biblical perspective. That God as Trinity may be said to be "our God in advance" and intratrinitarian relations be considered the foundation and archetype for creation[22] is a precious traditional insight.[23]

I confess serious misgivings, however, with the way these assets are used by "crucified God" champions. The most serious problem relates to the deity of the Son. Even in Jüngel's case (he is more subtle and ambiguous than Moltmann),[24] the probable interpretation is that Jesus is made the second of the Trinity *as man*, as the man (crucified) with whom God identifies himself, thus defining himself as love, thus differentiating himself as Trinity. Since this event acquires an eternal character, Jüngel can still speak of the eternal Son.[25] This is radically opposed to

22. Jüngel, *God as the Mystery of the World*, 347, 384 (*Gott als Geheimnis der Welt*, 475, 526), with Jesus Christ the archetype, "original image," of creation. Also Eberhard Jüngel, *The Doctrine of the Trinity: God's Being Is in Becoming* (Edinburgh: Scottish Academic Press; Grand Rapids: Eerdmans, 1976), 106, says that "God's being-for-himself makes itself known to us as a being which grounds and makes possible God's being-for-us," and he writes of "reiteration."

23. Thomas Aquinas expresses the thought several times, especially in his early *Scriptum super Libros Sententiarum* [*magistri Petri Lombardi*], as quoted and commented upon by Gilles Emery, *Trinity in Aquinas* (Ypsilanti, MI: Sapienta Press of Ave Maria College, 2003), 53–70, and *The Trinitarian Theology of Saint Thomas Aquinas*, trans. Francesca Aren Murphy (Oxford: Oxford University Press, 2007), 215–16, 239, 343–47.

24. Moltmann, *The Crucified God*, 239, 247, 255, shows that Moltmann agrees with Hegel on this aspect of the meaning of the Trinity: it introduces the human in God and thus provides the ground for *theopoiēsis*, "divinization." Romans 1:4 is understood in an adoptionistic way (177), and the construction based on Jesus's cry of dereliction (145–53) moves from the perfect faithfulness of the man Jesus to his God to the thesis that, in forsaking Jesus, God has divided himself against himself—the source of the trinitarian distinction.

25. Jüngel, *God as the Mystery of the World*, 37 (*Gott als Geheimnis der Welt*, 47): God's decision not to be God without man is "the sense of the New Testament statements about the preexistence of the Son of God identified with Jesus"; p. 77 (*Gott als Geheimnis der Welt*, 102): words of praise for Hegel's interpretation of the incarnation; p. 288 (*Gott als Geheimnis der Welt*, 394): "The mystery of the God who identifies with the man Jesus is the increase of similarity and nearness between God and man which is *more than mere identity* and which reveals the *concrete difference* between God and man in its surpassing mere identical being. It is *only in this sense* that the Easter confession may be risked, the confession that Jesus Christ is true God and true man" (italics added in the last sentence); the following pages interpret Jesus as the "parable of God"; p. 327 (*Gott als Geheimnis der Welt*, 447), on the antichrists in 1 John: "Whoever denies the identification of God with the man Jesus cannot be *of God*, which identification expresses itself in that this man merits to be called the *Son of God*. For in this identification, the being of God realizes itself as love"; p. 366 (*Gott als Geheimnis der Welt*, 498): God's self-distinction occurs for the sake of God's identification with Jesus, according to Goethe's dictum *Nemo contra deum nisi deus ipse* ("No one [can be] against God except God himself," also quoted, p. 119 and p. 346). Jüngel, 329n30 (*Gott als Geheimnis der Welt*, 450), does not imply a restoration of the Chalcedonian duality of natures but rather offers its radical reinterpretation (also see 367n54).

the truth of Nicaea, Constantinople, and Chalcedon, which was faithfully defined under the guidance, under the blessed constraints, of the
biblical testimony. For all his emphasis on the *communicatio idiomatum*,
"communication of properties," Luther explained that "God in his own
nature cannot die" and was only able to die through his union with the
human creature.[26] Luther remained in full accord with Tertullian[27] and
Constantinople II, which stressed that the "Lord of Glory," true God,
was crucified *in the flesh* (see also the careful wording of Rom. 9:5, that
the Christ, who is God above all, blessed for ever, belongs to the race of
Israel "as regards the flesh," *to kata sarka*). Direct consequences for the
divine nature are not easy to draw from Jesus's sufferings.[28]

The second major difficulty relates to God's independence from the
world if his being is *defined* by a worldly occurrence. Moltmann is ready
to let the old concern go, to soften the emphasis on God's freedom in
creation, to make some room for the idea of "emanation" and promote
"panentheism."[29] Jüngel, as Barth also had done, struggles to salvage the
freedom and ontological independence of God.[30] The question remains
whether he *can*. Hegel's shadow hovering over the enterprise does not
leave much hope of a satisfactory solution. (I candidly confess that orthodox theology has no *easy* solution to offer, either: God's decree being
eternal, its freedom, as opposed to the necessity of the divine essence,
is hard to conceive: from all eternity, the divine decision was made irrevocable; since it is coeternal with God's essence, can it be meaningfully
distinguished from it? Scripture, however, constrains us to maintain the
distinction, without which any notion of divine "willing" is emptied of
content; we reach the edge of our weak powers of understanding, and

26. Martin Luther, *Von den Konziliis und Kirchen*, Weimar Ausgabe 50 (Weimar: Her-
mann Böhlaus Nachfolger, 1914), 590, as quoted by Fleinert-Jensen, *Das Kreuz und die
Einheit der Kirche*, 23n12.

27. Jüngel, *God as the Mystery of the World*, 64–65 (*Gott als Geheimnis der Welt*, 85),
n. 27 (n. 26 castigates Moltmann's error), correctly perceives Tertullian's position.

28. Even John Stott yielded to Moltmann's influence in a way that called for the fine
critique by Donald Cobb, "Les deux natures du Christ au Calvaire," *Hokhma* 67 (1998):
19–44.

29. Jürgen Moltmann, *God in Creation: A New Theology of Creation and the Spirit of
God*, trans. Margaret Kohl, Gifford Lectures, 1984–1985 (San Francisco: Harper & Row,
1985), 80–103, esp. 82: "If we start from the Creator himself, the self-communication of
his goodness in love to his creation is not a matter of his free will. It is the self-evident
operation of his eternal nature"; p. 89: the difference between Creator and creature, without
which creation cannot be thought, is "embraced and comprehended by the greater truth
. . . that God is all in all"; pp. 303–4, 312–13, 317–20 relativize Old Testament traditions
and maintain panentheism.

30. Jüngel, *God as the Mystery of the World*, 37 (*Gott als Geheimnis der Welt*, 47); idem,
The Doctrine of the Trinity, e.g., 99.

we bow down obediently before the mystery—which remains mystery even in revelation.)

The third difficulty attaches to the relationship between ontology and history (with roots in Barth). If God's *being* is constituted or defined by the event in time, this supreme glorification of history is also its destruction. By doing ontological service, the event is transmuted into ontology itself: eternal, it no longer "happens."[31] The news of the cross becomes an eternal Idea (e.g., of deity as love). The nemesis is that ontology historicized breeds an ontologized history, which loses the true character of history. The true character of history demands the duality.[32]

Akin to the last difficulty, the *principium* question arises: can we derive a proper knowledge of God himself from the *event* considered as the exclusive locus of revelation? Undoubtedly, a person's actions can be most revealing regarding the person's character and even inner life, but not without a grid and framework of interpretation, not without some prior information available. The mere sight of what happened, the brute factual datum, is not enough; at best we are left with plausible hypotheses. Undoubtedly, the cross reveals God in truth—*if* we receive the God-given interpretation (1 Cor. 2:13!) together with the factual report. The need is most acute because inferences that might have plausibility in the case of fellow creatures are not certainly applicable to *God*. It is acute because the event is usually taken to involve both God *and* man; from the event itself (alone), it is impossible to decide what should be ascribed to God and what to the man. Theologians of the "crucified God" overlook the difficulty, since they make use of the God-given (biblical) interpretation, but they refuse to acknowledge its revelatory status, its intrinsic word-of-God nature and quality, and they adopt a critical stance over it. They thus forfeit the right to use it for theological decision and cannot escape frustrating arbitrariness.

I would plead that only a word spoken by God himself allows us to speak (as we confess, *homologoumen*, what he has said) of God himself. Whatever we draw from the event remains bound to the event, and we have no authority to claim that it is valid apart from it. The only "God," then, that can be conceived is "correlative" of some worldly reality (to use Cornelius Van Til's term). Only if God himself testifies about himself may we go beyond. That Jüngel (after Barth) remains a prisoner

31. Such was the complaint of Hans Urs von Balthasar, *Karl Barth: Darstellung und Deutung seiner Theologie* (Cologne: J. Hegner, 1951), 380, as quoted by Henri Bouillard, *Karl Barth* (Paris: Aubier-Montaigne, 1957), 2/1:102.

32. Oliver O'Donovan, *Resurrection and Moral Order: An Outline for Evangelical Ethics* (Leicester, UK: Inter-Varsity, 1986), 60, makes a similar point (against historicism): "When history is made the categorical matrix for all meaning and value, it cannot then be taken seriously *as history*."

of the correlation appears from his rejection of the *logos asarkos* as "abstract";[33] so must it be for his method, drawn from or out of (*abstrahere*) the event.

A theology of the cross, yes—but as interpreted under the guidance of all the Scriptures, the abiding word of God written!

God Capable of the Cross

With the issues of method and principle somewhat clarified (some controversial elaboration could not be avoided), I may sketch in more succinct form what profit in the knowledge of God we can gain from consideration of the cross—as biblically interpreted. Several passages explicitly refer to the demonstration of divine attributes in and through the event (e.g., divine righteousness, Rom. 3:25–26; love, Rom. 5:8), and I shall follow this path, but another line of inquiry also seems legitimate and nearer to the "crucified God" discussions: how was God *capable* of acquiring his church *by his own blood* (Acts 20:28)—perhaps the nearest biblical equivalent to the statement "God was crucified"?

The attempt to answer this question entails inferring from actuality to possibility, a procedure, I grant, fraught with danger. The major role the category of the "possible," in relationship with a hypostasized nothingness (*das Nichts*), plays in Jüngel's theology is worth a warning. Aristotle's category, the mongrel semireality (*to mē on*) between being and nonbeing worthy of the names,[34] smacks of mythology and seems to be alien to Scripture. At the same time, the theme of divine *power* is prominent indeed. Perhaps Karl Barth's distinction between *potestas*, the rightful power of God, and indefinite *potentia*, of which Barth suggests we should be rather suspicious,[35] points to the sounder approach. Since God himself teaches us that he *can* do what he does, we are free,

33. Jüngel, *God as the Mystery of the World*, 78 (*Gott als Geheimnis der Welt*, 103).

34. One remembers that the Greek language offers two particles for negation: one generally weaker (*mē*) and one stronger (*ou/ouk/ouch*). When the participle "being" is weakly negated, with *mē*, the phrase may be used for the idea of the "possible" as an intermediate category, that which does not exist actually (not being) and yet is not nothing. Jacques Maritain, *An Introduction to Philosophy*, trans. E. I. Watkin (New York: Sheed & Ward, 1937), 243, eloquently explains: "We have thus found something that does not deserve to be called being, on which that title can be bestowed only in a secondary and improper sense, as an alms, so to speak, but which nevertheless is real. It is what philosophers term *potency* or *potentiality*."

35. Karl Barth, *Réalité de l'homme nouveau: Trois conférences suivies d'entretiens* (Geneva: Labor et Fides, 1964), 95. Jüngel, *The Doctrine of the Trinity*, 50, comments on this theme in Barth (quoting from Karl Barth, *Church Dogmatics* [Edinburgh: T&T Clark, 1957], II/1:40, 49, 61–62) that God's ability is actually present as *Macht*, not as Aristotelian *dynamei on* contrasted with *energeia on*.

under biblical control, to ask about the traits that made the cross possible for God.

God cannot die in his own (divine) nature. This conviction, which, as we saw, was maintained in Luther's theology of the cross and which Hegel overthrew, has a strong scriptural backing. This we maintain against the (really Hegelian) theologies of the "crucified God." It is not only the original statement of Habakkuk 1:12a, *lō' tāmût*, "Thou diest not" (observing the *tiqqûn sōpĕrîm*)[36] and the clear implication of 1 Timothy 6:13–15; it should certainly, in the vision of the Bible, be understood as entailed by the title of the living God, the Alpha and the Omega, the One who has life in himself, I AM. For such a God, to die would be tantamount to denying himself, a forbidden thought (2 Tim. 2:13).

In order to die, God had to take on another nature without losing his own; therefore he must be capable of doing so. The New Testament and church doctrine of the incarnation follows this logic, which Anselm developed in his *Cur Deus homo* (*Why God Became Man*). It implies a union, without change and confusion, of the two natures, divine and human. If deity had been lost (as in the kenotic heresy), the one who died would no longer have been God; if humanity had been divinized, he could not have died. Contrary to widespread opinions, the New Testament already reflects the thought of the actual duality within the union. The argument of Hebrews 1–2 is built on this basis. Paul intimates the same in several passages, including Philippians 2:5–11, which does not say that Christ put off his *morphē theou* ("form of God"; the present participle *hyparchōn*, which just precedes the statement of his self-divesting and means "being" in the "form [i.e., nature or condition or mode of existence] of God," rather suggests the permanence of the divine "form," which, then, must coexist with that of serving humanity); Romans 1:3–4; Romans 9:5, already mentioned; Colossians 1:15–20 with its two panels, Christ as the divine Wisdom of Proverbs 8:22–31 in verses 15–17 (the Mediator of the first creation) and as the New Adam in verses 18–20; and Colossians 2:9. The prologue of the Fourth Gospel forcefully expresses the idea: though he was made flesh, the *logos* remains *monogenēs theos*, "God only-begotten" (John 1:18).[37]

The union of two created natures would not be possible without mixture; two sets of properties (*quidditates*) of the same ontological rank

36. A note which ancient scribes left in a margin indicating that they changed the text to avoid something incongruous in synagogue reading; it was not a fraud, not even a pious fraud, since they warn about the change.

37. Many scholars today criticize the traditional rendering of *monogenēs*, "only-begotten," *unigenitus*, arguing that it does not derive from *gennaō*, "beget." This is true of its etymology; in usage, however, it is very often linked with the genealogical relationship, and in the New Testament it is used only for the Son (we never read of a *monogenēs* brother).

would produce another set (one nature). Only the Creator, in his unique relationship with his creature, can protect the duality.

The mystery (we can hardly probe the "how") implies Rahner's proposal on divine immutability: God able to change *in another*. It also implies the original creation scheme: the world totally dependent on God's will and power and yet distinct from God; God the only *archē* of the world and yet distinct and independent from it. For dualism, with the world alien to God, the incarnation is either impossible or involves an *alienation* of God; not so in biblical, creational perspective, for God comes to his own. For monism, the incarnation cannot be free, and ultimately the duality of natures is resorbed.

The distinction between person and nature becomes foundational. If the two natures are united without merging, a third term appears to be required. This insight enabled orthodoxy in the fifth century to move beyond the disastrous opposition of Nestorian and monophysite Christologies, and so the distinct concept of the "person" emerged. Wolfhart Pannenberg, among others, has keenly perceived the Christian origin of this concept, which moderns tend to consider a self-evident datum.[38] The two natures are united in the person, or hypostasis, of the Son, which we must distinguish from deity as such (the essence).

Conceptual elaboration had to wait for a later stage, but we can argue that the New Testament already presupposes the distinction between nature and person inasmuch as it refers to the two natures (even in conscious thematization) and *never* suggests the presence of two persons in Christ, whose "I" is one. The one who dissolves (*lyei*) Jesus Christ is of the antichrist (the fascinating reading of some witnesses in 1 John 4:3).

The unity of the person is the foundation of the *communicatio idiomatum* in the classical sense (from which Luther departed), which Scripture freely practices, most clearly in Acts 20:28 and 1 Corinthians 2:8, and which validates the phrase "the crucified God."

Persons in the Godhead can be viewed only as subsisting relations. The distinction between person and nature also arises when Jesus Christ and his Father appear as two persons and the same deity (which can exist only once in monotheism) is ascribed to both; a plurality in the one Godhead is revealed. Presumably, it would be hard to conceive of a distinction between person and deity with one divine person only, but Scripture makes it clear that this is not the case. There are several

38. W. Pannenberg, e.g., thus introduces his article "Person" in *Die Religion in Geschichte und Gegenwart*, ed. Kurt Galling et al., 3rd ed. (Tübingen: Mohr Siebeck, 1961), 5:230: "Was man heute mit dem Wort P[erson] bezeichnet, dürfte der Menschheit erst durch das Christentum erschlossen worden sein. Die Antike unterschied noch nicht P[erson] von (geistiger) Individualität (so *hupostasis*; lat. *persona* bezeichnet die Maske, dann die Rolle eines Schauspielers, von da aus auch soziale Rolle und Charakter)."

persons of the one God, and the language of the "crucified God" must be explained as dealing with God the Son, whom God the Father has sent that he may take on human flesh and die in his flesh, in the weakness proper to human flesh (2 Cor. 13:4).

The oneness of the true God ('eḥād, Deut. 6:4) leaves only one option for persons sharing in absolute unity: they can distinguish from one another as *relations*. This insight of the Cappadocian fathers, Augustine, and the whole Catholic and Protestant tradition agrees with whatever hints may be found in Scripture on this subject. The data that compel us to distinguish between Father and Son (as God) are concerned with, and reveal, their mutual relations (most abundantly in the Fourth Gospel).

God is capable of the cross as the God of trinitarian and christological orthodoxy.

God Revealed by Means of the Cross

In the central event of the cross, biblically considered, all of God's attributes—which are one—shine forth in one way or other. Since however, Scripture, by its own use, validates the thought of their diversity (*in ratione, cum fundamento in re*),[39] we may focus on some of them.

The cross and sovereign singularity. Scripture often proclaims that the cross, the apparent failure of God, was the outworking of his sovereign purpose (as early as Acts 2:23 and 4:27–28). The theme of fulfilled prophecy and the necessity that it be fulfilled highlight this aspect of the cross. The most extensive presentations of God's plan put the cross in central position (Eph. 1:7; Col. 1:20; Rev. 5:6, and almost countless other texts). In the cross, God displayed the hidden determination of his wisdom in mystery (1 Cor. 2:7–8).

One aspect deserves to be singled out—*singularity*. God chose one small place in the whole universe, one day among myriads of possible days, to reconcile the world unto himself: *there and then*. This has been called "the scandal of particularity" (already for the incarnation), for it irritates the universalizing habits of reason and produces a dissonance in the present interreligious concert. Yet it is the brightest illustration of

---

39. This formula summarizes a middle solution (such as Aquinas's) in medieval debates: divine attributes are distinct for our intellectual apprehension, and validly so because the diversity is grounded in the reality of the divine being, though in this reality they are inseparable descriptions of the one essence of deity. This rules out, on the left, falsely humble agnosticism (the attributes are diverse for us but not in God, which means that our God-talk and that of the Bible are devoid of all true knowledge) and, on the right, the naive opinion (sometimes found in sophisticated garb) that our thought univocally corresponds to God's reality (forgetting God's transcendence and the limitations of our thought, 1 Cor. 13:12).

the sovereign freedom of a God who can choose any place and any time because he is not bound by cosmic regularities. He is the noncorrelative God. Such is the logic of Exodus 19:5: "Out of all the nations, you will be my special possession, *because* the whole earth is mine" (the particle used, *kî*, may very seldom bear an adversative meaning, but its usual one is causal, "for," "because," and I argue that it is appropriate here; accordingly, the Septuagint renders *gar* and the Vulgate has *enim*).

The cross and overflowing righteousness. Romans 3:25–26 insists on the demonstration (*endeixis*) of God's righteousness in the event of Calvary, and the prevalence of judicial language in the apostolic preaching of the cross (e.g., 2 Cor. 5:19–21) justifies an emphasis on this attribute or dimension of God's relationship with humankind.

In the light of convincing scholarly statements, I reach the conclusion that the root meaning of "righteousness," "justice" in the Bible is conformity to a norm, with an irreducible retributive element, and that the *dikaiosynē* exhibited on the cross according to Romans 3 is the satisfaction of the demands of retributive justice. Through the sacrificial substitution of the Redeemer for those who had deserved to die—through Christ's death on the cross—God shows himself righteous (inflicting the retribution of sins) and the justifier (acquitter) of the guilty who benefit from Christ's intervention.[40] This understanding best accounts for the range of biblical texts.

This is not to deny, however, the restorative facet of biblical righteousness/justice, which brings it very near to salvation, *šālôm*, and deliverance in many contexts. Justification through the blood of the cross is reconciliation and pacification (Col. 1:20), bringing back whoever takes refuge in Christ through faith in his name in conformity with the supreme norm of reality, in harmony with God's ordering of things (with cosmic extension, especially as the object of hope; cf. James 1:18, where the regenerate are the *aparchē* ["firstfruits"] of all creatures, and Rom. 8).

40. On the notion of righteousness, I found most helpful Mark A. Seifrid, "Righteousness Language in the Hebrew Scriptures and Early Judaism," in *Justification and Variegated Nomism*, vol. 1, *The Complexities of Second Temple Judaism*, ed. D. A. Carson, Peter T. O'Brien, and Mark A. Seifrid, Wissenschaftliche Untersuchungen zum Neuen Testament 2/140 (Tübingen: Mohr Siebeck; Grand Rapids: Baker Academic, 2001), 415–42. Likewise, on Rom. 3, Simon G. Gathercole, "Justified by Faith, Justified by His Blood: The Evidence of Romans 3:21–4:25," in *Justification and Variegated Nomism*, vol. 2, *The Paradoxes of Paul*, ed. D. A. Carson, Peter T. O'Brien, and Mark A. Seifrid, Wissenschaftliche Untersuchungen zum Neuen Testament 2/181 (Tübingen: Mohr Siebeck; Grand Rapids: Baker Academic, 2004), 147–84; the whole volume is relevant to the present topic, especially the contributions of Douglas J. Moo, "Israel and the Law in Romans 5–11: Interaction with the New Perspective," 185–216; and Moisés Silva, "Faith versus Works of Law in Galatians," 217–48; one can see my own remarks on righteousness in Henri Blocher, "Justification of the Ungodly (*sola fide*): Theological Reflections," 473–82.

 Chinese

Retribution and restoration are not mutually exclusive; the good news is the retribution, and the basis of restoration is in the person of the head and substitute. (It would be attractive to draw from Isa. 10:22 the image of the "overflow" of righteousness for this restoration effect, but exegetically the overflow seems to characterize judgment in that verse; the Septuagint loses the image, and Paul quotes in Rom. 9:27–28 from the Septuagint.)

The cross and unsurpassed love. Whether explicitly (Rom. 5:8) or more implicitly (John 3:16, though 1 John 4:10 shows that the gift and sending of the Son are orientated toward his sacrificial death), Scripture abundantly testifies to the tie that binds the cross and God's love for us. It was the *telos* of the love of God the Son for his own (John 13:1), a love greater than which cannot be conceived (John 15:13). It must be stressed that in strict orthodoxy the person of *God* the Son suffered and died; he did so through the possibilities of his human nature, but he was the subject to whom action and passion are ascribed.[41] Since the Father and the Son are one God with only one will (the will of Matt. 26:39, 42 is Jesus's human will), the love shown by Christ's self-giving on the cross cannot be severed from the Father's.

Moltmann stresses that for his theology of the cross, "God's being is in suffering and the suffering is in God's being itself, because God is love."[42] Jüngel even more impressively concentrates his interpretation of the cross—his theology of the cross—on love, and he claims that it entails the incorporation of death, suffering, and nothingness in God's being. Though his formulas may be breathtaking and rapturous in their condensed beauty—one is always impressed when a man speaks about love as if he knew what it is—their dialectical cast may be just a little too facile.[43] Perhaps the deepest methodological critique one could raise about Jüngel's achievement is that it rests on the anthropomorphic projection onto God of an analysis—an exceedingly brilliant one—of *human* love.[44]

41. To use Scholastic terms (precious accuracy!) the nature is only *principium quo*, that by which a person is what that person is; the person is the *principium quod*, the being who is (nominative case). Calvin grasped and expressed this rule of christological thinking and speaking (*Institutes of the Christian Religion*, II.14.3).

42. Moltmann, *The Crucified God*, 227; cf. 253–54, where he is conscious of the Hegelian stamp on his thesis.

43. König, "Le Dieu crucifié?" 94, mentions H. Berkhof's critique of Jüngel's phenomenology of love. König is not happy with Jüngel's definition of love as "the union of death and life for the sake of life" (*God as the Mystery of the World*, 299, 320); love is said to be the unity of power and weakness (206); the name of "this peculiar dialectic of being and nonbeing, of life and death," is love (220); it is fulfilled as selflessness and self-relatedness (298; cf. 322, 369); gift and loss.

44. Jüngel, *God as the Mystery of the World*, 315 (*Gott als Geheimnis der Welt*, 431), boldly states that what we say of God's love "may not contradict what people experience

What we may observe, lost in wonder, is that the presence of evil and death has been used by God's wisdom in mystery as the occasion of the greatest love, love greater than which cannot be thought. This does not explain (and therefore excuse, to some degree) evil; it reveals the fullness of God's victory over evil—not by might, not by mere power (as if evil were a creature with a quantum of power), but by love and righteousness.

In order to know God in accordance with the "theology of the cross," Luther affirmed in his twentieth thesis of the Heidelberg Disputation that one must behold the *posteriora Dei*, God's "back" or "back parts," which are seen after he has passed. This condition, laid down in Exodus 33:23, Luther interpreted as the requirement that theology be based on Christology, on the passage among us (beheld by faith) of the Incarnate and Crucified God—whereas natural or speculative theologies try to look God in his face.[45] Indeed, we begin to know God's love and righteousness, and his sovereignty, when we consider how he passed, in the person of Christ, through the death of the cross.

---

as love"; cf. 330 (*Gott als Geheimnis der Welt*, 542–43): "love is God" is "an allowable statement," as Karl Barth also granted. Moltmann also projects onto God what he sees valid at the human level and forcefully expresses: "Love makes life so lively and death so deadly. Conversely, it also makes life so deadly and death lively" (*The Crucified God*, 253); "Love is revealed in hatred and peace in conflict" (18).

45. Quoted by Fleinert-Jensen, *Das Kreuz und die Einheit der Kirche*, 20, and Jüngel, *God as the Mystery of the World*, 34n51 (*Gott als Geheimnis der Welt*, 42). Augustine already had meditated on the verse and identified God's "back, back parts," or *posteriora*, with Christ in his *De Trinitate* II.xvii.28.

This Chapter for Chinese

8

The Compassion of God

Exodus 34:5–9 in the Light of Exodus 32–34

PIERRE BERTHOUD

Introduction

The word "compassion" has become increasingly important within our culture. It is considered an essential value by many. Among those who promote it, one can mention the Buddhists. Indeed, one of the reasons why Buddhism has become so popular in the West is related precisely to its emphasis on compassion. In recent developments of contemporary thinking that have emphasized the need for spirituality, such philosophers as Luc Ferry have insisted on the importance of basic values essential to social community living: justice, truth, beauty, and love or compassion. These two outlooks favor a purely horizontal form of compassion. Buddhism offers a religious philosophy that has no clear transcendental reference point and therefore can plead for a type of spirituality which is well adapted to the humanism of our day, which has become aware of this need. As for the values put forward by Ferry, this in no wise means returning to the idea of the transcendent God of the Judeo-Christian tradition, which was given a fatal blow by the Enlightenment and especially by Nietzsche in the nineteenth century. Actually, Ferry relies heavily on the Judeo-Christian tradition, while rejecting its basis, in seeking to meet these newly expressed aspirations for the aforementioned values, including spirituality.[1] The protagonists of these two forms of compassion have at least one major point in common in the views they develop. As David the psalmist says, "they do not place God before themselves" (Ps. 86:14). In other words, they have no place for the transcendent, infinite, and personal God of Scripture and therefore for his wisdom in their appraisal of compassion! On the other hand, as we shall see, Islam seeks to maintain both the transcendence and the compassion—mercy—of God but in a way that differs from the biblical perspective.

We shall begin by considering the concept of compassion within an essentially horizontal world and life view in which humans are the measure of all things. If we take Buddhism as an example, it offers three scopes of motivation, ranging from the lowest to the highest:[2]

1. The first level is related to the realization of the problems one will encounter in the next life and is essentially concerned with worldly happiness—in other words, with the securing of a "good rebirth."
2. The second level enables one to come to the understanding "that within cyclic existence there is no real happiness" and that one must strive "for personal liberation or Nirvana."
3. The third level brings about a profound awareness "that all sentient beings are suffering within cyclic existence" and that one must make an effort "to free all beings from suffering." This is precisely where compassion comes into the picture. It must be understood as "wanting others to be free from suffering" and is therefore "the definition of the highest scope of motivation."[3] But Sharon Salzberg, a Buddhist, is eager to emphasize its dynamic aspect: "Compassion is the strength that arises out of seeing the true nature of suffering in the world. It allows us to bear witness to that suffering, whether it is in ourselves or others, without fear; it allows us to name injustice without hesitation and to act strongly, with all the skill at our disposal. To develop this mind state of compassion . . . is to learn to live, as the Buddha put it, with sympathy for all living beings, without exception."[4]

From these statements one can make the following remarks:

1. L. Ferry, *L'homme-Dieu; ou, Le sens de la vie* (Paris: Grasset, 1996); idem, *Qu'est-ce qu'une vie réussie?* (Paris: Grasset, 2002).
2. Cf. in particular Rudy Harderwijk, *A View on Buddhism: Compassion and Bodhicitta*, www.buddhism.Kalachakranet.org/compassion.html.
3. Ibid.
4. Sharon Salzberg, quoted ibid.

- It is essentially by human means—contemplation, meditation, and mind-training techniques—that human beings can "attain enlightenment for the benefit of all sentient beings."[5]
- When this state of mind—Bodhicitta—is attained, one can then experience freedom from suffering. It is compared to an "intoxicant that numbs us against pain and fills us with bliss."[6]
- Though there are some indications of personal compassion, it is viewed in general terms as showing "sympathy for all living beings, without exception." It corresponds to the wish of becoming an "omniscient Buddha" so as to "be of perfect help for others" in contributing to their liberation.[7]
- This view of compassion implies that suffering and evil are part of ultimate reality. This means that the freedom put forward can be identified with a renunciation of one's basic human nature.

Let us now consider how the Muslim faith conceives of love and compassion within a framework which insists on the centrality of transcendence. As J. Jomier says, among the many names given to the one God of the Qur'an, the most important are Allāh and al-Raḥmān. Noting that "all that is said of al-Raḥmān is said also of Allāh," he argues nevertheless that the former has a distinctive emphasis.[8] It occurs often in the Qur'an; in addition to "the ritual formula with which all the suras begin," it is used fifty-six times. It is related to the root rḥm, common to Semitic languages, which conveys the "idea of mercy."[9] This adjectival form is to be distinguished, says Jomier, from another adjective that derives from the same root, al-Raḥim, "the Merciful." This explains why al-Raḥmān "has been rendered in French as a special word: le Clément ('The Clement One'), le Bienfaiteur ('The Benefactor'), and the superlative le Très Miséricordieux ('The Most Merciful'), the emphasis being on 'the immense divine goodness.'"[10]

This implies that "the notion of love is found clearly in the Qur'an" but "the idea of giving love is rare."[11] When it is expressed, however, it

5. The Dalai Lama, quoted ibid.

6. Cf. Lama Thubten Yeshe, "Making Space with Bodhicitta," ibid.

7. "Bodhicitta," *Namo Dharmaya!* http://www.omplace.com/omsites/Buddhism/com passion.html.

8. J. Jomier, "The Divine Name 'al-Raḥmān' in the Qur'ān," in *The Qur'ān: Style and Contents*, ed. A. Rippin (Aldershot, UK: Variorum, 2001), 204.

9. Ibid., 197.

10. Ibid. Jomier goes on to show that in fact we have in al-Raḥmān more than an adjective and that as a consequence, the formula "designates God in his being," just like the French expression *le Bon Dieu* (198).

11. Ibid., 209.

earned love

is linked to the name al-Raḥmān. Thus we read, "Surely those who believe and do deeds of righteousness, unto them al-Raḥmān shall assign
love" (Qur'an 19:96). But it is not clear from the context whether this
love is related to the other life or if it applies also to this life. If in this
sura we have an independent clause, then we have a general statement
according to which "God loves the believers and loves them through the
angels, the creatures and the other believers."[12] Only two other passages
speak of a mutual love between God and humans (3:31; 5:54).[13] Such
a lack of references to love indicates that the Qur'an does not see the
need to emphasize a love relationship between God and humans as it
is presented within the biblical concept of the covenant.[14] Louis Gardet
makes interesting comments on this question:

> When in the ninth and tenth centuries the doctors and the jurists opposed
> the Sufis, it was to condemn the love of man for God, for, as some of the
> teachers maintained, love is an act of the will and human will, being finite,
> cannot have an infinite object. . . . Again in the fourteenth century Ibn
> Taymīyah, who was greatly concerned with the inner personal values of
> faith, said that love implied a correspondence between the Creator and
> the creature. The perfection of faith can and must find its fulfilment in the
> love of the law of God, in the commandment of God, in the kindness of
> God but not in the love of God himself and for himself. It is his concern
> for the faithful adoration of the divine majesty that leads Taymīyah to shy
> away from the personal love of God.[15]

It is thus the emphasis on the unity and the transcendence of God which
makes the Muslim teachers so reluctant to speak of the love of God and
for God. This means that the personal character of God is relegated to
the background of the classical expression of Muslim spirituality.

12. Ibid., 209n49.
13. "Tell them: 'if you love God, follow me'; he will love you, he will forgive you your
sins, he is indulgent and merciful" (Qur'an 3:31); "Oh you who believe, if you abandon
your religion, God will call others to take your place. God will love them and they will
love him. Gentle towards the true believers, they will be severe towards the unfaithful"
(5:54); *The Koran*, trans. N. J. Dawood (London: Penguin, 1990), 45, 85.
14. As Jomier indicates, the concept of covenant is not absent from the Qur'an. The word
for "covenant," 'ahd, is used especially with reference to the relationship between Israel
and God. "On the Day of Judgment, only those who have been received in the covenant
with al-Raḥmān will be able to intercede on behalf of others" (Qur'an 19:90/87, 81/78),
but only with the explicit permission of al-Raḥmān (20:108/109). See Jomier, "The Divine
Name 'al-Raḥmān' in the Qur'ān," 209. Jomier argues that this name for God (al-Raḥmān)
was probably already in use among the pre-Muslim Judeo-Christian dissident communi-
ties. This would explain why the Meccans felt an aversion, in the early period, to the use
of this name (cf. 200–203; 210–12).
15. L. Gardet, *Regards chrétiens sur l'islam* (Paris: Desclée de Brouwer, 1986), 56.

But can it be otherwise, within a concept of the unity of God that has no place for diversity, for the Triune God of the biblical perspective?[16] Indeed, the doctrine of the Trinity, in establishing the personal character of God, helps us to understand that the love which is in the Godhead from before the foundation of the world is the basis and fountain of God's love for creation and the creature made in his image (John 17:24). In order to grasp what true, authentic communication and love are, one only needs to be instructed by the Trinity. John's vivid description of the intimate relationship between the Father and the Son is the most significant example: God is love and all God does is motivated by love. The covenant God concludes with his people is a treaty and a relationship that is motivated by love. Created in the Creator's image, the creature, a personal being, is called to respond in love to God's loving initiative. Within this restored communion, diversity and personal communication are of vital importance. This is why the experience of God as proposed in Sufism is so different. In this type of mystical union with God, both mediation and personal communication are absent.[17]

In an article dealing with the different aspects of love in the Bible, Paul Wells distinguishes four sides to the love of God: the loving-kindness or goodness of God, the compassion of God, the grace of God, and the love of God. The Lord, being alone good (Mark 10:18) and a "river of delights" (Ps. 36:8 NIV), bestows his *loving-kindness* to all of creation and to all his creatures (Pss. 13:6; 145:9–10; Matt. 5:45). He extends his *compassion* to all those who bend under the weight of sin and human suffering and misery. His *grace*, undeserved and unconditional, brings deliverance from guilt to those who are aware of their unworthiness and are under divine judgment (Luke 15:21; Eph. 2:4–7; 4:24; Col. 3:10). Lastly, he lavishes his sanctifying *covenantal love* on his children, blessing them with his gifts and graces and arousing thankfulness in their joyful hearts (John 16:27; Rom. 5:5; 1 John 3:1).[18] Though these four facets of the love of God are related and it is therefore difficult to separate them, nevertheless we shall limit our study, as requested, to the compassion of God. We shall pay special attention to the theophany that Moses witnessed when the Lord renewed his covenant with the people of Israel, as it is recorded in Exodus 34. Other passages will also help us grasp the scope and depth of

16. P. Berthoud, "Le Dieu du Coran est-il le Dieu de la Bible?" *La Revue réformée* 174 (1992): 52–55.

17. R. Poupin, "Is There a Trinitarian Experience in Sufism?" in *The Trinity in a Pluralistic Age*, ed. K. J. Vanhoozer (Grand Rapids: Eerdmans, 1997), 72–87. In this interesting and thought-provoking article, Poupin underestimates the difference in the mystical union that a trinitarian concept of God implies.

18. P. Wells, "Les différents visages de l'amour selon la Bible," *La Revue réformée* 229–230 (2004): 130–43.

this fundamental notion. Though the question of creation has its place in this discussion,[19] we shall concentrate essentially on the compassion of God toward the sinner in spite of, and even because of, his sin.

Exodus 34:5–9 within Its Immediate and Larger Context

This theophany or manifestation of God's glory to Moses (Exod. 34:5–9), accompanied as it is by yet another dialogue between the Lord and the mediator, is related to both the immediate and the larger contexts. On the one hand, it comes as God's answer to Moses's request to see God's glory or God's face (Exod. 33:18, 20), as summarized in the report given of their conversation in Exodus 33:12–23. On the other hand, it comes at the end of a process originating with the dramatic incident of the golden calf, which is related at the beginning of Exodus 32. In a very thorough study, R. W. L. Moberly argues in favor of the literary and theological coherence of Exodus 32–34 in its final and present form.[20] He also holds that this "clearly defined unit" is linked to both the material preceding it (Exod. 25–31, the instructions concerning the tabernacle) and the material following it (Exod. 35–40, the building of the tabernacle).[21] As we seek to understand the significance of the compassion of God as revealed in God's theophany to Moses, it is thus important to take into consideration the broader context, but

19. Cf. Ps. 145:8–9. Mary Douglas, *L'anthropologie de la Bible: Lecture du Lévitique* (Paris: Bayard, 2004), 21–22, 161–62 (translation of *Leviticus as Literature* [Oxford and New York: Oxford University Press, 1999]), argues that God's compassion for creation is essential to a proper understanding of the legislation applying to the animals. She considers that the Genesis narratives underlie these laws (Lev. 11) and mentions in particular the covenant that God established with Noah (Gen. 9).

20. R. W. L. Moberly, *At the Mountain of God: Story and Theology in Exodus 32–34*, Journal for the Study of the Old Testament Supplement Series 22 (Sheffield, UK: University of Sheffield Press, 1983); cf. esp. ch. 2, "An Exegesis of Ex 32–34," 44–115. J. A. Motyer, *The Message of Exodus: The Days of Our Pilgrimage* (Leicester, UK: Inter-Varsity; Downers Grove, IL: InterVarsity, 2005), 205, 294, identifying a concentric structure, recognizes the literary coherence of these three chapters.

21. Moberly, *At the Mountain of God*, ch. 2, consistently indicates the links with the material that precedes and also pays brief attention to the chapters that follow (Exod. 25–31). The relation of these chapters with Exod. 32–34 is confirmed by the following factors: (a) The building of the tabernacle is possible only because of the restoration of the covenant between the Lord and the people. (b) "The glory of the Lord filling the tabernacle" (Exod. 40:34) is directly linked to "the Sinai experience" and confirms that the presence of God revealed on Mount Sinai is to accompany the covenant people in the tabernacle as it journeys toward the promised land. The question of the presence of the Lord in the midst of Israel is a central theme of Exod. 32–34. (c) The eagerness of the people to partake in the building of the tabernacle (35:20–29; 36:2–7) is probably to be understood as their response to what the Lord had done in restoring Israel to its covenantal relationship (cf. pp. 109–10).

especially the fact that Exodus 32–34 is a carefully constructed literary entity building up to the restoration and the renewal of the covenant. The major actors of this ensemble are God, Moses, Aaron, and the people. The covenant has hardly been concluded and Moses is still on the mountain with God when Israel brings upon itself a major crisis that threatens its existence as the covenant people and the realization of the divine plan of redemption. We shall briefly deal with some of the aspects of this dramatic narrative, which leads to the sublime revelation of God's compassion toward his people: the nature and the consequences of Israel's sin and the significance of the role of Moses as mediator in the ongoing conversation between him and the Lord, which brings about the ultimate resolution of the crisis.

The Nature and the Consequences of Israel's Sin

We are told that Moses stayed on the mountain in the presence of God a long time, "forty days and forty nights" (24:18 NIV). As the narrative begins, Moses has not yet returned. He is receiving the instructions concerning the building of the tabernacle destined to accommodate the presence of the Lord in the midst of Israel. But the people are impatient! This impatience reflects the unbelief of a natural heart or state of mind. Moses had told the people that during his absence they could speak to Aaron and Hur concerning current affairs (24:14). The prolonged absence of Moses has led the people to doubt that he will return (32:1b). With his disappearance, "the protecting help of God and his presence had vanished." Indeed, the people consider themselves abandoned by God because "His help is not visibly and outwardly at hand."[22] After all, Moses, the mediator of the leadership, the guidance, and the presence of God, he who had brought up the people out of Egypt, is but a man (32:1). Who knows what has happened to him? So they press Aaron, threateningly demanding that he "make them gods who will go before them" (32:1b). In other words, the golden calf is meant to mediate the divine leadership and presence instead of the absent Moses. But "the calf was actually intended as a symbol of the divine presence in a more real and direct way than Moses could be"; it "was seen as a real embodiment of the divine presence."[23] In their concern to maintain the continuity be-

22. C. F. Keil and F. Delitzsch, *The Pentateuch* (Grand Rapids: Eerdmans, 1971), 2:220.

23. Moberly, *At the Mountain of God*, 47. In favor of this interpretation, Moberly mentions the expression "festival to the Lord"; the designation of the bull as *'ĕlōhîm* (Exod. 32:1, 4, 8); and the parallel with 25:1–9, specifying the offerings the people are to bring in view of constructing the tabernacle, the dwelling place of the presence of the Lord in the midst of his people.

tween "the past experience" and "the present representation," the people go on to acclaim the "calf as the divine agent of the Exodus." In short, they believe the golden bull to be identical with the Lord (Yahweh).[24] In so doing, the people introduce into the true worship of God rites and practices that are foreign to it. The form of apostasy they adopt can be compared to syncretism. This indeed was to be the temptation of Israel and Judah all through their history: to introduce the worship of other gods, more specifically the Canaanite divinities and their religious customs, while maintaining their allegiance to the Lord, the one and only true God.[25] In this passage of Exodus, we are told that the people of the covenant confuse the Lord with a bull, the symbol of power and fertility.[26] The apostasy of the people, with which Aaron complies, can be summarized as follows:[27]

- the practical denial of the inimitable nature of the glory of the true God, which inevitably leads to falling back to a pagan religious mind-set;
- rejection of the first and second of the Ten Commandments, concerning the making of idols, resulting in the breaking of the covenant with the Lord (symbolized by the shattering of the two tablets of the testimony, Exod. 32:19);
- forgetfulness of the great saving acts of God as he delivered the people from Egypt through the Sea of Reeds to Mount Sinai, thus denying that the Lord is a living, faithful, and merciful God (Ps. 106:19–22);

24. Ibid. Cf. the preceding references to "the Lord who has brought you out of Egypt" (Exod. 20:2; 29:46). As to *'ĕlōhîm*, constructed with a plural verbal form, it is generally "used to convey a pagan understanding of deity" (Gen. 20:13; 1 Sam. 4:8). There are, however, instances of such a usage where there are no pagan connotations (Gen. 35:7; Deut. 4:7; 2 Sam. 7:23); cf. Moberly, *At the Mountain of God*, 46, 48n16, for further indications.

25. P. Berthoud, "The Covenant and the Social Message of Amos," *European Journal of Theology* 14 (2005): 99–109.

26. The traditional interpretation of the apostasy has usually emphasized its "orgiastic nature," but it also has been argued that the worship was "an orderly ritual following known practices"; cf. Moberly, *At the Mountain of God*, 196n7. John Calvin, *Commentaries*, ed. and trans. John King et al. (Edinburgh, 1845–1856; repr., Grand Rapids: Baker Academic, 1981, 2003), 3:336, adopts the latter interpretation. For Calvin, the sin is essentially the idolatry of the people and not the rituals and practices they performed (cf. Exod. 15:20–21). He also thinks that Paul refers to this passage when the apostle argues that syncretism is the negation of the worship of the one and true God (1 Cor. 10:18–22). Indeed, to eat meat sacrificed to idols during a pagan temple feast is to partake in idol worship and become "participants with idols" (1 Cor. 10:20).

27. Aaron, too, is guilty of transgression against the Lord. He reveals sinful weakness in his failure to resist the evil intentions and determination of the people. He thus betrays his calling as priest and is also threatened with destruction (Deut. 9:20).

- exposition of themselves to the mockery of the surrounding nations because of their betrayal of the one and only God as they turned away from the covenant blessings and protection (Exod. 32:25).[28]

All through these three chapters, the emphasis is upon the grievous rebellion, stubbornness, and corruption of the covenant community (32:8–9, 22, 30–31; 33:3, 5; 34:9). Indeed, the expression "this is a stiff-necked people" is used four times to describe the unresponsive attitude and determined resistance of Israel to the Lord (32:9; 33:3, 5; 34:9).[29] In the first three instances, it is presented as the reason for the Lord's threat to destroy the people. Thus a grievous offense on the part of the people calls for God's ultimate judgment, the capital punishment. By despising and disdaining the honor and glory of the Lord, they have struck at the very heart of the covenant. Indeed, as the episode of the Levites reveals, the penalty for being unfaithful to the Lord and for turning away from the covenant and its stipulations is death (32:26–28).[30] The rebellion and sin of the people are incompatible with God's holy and just character. This is emphasized in a number of passages throughout this narrative and signified specifically by the Lord himself:[31] his resolution to destroy Israel (32:10); his will

28. Cf. n. 31 for a discussion of this verse.

29. We have in this expression either a metaphor of an animal that rejects the yoke imposed upon it and thus opposes resistance to its master or the opposite of the expression "to incline one's ear," meaning "to listen and obey" (Deut. 9:6, 13; 10:16; Neh. 9:16, 29; Prov. 29:1; Isa. 48:4; Jer. 7:26; Acts 7:51).

30. On the other hand, God's blessing is bestowed upon those who are dedicated to the Lord and remain faithful (Exod. 32:29).

31. The narrative also speaks of the mediation of God's judgment through Moses, who destroys the bull, reduces it to powder, and scatters it on the flowing stream of drinking water (Exod. 32:20; Deut. 9:21). In Num. 5 the emphasis is on determining guilt; here it is on administrating judgment, though Umberto Cassuto gives to this practice the same meaning as in Num. 5 in *A Commentary on the Book of Exodus* (Jerusalem: Magnes Press, 1967), 419. The Levites, too, are instruments of the Lord's punishment as they "go back and forth in the camp . . . killing their brother and friend and neighbor" (Exod. 32:27b). The purpose of this judgment seems to have been to restrain the sinful carelessness and extravagance of the Israelites (32:25) and to ward off the destruction of the nation, the faithful Levites inflicting a terrible punishment on the people who persevered in rebellion. Cf. Keil and Delitzsch, *The Pentateuch*, 2:227. Calvin considers 32:25 to mean that Israel was "not only deprived of God's assistance . . . but also abandoned to ignominy, whilst they were surrounded on all sides by enemies" (*Commentaries*, 3:352). This is certainly one of the consequences of their "great sin," but the reading indicating that the people were "running wild" because "Aaron had let them get out of control" is more appropriate in the immediate context. As to the hapax legomenon šimṣâ, the versions translate it as "gloating," "mockery," "ridicule," "disgrace," "dishonor," "bad reputation." The former meaning is generally retained among modern commentators. Thus, for example, J. I. Durham translates 32:25, "Thus Moses saw the people, that they were out of control, because Aaron had let them get out of control, fair game for the whispered slander (the criticism) of those who are set against them." B. S. Childs has "to be a derision among

to blot the sinner out of his book (32:33); his striking the people with a plague (32:35); that his presence in the midst of a sinful people would have disastrous consequences (33:3, 5); and the inability of anyone, including Moses, to survive the contemplation of his face (33:20b). Moses was to recall later that the Lord was angry enough with Israel to destroy both the people and Aaron (Deut. 9:18–20). The tension is extreme.

Moses as Mediator and Intercessor

It is within this dramatic situation that Moses intervenes both as mediator between God and Israel and as intercessor in favor of the people. Commenting on the phrase "from everlasting to everlasting you are God," John Calvin writes in his exposition of the Psalm of Moses (Ps. 90:2), "Thus the everlastingness of which Moses speaks is to be referred not only to the essence of God but also to his providence by which he governs the world. Although he subjects the world to many alterations [*mutations*], he remains unmoved [*coi et paisible*]; and that not only in regard to himself but also in regard to the faithful, who find from experience that instead of wavering [*mutable*], he is steadfast [*constant*] in his power, truth, righteousness, and goodness, even as he has been from the beginning."[32] In this quotation, Calvin captures, as in a nutshell, the fundamental principle that underlies the dialogue between the Lord and Moses and specifically the argumentation of the latter: the conviction that God is "steadfast in his power, truth, righteousness, and goodness." In other words, God is "thoroughly self-consistent and reliable" in his dealings with the world, humanity, and especially the covenant people.

Without ignoring or setting aside God's power, truth, and righteousness, Moses appeals primarily to God's goodness, for it "alone can move God's will." This fundamental divine attribute is suggested by the Lord himself. When confronted with the sinful rebellion of the people, he says to Moses, "Now leave me alone so that my anger may burn against them and that I may destroy them" (Exod. 32:10 NIV). In asking the

---

their enemies," and J. A. Motyer, "to [their] belittlement among their opponents." W. Jacob suggests, "through rumours among their rebels," and considers that it was an occasion for the enemies to point out "the disloyalty and lack of belief in God" of the people of Israel, but his translation is unclear. Cf. L. Köhler and W. Baumgartner, *The Hebrew and Aramaic Lexicon of the Old Testament* (Leiden and Boston: Brill, 1994–2000), 3:970; 4:1580–81; J. I. Durham, *Exodus* (Waco: Word Books, 1987), 424, 426, 431; B. S. Childs, *The Book of Exodus* (Philadelphia: Westminster, 1974), 555, 557; Motyer, *The Message of Exodus*, 297, 315; B. Jacob and W. Jacob, *The Second Book of the Bible: Exodus* (Hoboken, NJ: KTAV, 1992), 950, 952–53.

32. John Calvin, *Commentaire du livre des Psaumes* (Paris: Librairie de C. Meyrueis, 1859), 2:184.

mediator to refrain from interfering with him[33] and his resolution to exercise his righteous judgment, God actually leaves the door ajar for an appeal to his goodness. The Lord refers to it explicitly when, in answer to Moses's request to see his glory, he says, "I will cause all my goodness to pass in front of you" (33:19 NIV). In fact, the mediator had a further reason not to intervene in favor of Israel. Although God suggests destroying this stiff-necked people, he offers to "make *him* [Moses] into a great nation" (32:10b). Who would not be tempted by such a gratifying proposal? But Moses, having been put to the test, chooses to assume his calling as mediator. "The preservation of Israel was dearer to him than the honour of becoming the head and founder of a new kingdom of God."[34] In the words of the psalmist, he "stood in the breach before [God] to keep his wrath from destroying them" (Ps. 106:23 NIV).

What a contrast with Aaron's behavior toward Israel! Not only does Aaron give in out of moral weakness to the pressure of the rebellious and threatening people who ask him to make them an idol (Exod. 32:1–6); when questioned by Moses on what had happened, Aaron's answer is pathetic. Like Adam and Eve in the garden of Eden, he shifts responsibility from himself as he recalls that the people are prone to evil (32:22; Gen. 3:11–15). Aaron thus avoids recognizing his portion of responsibility in the "great sin" committed by the people (32:21). On the other hand, while acknowledging the gravity of Israel's sin and the appropriateness of the Lord's righteous indignation and sentence, Moses, as the go-between, appeals to the Lord's goodness, fountain of his mercy and compassion (33:19).[35] As U. Cassuto remarks, there are three stages to the process of forgiveness that the mediator instigates in view of the restoration of the covenant between the Lord and his chosen people. These are discussed in the next sections.

THE FIRST STAGE: MITIGATION OF THE DIVINE SENTENCE (32:9–14)

Confronted with the divine intention to annihilate the rebellious people, Moses seeks to mitigate the sentence in order to avert such a calamity. "He entreats the favor of the LORD *his* God" (32:11). In other words, he

---

33. Cf. also Hos. 4:17, where the sin of Ephraim is so rampant and persistent that nothing could be done to prevent him from experiencing divine retribution (2 Sam. 16:11).

34. Keil and Delitzsch, *The Pentateuch*, 2:224. W. H. Gispen, *Exodus*, ed. Ed van der Maas (Grand Rapids: Zondervan; St. Catherines, ON: Paideia, 1982), 295, notes that "the Lord could not do what He suggested here to Moses, unless Jacob turned out to be a false prophet" (Gen. 49:10; Exod. 2:1–21).

35. Moses does not question the divine sanction but attracts the Lord's attention to the consequences of wiping out the people.

induces him to show favor in place of wrath and chastisement.[36] From the start, his appeal is to the mercy and compassion of God for his creatures, for his people. As he intercedes on behalf of Israel, the mediator brings in two other arguments. First, to wipe the covenant community "off the face of the earth" (32:12 NIV) is to jeopardize all that the Lord has done in its favor by bringing it "out of Egypt with great power and a mighty hand" (32:11 NIV) and, as a consequence, to undermine the divine glory and honor among the nations and especially among the Egyptians (32:12). Second, Moses recalls the promise God had made on oath to the patriarchs, Abraham, Isaac, and Jacob, to give them a numerous offspring and a land. His appeal is to the steadfastness, the self-consistency, and the reliability of the divine character. As one looks more closely at the text, one is struck by the audacity of the mediator, who questions the Lord twice (32:11, 12a) and uses the imperative as he speaks to him: "turn from your fierce anger," "relent [from evil]," "do not bring disaster" (32:12b NIV), "remember your servants" (32:13 NIV). The plea of Moses for this sinful people is poignant. But his appeal is essentially to God's character and attributes, to God's favor, to the honor of God's name, and to his faithfulness. This first encounter ends with the narrator's comment: "Then the LORD relented and did not bring on his people the disaster he had threatened" (32:14 NIV). Like Jacob, who had wrestled with God (Gen. 32:22–31), Moses had overcome. But this he did not know. It is important to remember this as we move further on into the heart of the mediator's intercession. But what does it mean that "God relented"? It does not presuppose any change in God's nature or his purposes. This is forcefully expressed by Samuel to Saul, who has just been rejected as king over Israel: "He who is the Glory of Israel does not lie or change his mind; for he is not a man, that he should change his mind" (1 Sam. 15:29 NIV). In this sense, God never repents of anything. But as Keil and Delitzsch have noted, it is more than "an unexpected change in the things which God has put in his own power."[37] Within this context, it is an "anthropomorphic description of the pain which is caused to the love of God by the destruction of His creatures."[38] The

36. Such is the meaning of the verb *ḥlh* (cf. 1 Kings 13:6; 2 Kings 13:4; 2 Chron. 33:12; Jer. 26:19; Dan. 9:13; Mal. 1:9). In all these passages the faithful are faced with dramatic circumstances.

37. Cf. Keil and Delitzsch, *The Pentateuch*, 2:225, who quote Augustine, *Contra adversarium legis et prophetarum* 1.xx (*Oeuvres complètes de s. Augustin* [Paris: Louis Vivès, 1870], 26:493).

38. Keil and Delitzsch, *The Pentateuch*, 2:225. God, as a personal being, is not indifferent to human misery, plight, and sin, though not changing in his nature and purposes (cf. also Num. 23:19; Ps. 110:4; Jer. 4:28; Mal. 3:6). In Gen. 6:5–7 the proximity of the verb *nḥm* in the Niphal with the verb *ʿṣb* in the Hitpael expresses "the pain of the divine love at the sin of man." As Calvin says so well, "God is hurt no less by the atrocious sins of men than if

appeal to the Lord's goodness and favor has had a decisive effect. He is
"a God both of judgement and mercy."

THE SECOND STAGE: THE ATONEMENT FOR SIN (32:30–33:6)

We have seen that Moses was aware of the people's great sin and that
he and the Levites had been the instrument of the divine judgment. In
32:30–33:6, his second dialogue with the Lord, he confesses specifically
the sin of the people (32:31) and asks the Lord to forgive them their
sin (32:32a). In this encounter with God, Moses is both cautious and
insistent. He is cautious in saying to the people, "*perhaps* I can make
atonement for your sin" (32:30 NIV), and in the way he prays to God,
interrupting the flow of his thought, "And now if you will forgive their sin
. . ." (32:32a). He is insistent in requesting to be blotted out of the book
the Lord has written (32:32b). Did Moses think that he could atone for
the "great sin" of the people? Just like Paul later on (Rom. 9:3), Moses
is no doubt expressing self-sacrificing love towards his fellow citizens.
He even stakes his own life in the hope of obtaining their deliverance.
But actually he is simply stating, in the case of a negative response, that
he wants to share the fate of his people. As the mediator, he shows such
solidarity with sinful Israel that if God refuses to forgive, he is willing to
share in its predicament, not to live before the Lord. By using the verb
kipper, "atone," Moses recognizes the need of both propitiation and expiation in order that forgiveness be effective.[39] It is no less than holy love
that is required for genuine reconciliation to take place. The response of
the Lord is significant: he will ensure the continuation of the covenant
people under the leadership of Moses; he will send his protective angel,
who will go before Israel; and he will suspend the punishment until the
day of his visitation.[40] In other words, the Lord gives a positive answer
to Moses's request and grants the people forgiveness, though with some
reservation; God is sensitive to the intercession of the mediator, but
sin and divine holiness remain incompatible. How can the Lord live
in the midst of a stiff-necked people (Exod. 33:3, 5)? Thus the tension

they pierced His heart with mortal anguish." Calvin speaks of an "anthropopathic figure
of speech." God applies to himself a human affection in order to touch and transform the
depths of the hearts of human creatures. Cf. Keil and Delitzsch, *The Pentateuch*, 1:139–40;
John Calvin, *Le livre de la Genèse* (Geneva: Labor et Fides, 1961), 130–31.

39. This idea is strongly emphasized throughout the narrative as well as by the fact
that Exod. 32–34 is preceded by the instructions concerning the tabernacle (25–31) and
followed by the building of the tabernacle (35–40). There is no indication whatsoever in
this passage that forgiveness and reconciliation could take place without atonement. For
a detailed discussion of the concept of atonement, cf. R. E. Averbeck, "כִּפֶּר," in *The New
International Dictionary of Old Testament Theology and Exegesis*, ed. W. A. VanGemeren
(Carlisle, UK: Paternoster, 1997), 2:689–710.

40. Keil and Delitzsch, *The Pentateuch*, 2:232.

remains. Even the people are distressed and overwhelmed by this state of affairs (33:4–6).

Indeed, one can see a change in the mentality of the children of Israel. The judgment as mediated by Moses and the Levites has curbed the wild and illicit behavior of the people; when they become aware that the presence of the Lord in their midst could bring calamity on them, a rebellious nation, they take to mourning because of divine displeasure; later, as they witness the interaction between the Lord and Moses in the tent of meeting that the latter had set up outside the camp, the people show deference toward the mediator, and they honor and worship God (33:7–11). The realization of the horror of sin and the separation from the Lord that it entails, bringing sorrow and repentance,[41] is one of the factors that contributes to further divine action. This leads us to the next stage.

THE THIRD STAGE: THE PRESENCE AND GLORY OF THE LORD (33:12–34:9)

The grievous sin of Israel had led to the breaking of the covenant and the withdrawal of God. The construction of the tabernacle, the dwelling place of the Lord in the midst of his people, was suspended indefinitely. Henceforth the tent of meeting was pitched outside the camp at some distance (33:7). The narrator lays great emphasis on this point. The role of the mediator is all the more important in that the community is separated from God.[42] Moses could have been content with this new setup. The worst had been avoided, forgiveness had been offered provisionally, and he had been confirmed as mediator. It was evident to all that his communication and fellowship with the Lord were unique. They were so unique that they made a deep impression and were remembered in subsequent generations as characteristic of the fundamental role he played in the history of revelation. We are told that "the LORD spoke with Moses face to face, as a man speaks with his friend" (33:11; cf. Num. 12:6–8; Deut. 5:4; 18:14–22; 34:10–12).[43]

But Moses, as the faithful and true intercessor he was, had the audacity to go one step further. Indubitably, the promises the Lord had made to Abraham, Isaac, and Jacob would be fulfilled, but Moses wanted more than an angel guiding the nation to the promised land (Exod. 32:34), he wanted more than to be the lone and special go-between. He prayed

41. The word "repentance" is not used in the passage that mentions the distress of the people (Exod. 33:4–6) but is implied by the context.

42. Cf., among others, Cassuto, *Exodus*, 429–32. Moberly speaks of remorse (*At the Mountain of God*, 60–61).

43. "Although the Lord showed Himself to Moses in some particular form of manifestation, He never appeared in His own essential Glory, but only in such a mode as human weakness could bear" (Keil and Delitzsch, *The Pentateuch*, 2:234).

for the presence of the Lord in the midst of his people, and he begged the
Lord to restore the covenant relationship with Israel. But how can "a holy
God abide with a sinful people?"[44] The leader of Israel was confident that
the Lord would respond to this request and display once again his presence in the midst of his people without the threat of "further wrath and
judgement against them as the inevitable result of any future sin."[45] But
in order for this to happen, it was vital that the Lord reveal and manifest
to Moses and to the community the fundamental goodness, mercy, and
compassion of his character. We shall now proceed by considering more
specifically both requests of Moses: the presence of the Lord in the midst
of his people and the theophany of the divine glory.[46]

The Presence of the Lord in the Midst of Israel (33:12–17)

In this third dialogue, Moses begins by stating the problem (33:12a).[47]
He refers back to the two passages that indicated that he was to lead
the people and that an angel would act as guide while the Lord would
remain at a distance (32:34; 33:1–6). The use of the preposition 'im
("with") is significant in this verse (33:12a), as it will also be in 33:16:
"You have told me to lead these people but you have not informed me
whom or what[48] you will send with me." Note that the emphasis is on
the personal relationship between the Lord and the mediator. Perhaps
the words of Moses are an echo of God's promise made to him on the
occasion of his calling: "I will be with you" (3:12 NIV). In the eyes of
the go-between, this "general indirect assistance," which maintains the
people at a distance, is unsatisfying and inadequate. The proximity of
the Lord is not only vital for Moses but also for the Israelites: "See that
this nation is your people" (33:13b). Moses's prayer shows both finesse
and sensitivity, openness and confidence. It reveals the intimate nature
of the relationship he lived with his ultimate counterpart.

44. Moberly remarks that the problem in the present context is not "spatial or metaphysical . . . but the moral problem of how a holy God can abide with a sinful people" (*At
the Mountain of God*, 67).

45. Ibid., 68.

46. In Exod. 33:12–23 *rā'â* ("see") occurs seven times: vv. 12, 13, 18, 20 (2x), 23 (2x).
In 33:12 the words of Moses to the Lord begin with *rā'â*, which forms an inclusio with
33:23, in which *rā'â* is used twice by the Lord; *ḥānan* ("show favor," "be gracious") or *ḥēn*
("grace," "favor") occurs seven times: vv. 12, 13 (2x), 16, 17, 19 (2x); *pānîm* ("face") occurs
seven times: vv. 14, 15, 19 (2x), 20, 21, 23.

47. In Exod. 33:12–17 *yāda'* occurs six times: vv. 12 (2x), 13 (2x), 16, 17. The expression
"find favor in the eyes of someone" occurs five times: vv. 12, 13 (2x), 16, 17. The repetition of these words and expressions are not without significance. It indicates that we are
entering into a crucial moment of the narration that will find its ultimate resolution in
the first verses of Exod. 34.

48. Cf. Cassuto, *Exodus*, 433; Moberly, *At the Mountain of God*, 69. The reference is to
a person or an object or perhaps both: the presence of the Lord in the tabernacle.

The intercessor introduces, however, a new element to his reflection. He appeals to the Lord's gracious and sovereign intervention on his behalf when he says, "You have said, 'I know you by name,' and, 'you have found favor in my eyes.'" This double statement is found both at the beginning (33:12b) and at the end (33:17b) of the first part of this dialogue. In the latter declaration, the Lord confirms what Moses had said and acknowledges that his calling and special position within the covenant are the consequence of a divine, merciful initiative. In the expression "know by name," the verb "know" means to have a personal relationship with someone, and when used with God as subject, it can have the connotation of choice or election (Gen. 18:19; Jer. 1:5; Hos. 13:5; Amos 3:2).[49] When the formula "by name" is added, it suggests the "intimate knowledge of a person and his character."[50] This is the only time in the Hebrew Bible that the two words "know" and "name" are brought together. N. M. Sarna proposes to translate this phrase, "I have singled you out by name," and indicates that it "connotes a close, exclusive, and unique association with God."[51]

As for the expression "find favor in someone's eyes," it can have a variety of meanings,[52] but within this specific context, especially as it is used at the beginning of Moses's intercession (Exod. 33:12b) and in God's second response (33:17), it has a strong connotation and emphasizes the Lord's goodwill toward Moses and approval of him. This formula thus stresses the mediator's special election. As Moberly notes, Noah (Gen. 6:8) and Moses are the only two examples in the Old Testament "where it is said absolutely of individuals that they 'found favour' with God."[53] In the case of Noah, we also read, "Noah was a righteous man, blameless among the people of his time, and he walked with God" (Gen. 6:9 NIV). This statement may be considered a commentary of the formula at hand. "To find favor in the 'eyes of the Lord'" means to be the object of the sovereign and free divine grace, to be just and upright, to put on religious and moral integrity, and to enjoy a deep and personal fellowship with the Lord.[54] Moses's position as mediator is thus essentially due to

49. For a study of the different meanings of *yāda'* ("know"), see P. Berthoud, "L'autorité et l'interprétation de l'Ancien Testament," *La Revue réformée* 135 (1983): 100–110.

50. Moberly, *At the Mountain of God*, 70. The formula "call someone by name," in relationship to election, is more frequent (cf. Exod. 31:2; Isa. 43:1; 45:3, 4; 49:1).

51. N. M. Sarna, *Exodus*, JPS Tora Commentary (Philadelphia, New York, and Jerusalem: Jewish Publication Society, 1991), 213.

52. For a brief and comprehensive summary of the evidence, see Moberly, *At the Mountain of God*, 70–71, 202.

53. Ibid., 70–71.

54. Noah's righteousness and integrity are therefore the fruit of the Lord's favor and of the intimate fellowship he enjoys with his divine partner (cf. also Gen. 5:22, 24 with reference to Enoch); cf. Calvin, *Genèse*, 132–33; G. C. Aalders, *Genesis* (Grand Rapids:

God's free initiative and decision. This, however, within the context of the covenant, not only entails a continuous, intimate fellowship with the Lord and a knowledge of his ways (Exod. 33:13) but has consequences for the people who have been entrusted to his leadership and care (33:14).

The argument of the intercessor is forceful, for it refers back to a previous and decisive encounter, whether it be Moses's initial call (3:3–4), or God's desire "to make [him] into a great nation" (32:10 NIV), or the special relationship Moses had with the Lord (33:11), or all three occasions.[55] The request is all the more warranted, as Moses is careful to place it within the context of the covenant. It is appropriate for the mediator to know the Lord's ways, to understand God's character and the attributes which govern God's intention and action within the present circumstances of the life of Israel.[56] A few centuries later, Amos expressed a similar thought: "Surely the Sovereign Lord does nothing without revealing his plan [sôd] to his servants the prophets" (Amos 3:7 NIV). It is important, however, to realize that the emphasis is not on the special position of the intercessor but on the character of the Lord, the steadfast, faithful, and reliable character of the One who has initiated the covenant.

The response of God is to the point but remains somewhat ambiguous: "My Presence ['face'] will go and I will give you [singular] rest" (Exod. 33:14).[57] The word pānîm ("face") is an important term. As F. Michaeli notes, it gives a personal touch to the presence of God, and when it is used with a suffix, it is the equivalent of the personal pronoun (2 Sam. 17:11). "I will go," says the Lord, thus assuring Moses of his accompanying presence. In his compassion, God offers his human partner peace of mind[58] and promises to bring him to Canaan, the resting place.[59] F. Michaeli adds that pānîm is also used within the context of worship. "To celebrate the worship service is to seek after his face," the sanctuary being the place where the Lord usually manifests himself. There is therefore a link between a theophany and the face of the Lord. In saying that "his presence will go," God may also be suggesting implicitly that

---

Zondervan, 1981), 1:159; G. J. Wenham, *Genesis 1–15* (Waco: Word Books, 1987), 169–70; B. K. Waltke, *Genesis: A Commentary* (Grand Rapids: Zondervan, 2001), 119, 133.

55. Moberly, *At the Mountain of God*, 71–72.

56. And not only generally, as some commentators suggest (cf. S. R. Driver).

57. God's response is not a question (Gispen, *Exodus*, 309) but, as the immediate context strongly suggests, a positive affirmation (Cassuto, *Exodus*, 434; Moberly, *At the Mountain of God*, 74).

58. Cassuto, *Exodus*, 434.

59. Gispen, *Exodus*, 309; cf. Deut. 3:20; 12:10; Josh. 22:4. Sarna translates, "lighten your burden," and notes that this phrase is "found in the context of giving relief from national enemies, especially in relation to the occupation of the land" (*Exodus*, 213, 261). Cf. also Deut. 26:10; Josh. 1:13, 15; 21:43ff.; 23:1; 2 Sam. 7:1, 11; 1 Kings 5:18; 1 Chron. 22:9, 18; 23:25; 2 Chron. 14:5, 6; 15:15; 20:30.

the tabernacle and the divine services will find their place in the midst of the people.[60]

The Lord's response to Moses indicates his decision to be directly and personally involved once again, at least with the mediator. Indeed, the personal pronoun "you" is used only once, and it is in the singular. Understood as a collective, it could refer to Israel as a whole, but the immediate context calls for a singular. This explains Moses's response and his desire to avoid any misunderstanding that might remain. In his comment Moses uses the first person plural of the personal pronoun "us" three times and the formula "me and your people" twice, thus identifying himself with the people. The uniqueness of Israel and of its witness lies not in its ethnic, cultural, and social differences but in the intimate presence of the divine Partner. Unless the Lord tabernacles in the midst of his people, there is no calling, no moving forward, no testimony to the glory of the one living God among the surrounding nations (Exod. 33:15–16). This time the Lord's answer allows for no ambiguity. He confirms explicitly what he had already stated implicitly. Because of his fundamental goodness, because of his unchanging engagement and commitment to Moses the mediator, the Lord has chosen to restore the broken relationship with Israel. Moses, the intercessor, has wrestled with the merciful and compassionate God of Abraham, Isaac, and Jacob and has won the victory of faith. אִנִ

"Show Me Your Glory" (33:18–34:4)

One would think that after such a passionate plea so full of dramatic intensity and the reassuring answer of the Lord, who has decided to withhold his judgment, to forgive, and to reside in the midst of his people as they journey toward the promised land, Moses would have been content with such an expression of divine mercy and compassion. Not so! He makes a last request. He asks the Lord to show him his glory that he may contemplate his face, the radiance of his beauty and loving-kindness—not according to a manmade sacrilegious image and caricature but according to the Lord's self-manifestation. After laying hold of God's words of mercy and compassion by faith, Moses seeks for an existential encounter with God, "a deeper and fuller revelation of the character of the Lord whose very nature it is to be gracious, merciful,"[61] and compassionate. What he desires corresponds in many ways to what Job had experienced: "my ears had heard of you but now my eyes have seen you" (Job 42:5 NIV).

The "glory" of God usually means his majesty. It is the visible and powerful manifestation of his radiant presence (Exod. 16:7, 10). In Isaiah

60. F. Michaeli, *Le livre de l'Exode* (Neuchâtel, Switz., and Paris: Delachaux & Niestlé, 1974), 279–80. Cf. also Cassuto, *Exodus*, 434; Moberly, *At the Mountain of God*, 74, 68.

61. Moberly, *At the Mountain of God*, 68.

6:3, for example, it is the manifestation of the Lord's holiness. It gener-ates both awe and worship. The immediate context will help us clarify the meaning of Moses's request. In Exodus 34:6 (NIV) we are told that "the *Lord passed* in front of Moses ['before his face']." Coming back to Exodus 33:22 (NIV), we read, "When my *glory passes by*, I will put you in a cleft in the rock and cover you with my hand until *I have passed by*." In the light of these passages, it becomes clear that Moses is requesting to contemplate the Lord himself (Yahweh). Moberly suggests that he may also be "seeking an experience of God such as will characterise the regular cult where Yahweh will meet with His people in both judgement and mercy."[62] This can only be inferred, for there is no explicit mention of this in the passage. Keil and Delitzsch suggest that Moses wants to see a revelation of the glory of God that surpasses all the previous ones (16:7, 10, the manna and quail; 24:16–17, the covenant confirmed) and that is even more significant than his talking face to face with the Lord, for then he only saw "the form of the LORD" (Num. 12:8 NIV). In other words, he seeks to contemplate the glory or the essential being of God without a veil and without a form or figure.[63] One could add that it is the essential being of God as it is characterized by grace, mercy, and compassion. Such a theophany would confirm Moses in his calling as mediator and intercessor and would be the basis of the restoration and renewal of the covenant of the Lord with a sinful people.

We are told by the narrator that Moses's request was granted but within limits, those existing between the infinite and holy God and the finite and sinful man. Moses had asked to see God's glory; the Lord was to show him his goodness. The verb "pass" ('*br*) is used for both the glory and the goodness of God: "I will cause all my goodness *to pass*" (Exod. 33:19 NIV) and "when my glory *passes by*" (33:22 NIV). This parallel is most significant. This manifestation of God's glory will not emphasize primarily the Lord's righteous judgment but his goodness (Jer. 33:11), the fundamental spiritual and moral characteristic of God's divine being, fountain of the benefits his people are to enjoy over and over again in their history (Ps. 27:13; Isa. 63:7; Jer. 31:12, 14; Hos. 3:5; Zech. 1:17). Sarna suggests, in the light of ancient Near Eastern treaties, that the word *ṭôb* could have a "technical, legal meaning of covenantal friendship" which was established at "the conclusion of a pact." Among the biblical pas-sages indicated, he mentions this verse (Exod. 33:19), which would then contain "an intimation of the renewal of the covenant between God and Israel."[64] The further reference, in the same verse, to both the character

62. Ibid., 76.
63. Keil and Delitzsch, *The Pentateuch*, 2:237.
64. Sarna, *Exodus*, 214. The biblical passages are Gen. 32:9; Deut. 23:6; Josh. 24:20; 1 Sam. 25:30; 2 Sam. 2:6; 7:28; Jer. 18:10; 33:9, 14. Sarna mentions M. Fox, "Ṭôb as Covenant

and the nature of the Lord and to his merciful initiative brings weight to this interpretation.

In addition to the manifestation of his goodness, God says to Moses, "I will proclaim my name, the LORD [Yahweh], in your presence ['before your face']" (33:19 NIV). In the Hebrew Bible, the believer who calls upon the Lord as he worships him is said to proclaim the name of God. This is the unique example (cf. also 34:5–6) in which the Lord himself is the subject. It is a beautiful and forceful way to emphasize the divine initiative. Without a specific disclosure of God's character in space and time, how could people truly call upon the name of God and invoke his attributes, whether individually or at the sanctuary? Only God can reveal the content of his name as he manifests himself. This is of crucial importance, for his initiative and action are directly related to who he is. The gracious character of God is the basis of Moses's confidence and assurance as he anticipates the Lord's intervention in favor of a stiff-necked people.[65] Exodus 33:19 ends with the emphatic double *idem per idem* formula: "I will grant grace *on whom* [literally, 'that'] I will grant grace, and show compassion *on whom* ['that'] I will show compassion." The emphasis is on the verbal action in both cases, and the bestowal of divine mercy depends entirely on the initiative of the Lord himself. As Paul says, quoting this passage, "it does not, therefore, depend on man's desire or effort, but on God's mercy" (Rom. 9:16 NIV). The mystery of divine election is both sobering and reassuring.

J. A. Motyer has identified a concentric pattern in the passage under discussion (Exod. 33:18–23), 33:20 (NIV) being the turning point: "you cannot see my face, for no one ['man'] may see me and live."[66] This statement reiterates emphatically the limits that exist between the infinite and holy God and the finite and sinful man. The stress does not

---

Terminology," *Bulletin of the American Schools of Oriental Research* 209 (1973): 41–42. It has also been noted that the vocabulary of love can have both a personal and a political connotation and thus implies a covenantal dimension. Cf. J. A. Thompson, "The Significance of the Verb *Love* in the David-Jonathan Narratives in 1 Samuel," *Vetus Testamentum* 24 (1974): 334–38; P. K. McCarter Jr., *II Samuel*, Anchor Bible 9 (New York: Doubleday, 1984), 77.

65. Moberly, *At the Mountain of God*, 78–79, stresses rightly that the meaning of the name of the Lord must be derived from usage as reflected in the texts themselves. He thus brings together Exod. 3:14; 33:19; and 34:14 ("Do not worship any other god, for the LORD, whose name is Jealous, is a jealous God"). In 3:14 "the emphasis is on Yahweh's triumphant acts of deliverance" whereas in 33:19 it is "on Yahweh's character revealed entirely in moral terms" as he deals with sin and forgiveness.

66. The concentric structure is as follows (Motyer, *The Message of Exodus*, 308):

A¹ Moses's prayer: "show me" (18)
B¹ Promised divine self-revelation: goodness and name (19)
C   The unbearable reality (20)
B² Promised divine self-revelation: glory and care (21–22)
A² The Lord's reply: "you will see" (23)

lie on the ontological or qualitative difference, as Moberly suggests,[67] but on the moral separation. This is not to deny the radical difference between the Creator and the creature or to minimize the limits inherent to terrestrial human bodies, but man is created in the image of God. The emphasis is thus, as we have noted already (32:10; 33:3, 5, 17–23) and as will be suggested again in the next chapter of Exodus (34:9), on the disastrous consequences of rebellion against the Lord. Since the fall, sin has contaminated the nature of all people, including the mediator, and to seek to contemplate the essential being of the Lord could be fatal. This is why God, in his concern for the creature, is careful to protect Moses from the fullness of his presence. The dynamic image of "the Lord passing by" emphasizes the sovereign freedom and activity of the Lord and indicates, by the means of a daring anthropomorphism, the extent or degree of the divine manifestation. Though Moses cannot contemplate the Lord's "face," he will nevertheless see "his back," see him from behind.[68] In other words, he will contemplate the traces of God's presence, the afterglow of his passage. But this glimpse of the ultimate counterpart as he manifested himself to the mediator would be sufficient to restore and renew the covenant relationship of the Lord with his people. It contained the revelation of divine grace, compassion, and faithful loving-kindness.

The Theophany (34:5–9)

This leads us to the theophany itself as related in Exodus 34. As in the preceding section, from the moment Moses asks to see God's glory, the Lord continues to have the initiative while the mediator remains passive as the attentive and receptive servant. More than ever Moses's and the people's future depends on the Lord himself, on his goodwill, decision, and action. Moses is fully aware of this as he goes up onto Mount Sinai in order to take part in the renewal of the covenant.[69]

---

67. Moberly, *At the Mountain of God*, 81.

68. Ibid., 81–82. Moberly notes that the word "back" (*'āḥôr*) actually means "hinder part," thus the paraphrase "you will see me from behind." The usual word for "back" is *gab* or *gaw*.

69. See Motyer, *The Message of Exodus*, 299, for an analysis of the literary structure of this chapter and its covenantal profile. R. W. L. Moberly, "How May We Speak of God? A Reconsideration of the Nature of Biblical Theology," *Tyndale Bulletin* 53 (2002): 177–202, esp. 191–202, takes Exod. 34:6–7 as an outstanding example of a truthful speech about God. Moberly emphasizes the need to take into consideration the narrative context of this passage and especially the significance of Moses's intercession. He argues convincingly that God's revelation must not be conceived independently of human responsiveness and "is generative of a new form of life which is under-girded by grace." The emphasis on the theological dimension of revelation is welcome, but Moberly seems to sidestep two aspects of the biblical perspective: (a) the fundamental historicity of the biblical narrative and therefore of divine revelation; (b) the possibility

In the light of what has already been said above, we need only stress the following points:

1. Whatever may be the intensity of the experience the theophany initiates, the central factor remains the verbal divine communication. The content of the revelation is of paramount importance. The Lord, as he proclaims his name, presents and discloses himself to Moses as "God of compassion [*raḥûm*] and grace [*ḥannûn*]" (34:6a). Compared with the other passages (20:5–6; Num. 14:18–19; Deut. 7:9–10)[70] that have a similar context, this passage is the only one to use the nouns "compassion" and "grace/favor." In those parallel texts, one finds repeatedly "faithful loving-kindness"[71] and occasionally "love" (*ʾahăbâ*). These revelations of the Lord's character thus highlight his love in terms of compassion, grace, and faithful loving-kindness. The term *raḥûm* lays the emphasis on God's deep appreciation and understanding of the misery and suffering of the creation including man; *ḥannûn*, on God's favorable predisposition; and *ʾahăbâ*, on the fidelity of the Lord as he offers his loving-kindness.[72] In this specific context, this love is freely and sovereignly manifested and bestowed by the Lord. As we further discover the content of this theophany, God is careful to specify and qualify the nature of his compassion and favor. The Lord is patient or long-suffering (Exod. 34:6b) and thus slow to inflict punishment on the sinner. He is generous in his faithfulness and truth (34:6b) and thus steadfast to his character and promises. God's kindness is enduring (34:7a), and he is prompt to forgive or to take away (*nāśāʾ*; cf. 32:32) wickedness, rebellion,

---

of divine communication within the categories of human language. Since God is both infinite and personal, his communication is both objective and personal. Notwithstanding this sidestepping, there is much with which I am in agreement, as will be seen from the present study. His approach toward revelation is both thought-provoking and refreshing.

70. For other Old Testament references, cf. Neh. 9:17; Pss. 86:15; 103:8; 145:8; Joel 2:13; Jon. 4:2.

71. The word *ḥesed* is also found twice in the passage under discussion (Exod. 34:6–7).

72. For a comprehensive study of *ḥesed* in the Hebrew Bible, cf. F. I. Anderson, "Yahweh, the Kind and Sensitive God," in *God Who Is Rich in Mercy*, ed. P. T. O'Brien and D. G. Peterson (Homebush, NSW: Lancer Books; Grand Rapids: Baker Academic, 1986), 41–88. Anderson argues that this word conveys the idea of an unrequired beneficial action rather than the formal and legal idea of obligation and duty. I tend to agree with this analysis, but because of the covenantal aspect of biblical revelation, the notion of faithfulness should be included. On *ḥesed* meaning mercy, cf. also C. H. Dodd, *The Bible and the Greeks* (London: Hodder & Stoughton, 1954), 59–65.

and sin (34:7a).[73] Indeed, God is love, the kind of love in which compassion, grace, and kindness go hand in hand with patience, generosity, faithfulness, truth, and forgiveness. Such is the expression of his inherent goodness. But just in case the recipients of this overwhelming and astounding revelation might be tempted to say, "Let us 'go on sinning so that grace may increase'" (Rom. 6:1 NIV), the Lord adds abruptly that the positive divine attributes are not signs of weakness and do not imply a perversion of justice. He "will by no means clear the guilty" (Exod. 34:7a).[74] The person who perseveres in the rejection of the Lord will not experience his mercy but a just retribution, and the consequences of his folly will endure until the fourth generation (34:7b). The Lord's compassion, grace, and favor are juxtaposed, even united to his holiness and justice. In Exodus 20:5–6, the emphasis is on God's judgment, but in Exodus 34:6–7, his love is in the forefront, for it far exceeds the Lord's just indignation, wrath, and judgment (34:7a–b). In his innermost being, the Lord is goodness, compassion, favor, and kindness. He is love, holy love. This is why, because of their sin, the dilemma of Moses and the people remains, and the tension persists, for the threat of judgment continues to hover over their heads. This explains the final intervention of Moses as he bows down before the Lord in awe and adoration (34:8).

2. Because of the Lord's favor toward him, Moses the mediator pleads for the last time the cause of a sinful people with whom he identifies himself completely. Four times he uses the first person plural of the personal pronoun.[75] The request of the intercessor is threefold: the presence of the Lord in the "midst of the people," the forgiveness of a sinful people, the taking of the people as his inheritance. This last request corresponds to the idea that Israel is the inheritance of God (1 Kings 8:51, 53). It probably reflects a covenantal connotation similar to the one expressed by the phrase "his [the LORD's] treasured possession" (Deut. 7:6; 26:18 NIV). The first and the third requests are dependent on the second, which is formulated in a unique and most significant way: "Because this is a stiff-necked

---

73. These three words are used here to cover the entire range of wrongdoing (cf. also Pss. 32:1–2; 51:1–3; Dan. 9:24), which, according to a careful concordance study, is defined in terms of moral rebellion against God and disobedience to God's covenantal law as summarized in the Ten Commandments. For a short and complete synthesis of the question, cf. H. A. G. Blocher, "Sin," in *The New Dictionary of Biblical Theology*, ed. T. D. Alexander and B. S. Rosner (Leicester, UK: Inter-Varsity; Downers Grove, IL: InterVarsity, 2000), 781–88.

74. See also Cassuto, *Exodus*, 440.

75. "Let the Lord go with *us*"; "forgive *our* wickedness and *our* sin"; "and take *us*."

people, forgive our wickedness and sin" (Exod. 34:9b). The way the particle *kî* is identified will determine the interpretation of this request. Moberly suggests "three possible ways of construing it."[76] It can be understood as

a. a causative, "for" or "because." It has already been used with this meaning in the preceding chapters in relation to the formula "a stiff-necked people" (Exod. 33:3)
b. a concessive "although": "although this is a stiff-necked people . . ." (cf. the NIV)
c. an emphatic concessive, "however much," "although indeed" (cf. JB)

Considering the paradoxical nature of Moses's prayer, the second option seems to sidestep the issue and weakens the audacity of Moses's request. This leaves us with the first (causative) and the third (emphatic concessive) readings. Moberly considers that they are both possible, as they draw attention to and stress that the Israelites are still a stiff-necked people. Having retained the emphatic concessive option, he translates this petition as follows: "Although they are indeed a stiff-necked people, yet forgive our wickedness and sin."[77] As we have seen, a central theme of these chapters is sin and forgiveness. Moses recognizes that Israel (the people and the mediator himself), as it is placed before the God of holy love, can only become aware of its sinfulness and seek God's forgiveness, his presence, and the renewal of the covenant relationship entirely on the basis of the Lord's character. To state it even more sharply, the mediator is pleading that the people's sin is *the reason* why God should forgive them, go in their midst, and take them as his treasured possession.[78] As Moses contemplates the divine manifestation, he is convinced that only the goodness of God, as revealed in his compassion, grace, and faithful loving-kindness, can bring about reconciliation and the restoration of the covenant. Thus the Lord, in answer to the prayer of Moses, withheld his wrath and judgment and indicated implicitly that the Mosaic era was a time of reprieve and patience. Moses was confirmed as mediator-intercessor, the tabernacle was built, and the cult was effectively put into place.

76. R. W. L. Moberly, *At the Mountain of God*, 90.
77. Moberly (ibid., 91–92) mentions another significant passage that expresses the same idea. After Noah sacrificed burnt offerings and he again had found favor before God, the Lord says, "I will not again add to the curse of the ground, because of man although every inclination of his heart is indeed evil from childhood" (Gen. 8:21). The only hope of Noah and his descendants lies in the character of the Lord and in his gracious promises.
78. Ibid., 89–93.

But these forms of mediating the presence of the Lord, though of great significance, were only the type and shadow of things to come, of him in whom "faithful loving-kindness and truth meet together, righteousness and peace embrace each other" (Ps. 85:10). As the apostle John expresses it so well, Jesus of Nazareth, the Christ, has fully made known the Father: "The Word became flesh and made his dwelling among us. We have seen his glory, the glory of the One and Only, who came from the Father, full of grace and truth" (John 1:14 NIV). As the Messiah walked the roads of the world, not only did he bear with and heal the misery and suffering of those who live in the shadow of death (Matt. 9:36–37; 15:32; 20:34; Mark 1:41; Luke 7:13); he also gave himself on the cross and thus delivered them from sin, the power of death. Such was the extent of his compassion.

Conclusion

As we contemplate the Lord's amazing grace, we can only be struck by the richness of his compassion. Compared with both Islam and Buddhism, this passage brings to the forefront that the Triune God is

- sovereign, free, and steadfast in both his purposes and actions
- close to his people and eager to establish a personal relationship with them
- the fountain of, and model for, human compassion and kindness
- alone the remedy to the disastrous human predicament occasioned by man's rebellion and sin (in other words, his dilemma is not metaphysical but moral)
- the initiator of both a liberation and a forgiveness that are effective here and now in the midst of human existence, the guarantee of a substantial healing within a broken reality, and the promise of the transfiguration of all things when the Messiah returns in glory

The words of the apostle Paul, who so magnificently states how the holy love of God was fully manifested in Jesus Christ, constitute a fitting conclusion:

But now a righteousness from God, apart from law, has been made known, to which the Law and the Prophets testify. This righteousness from God comes through faith in Jesus Christ to all who believe. There is no difference, for all have sinned and fall short of the glory of God, and are justified freely by his grace through the redemption that came by Christ Jesus. God presented him as a sacrifice of atonement,[79] through faith in his blood. He did this to demonstrate his justice, because in his forbearance [patience] he had left the sins committed beforehand unpunished—he did it to demonstrate his justice at the present time, so as to be just and the one who justifies those who have faith in Jesus. (Rom. 3:21–26 NIV)

79. The Greek word *hilastērion* can also be translated "place of atonement," but within the immediate context "sacrifice of atonement" is to be preferred. Cf. Averbeck, "כפר," 708.

9

The Sovereignty of God

Stephen N. Williams

"As clowns yearn to play Hamlet, so I have wanted to write a treatise on God." So J. I. Packer introduced his book *Knowing God*.[1] It is in the spirit of this observation that I approach the question under consideration.

The sovereignty of God, from whom, through whom, and to whom are all things (Rom. 11:36), is the grand theme of Scripture and cause for the highest praise of which the human heart is capable and for which the human heart was created. Yet for many, the notion is one that darkens the horizon and causes the furrowed brow. For "sovereignty" connotes authority and fiat, direction and control, not to mention insuperable power. It cuts across a sensibility that it has taken us ages to attain. "The history of the world," Hegel famously remarked, "is none other than the consciousness of the progress of freedom," and this was a shrewd enough analysis of at least the world familiar to him.[2] Hegel himself was a complex, nuanced, and many-sided thinker, but the heirs of the Enlightenment and the postmoderns who have quarreled with those heirs might gladly seize his hint that their labors have been in vain if they have overthrown kings and princes just to remain in thrall to a sovereign God. And those who doubt whether intellectual illumination has brought much spiritual or political freedom will nonetheless be

1. J. I. Packer, *Knowing God* (Downers Grove, IL: InterVarsity; London: Hodder & Stoughton, 1973), 5.
2. G. W. F. Hegel, introduction to *Lectures in the Philosophy of History* (New York: Dover, 1956).

disturbed that religious believers speak positively of the sovereignty of
God in the face of misery, suffering, and injustice—what the religious
themselves call "evil." Sovereignty coexists felicitously with neither evil
nor freedom. We glance at these in turn.

Evil

The scriptural notion of divine sovereignty broadly takes in the notions of kingship and rule. Just more than fifty years ago, Edmond Jacob
opened the first part of his Old Testament theology with the characteristically bald statement that "what gives the Old Testament its force and
unity is the affirmation of the sovereignty of God," which pertains both
to the present exercise of divine power in the world and to the messianic
future.[3] "How awesome is the LORD Most High, the great King over all the
earth," the psalmist exclaims, dwelling on the here and now (Ps. 47:2).
"The LORD will be king over the whole earth. On that day there will be
one LORD, and his name the only name," proclaims Zechariah in eschatological counterpoint (Zech. 14:9). The revelation of God's sovereignty
in the New Testament is astonishing on at least two scores. First, in the
Old Testament, God is the ever-present speaker and actor, director of
the ins and outs of history, while greater or lesser human figures come
and go in the pages of the text. But in the Synoptic accounts, although
God is heard uttering words at the baptism and the transfiguration of
His Son and we are reminded of what He said through prophets, it is
the voice of Jesus that we constantly hear.[4] Jesus is raised from the dead
and exalted as Lord. The book of Revelation graphically testifies to the
fact that he shares the throne of God Himself. After God has announced
Himself as the "Alpha and Omega" (Rev. 1:8), Jesus designates himself
ho prōtos kai ho eschatos (Rev. 1:17) and then *to alpha* and *to ōmega* at

3. Edmond Jacob, *Theology of the Old Testament*, trans. A. W. Heathcote and P. J. Allcock
(London: Hodder & Stoughton; New York: Harper, 1958), 37; translation of *Théologie de
l'Ancien Testament* (Neuchâtel, Switz.: Delachaux & Niestlé, 1955).
4. W. Pannenberg is not quite right, however, to say that the "Father acts in the world
only through the Son and Spirit. He himself remains transcendent" in *Systematic Theology*
(Edinburgh: T&T Clark, 1991), 1:328. At least in John's Gospel, the mutual indwelling of
Father and Son requires us to modify this claim. (I capitalize the pronouns or possessive
adjectives for God as "He," "His," etc. This is not only because I agree with Helen Oppen-
heimer that the capital form secures us against the claim that God is "anthropomorphi-
cally masculine" [preface to *The Hope of Happiness: A Sketch for a Christian Humanism*
(London: SCM, 1983)]. It is also because I turn to a brief consideration of Islam near the
end of this chapter, where references to Allah are appropriately capitalized as "He," and
there are advantages to interreligious consistency in capitalization.)

the climax of the Apocalypse (Rev. 22:13). The sovereignty of the one God is shared with one who is other than the Father.

The theme of sovereignty is more directly connected with the question of evil than with the question of freedom on the surface of Scripture, and the second cause of astonishment is the manifestation of evil in connection with the New Testament witness to Jesus Christ. It is not just that we learn of a "ruler of the kingdom of the air" (Eph. 2:1), a "prince of this world" (John 12:31), and a dragon empowered to give his throne to the beast (Rev. 13:2). More than this, in the Gospel accounts the conflict between God and evil is visible, onstage, before us. Before he has arrived at the so-called parables of the kingdom in the fourth chapter of his Gospel, Mark has alluded to or focused on exorcisms six times. Matthew and Luke depict the satanic temptation early in their Gospels in greater detail than does Mark. In, through, and after conflict, the "kingdom of this world" becomes the "kingdom of our Lord and of his Christ" (Rev. 11:15).

Biblical testimony to God's sovereignty in its relation to evil is designed to remove neither deep perplexity of mind nor deep anguish of spirit in relation to the origins, presence, form, sphere, permission, or ordination of evil. What we receive is assurance that it is not out of control and that it is destined to perish. So long as we maintain the belief in God's power and His sovereignty, everywhere expressed in the Bible, perplexity will remain in relation to the question of evil, even if this or that might be said which brings some measure of relief to this or that aspect of the problem.

Just as biblical testimony does not provide the answers, theological reflection likewise displays no special ability to discover where the serpent came from, how he got where he did, how evil became omnipresent, or why its ravages are allowed. The word "allowed," like the word "permission" used earlier, invites connection with the question of freedom. Is speaking of "allowance" at least an improvement over speaking of "ordination," so that it is necessary to stipulate freedom if we wish to relate sovereignty and evil aright? Is sovereignty a matter of divinely giving permission? Here we must pass over the primary task of biblical exegesis. But even if we do work provisionally with a rough-and-ready categorical distinction between permission and ordination, we shall surely bring little, if any, relief to the problem of sovereignty in relation to evil by insisting on permission rather than ordination. Sustained, daily, regular permission of a vast multitude of particular evils over centuries of time on the part of One who is presumably possessed of the power to prevent them constitutes an active decision that these things should happen. Is such a decision less problematic than ordination? Indeed, just how different is it from ordination? Many opponents of Christianity,

Clement of Alexandria testified long ago, urge that anyone who does not prevent something is culpably responsible for it in a strong sense.[5] We might demur, of course. We might deny that evil, qua evil or qua sin, is the direct creation of God or something that He causes. "In his heart a man plans his course, but the LORD determines his steps" (Prov. 16:9): taking this statement as a conceptual guide instead of strictly exegeting it, we might say that when the human heart is filled with an evil that is constitutionally pregnant with action, the sequence that takes us from disposition through to desire, intention, plan, and execution of evil is one that is not allowed to run its own untrammeled course. In such a case, God might be said to direct sovereignly the evil action without causing its evil. But even if we take this line, the problem of sovereignty in relation to evil is not disposed of.

I am not arguing theologically on behalf of any one form of sovereignty—decretive or permissive—over the other or even maintaining the coherence or otherwise of the different conceptual possibilities. The only point being made is that if there exists a God of sufficient power and goodness to make it the case that evils do not *have* to occur, then opting for "permission" rather than "ordination" does not necessarily or greatly help matters when we face the question of evil; at least, significant perplexity remains. It is not surprising that various theological and philosophical attempts have been made, especially in modern times, to rethink radically the notions of divine power and goodness in order to relieve the problem. We might sympathize with the pressure to do this, yet such attempts can succeed (in principle) only in deflating the problem if the connection with the biblical mode of ascribing sovereignty to God is strained to breaking point. If God is capable of creating and speaking, of becoming incarnate, and of securing the ultimate future that He desires, then it is hard to see how depotentiating or reenvisaging His deity in order to resolve some of our difficulties coheres with these convictions. If God is *not* perpetually able to excise evil, we have apparently changed the rules of the grammar of a faith riveted to the capacity of God to create, reveal, be incarnate, and rule eschatologically. It may be protested that I have lapsed into handling divine power abstractly instead of speaking of divine covenanted dealings with a human race, God's *potentia ordinata*. Granted. But our original difficulty will remain even if we review our approach. For the terms of God's covenant and the actual exercise of His power still leave us with the coexistence of evil with mighty works of constructive power in the course of history and on behalf of lost humanity. And this is the problem.

5. Clement of Alexandria, *Stromata* 1.82, *Stromateis: Books One to Three*, trans. John Ferguson (Washington, DC: Catholic University of America Press, 1991).

Maintaining the sovereignty of God does not get us away from what is grim and dark. We can only confess that we believe in the coexistence of one who is light, in whom there is no darkness, with that which is dark, in which there is no light. We confess Jesus Christ, worthy of service, love, and praise, in whom there is no shadow of evil, through whom we worship the Father. We give reason for this confession. We shall not see things in the hereafter as we see them now. Now we see Jesus, who reveals to us the form in which God wills to exercise His sovereignty over humankind here in the present evil age.

It may nevertheless be said that even if an appeal to "freedom" and "permission" do not markedly alleviate the ultimate problem of evil, we increase the offense or the difficulty caused by divine sovereignty if we do not maintain human freedom for other reasons. To these we now turn.

Freedom

Must sovereignty mean control? Some, believing that the very notion of God entails sovereign control, reject this God. Others maintain that sovereignty does not entail control and that human freedom is protected and propagated in the divine-human relationship; thus we may believe and trust in God. Still others are glad to affirm control and deny freedom as long as freedom is understood as the indeterminate and libertarian antithesis of control. We skip over the primary task of exegesis here, as we did in relation to sovereignty and evil. Similarly, again, I make just one point in connection with this question.

Theological discussion of how to plot sovereignty in relation to free-dom seems either to begin at or to move swiftly to a point where God is pictured as an individual person far greater than ourselves. This may be the case for protagonists on different sides of the debate.[6] To sim-plify: one party likens the controlling God to a tyrannical despot who effectively dictates what we do, and so rejects a sovereignty which is absolutely controlling. Another likens the controlling God to a righteous king whose right, not just power, to control is fundamental and absolute, and so accepts and submits to His authority. In both these ways of put-ting things, I, as a person down here, am placed vis-à-vis God, a person naturally pictured as being elsewhere, though a person overarchingly transcendent and pervading His creation. Such a picture is naturally

6. See A. B. Caneday, "Veiled Glory: God's Self-Revelation in Human Likeness—a Biblical Theology of God's Anthropomorphic Self-Disclosure," in *Beyond the Bounds: Open Theism and the Undermining of Biblical Christianity*, ed. John Piper et al. (Wheaton, IL: Crossway, 2003), 149–99.

derived from the Scriptures. Yet in deploying it as we do in this discussion, we can be conceptually misled by a picture, to use Wittgenstein's phrase.[7] Other pictures need to be superimposed.

God is seen "seated on a throne, high and exalted, . . . the train of his robe" filling the temple (Isa. 6:1).[8] He has the appearance of jasper and carnelian (Rev. 4:3). When so seen, He is worshiped. Richard Bauckham, who finds in its distinctive doctrine of God the book of Revelation's "greatest contribution to New Testament theology," comments that "its most elemental forms of perception of God not only require expression in worship: they cannot be truly experienced except as worship."[9] He goes on to describe, in an argument that we cannot trace here, how Revelation "suggests the incomparability of God's sovereignty" by its studious avoidance of anthropomorphism. We are discouraged from imaging God along the lines of human personhood. It is well to mention George Caird's telling formulation applied to another biblical book: Ezekiel, speaking of "the appearance of the likeness of the glory of God" (Ezek. 1:28), provides "a triple guard against literality" in this representation.[10] The question of sovereignty as control takes on a different shape when we move away from the picture of one person confronting another. Yet must not theology be done, as far as is possible, before the throne as envisioned in the Apocalypse?

A powerful passage in Luther's writing is instructive here. In *Contra Latomum* he is discussing whether any of our good works is free of sin:

> Let us take St. Peter or Paul as they pray, preach or do some other good work. If it is a good work without sin and entirely faultless, they should stand with appropriate humility before God and speak in this fashion: "Lord God, behold this good work which I have done through the help of Thy grace. There is in it neither fault nor any sin, nor does it need Thy forgiving mercy. I do not seek this, as I want Thee to judge it with the strictest and truest judgement. In my work, I can glory before Thee, because Thou canst not condemn it without denying Thyself. The need for mercy which, as the petition teaches, forgives the trespass [alluding to the Lord's Prayer] in this deed is cancelled, for here is only the justice which crowns it." Latomus, doesn't this make you shudder and sweat?[11]

7. Norman Malcolm, *Ludwig Wittgenstein: A Memoir* (New York and London: Oxford University Press, 1958), 53–54.

8. Scripture quotations in this chapter are from the NIV.

9. R. J. Bauckham, *The Theology of the Book of Revelation* (Cambridge: Cambridge University Press, 1993), 32–33.

10. George B. Caird, *The Language and the Imagery of the Bible* (London: Duckworth, 1980), 175.

11. Martin Luther, *Works* (Philadelphia: Muhlenberg, 1958), 32:190.

Luther's theology of justification is not our quarry here. But we learn this from him: while pure *thought* concentrates on the questions of sin, freedom, and justification, it might toy with different possibilities, including that I might produce a good work free from sin. In the presence of God, however, the thought is exposed for its unworthiness and expelled. I am not directly drawing or inferring any conclusions about human action from this passage in Luther's work. But he rightly forces us to envision aright the sphere within which theological reflection takes place. Before *this* presence, so imagined in Scripture as to convey that the image can *not* convey the greatness of God, the question of my freedom vis-à-vis God the King tends to shrivel up or appear a little shabby in the form in which I most naturally pose it. *This* God may control meticulously without a hint of human despotism. Alternatively, He may choose to grant any form of freedom that He wills without a hint of compromise of His sovereignty. The greatness of His sovereignty does not lie directly either in meticulous control or, alternatively, in the donation of a space that He does not determine. In worship we find that sovereign greatness lies in God's sheer being. Worship is the proper context of theological thought, and when apprehension of sovereignty lies at the heart of worship, it can look as though the control-versus-reciprocity sort of battle that we sometimes find in theology is fought on the ground of an excessively anthropomorphic sense of God.

It may be protested that in order to avoid an excessively anthropomorphic picture of the relation between God and humans, I have moved unidirectionally and attained theological imbalance. Sovereignty, it may be argued, should be primarily interpreted by moving the other way, in the direction of the humility of incarnation; it must be understood christologically. The point is well taken. But what do we find in the Gospels that witnesses to divine humility? Both Matthew and Luke record the worship of Christ at the climax of their Gospels, and Thomas's confession of Jesus as Lord and God comes at the end of the penultimate chapter of John's Gospel. (Mark climaxes either with resurrection and fear or, in the longer ending, ascension and proclamation.) It is instructive to follow just Luke for a moment. The first recorded words spoken to Jesus by a disciple are by Simon Peter: "Master, we've worked hard all night and haven't caught anything. But because you say so, I will let down the nets" (Luke 5:5). The second set of recorded words are spoken by the same person a short time later, this time from a kneeling position: "Go away from me, Lord; I am a sinful man!" (5:8). At least he knew what he was saying, unlike on another occasion when Jesus appeared transfigured before him and he proposed the construction of shelters for Jesus, Moses, and Elijah (9:33). One way or another, the account of the transfiguration is a turning point in Luke's narrative, as it is with

Matthew and Mark. Surveying the scenes that feature Peter on the shore and Peter on the mountain, let us ask, What kind of freedom should he have coveted? What kind of freedom should we covet? And what kind of freedom do we possess before *this* sovereignty? One answer seems appropriate at those scenes: the freedom to worship and to obey. Nor is such a conclusion abstracted from the whole of Jesus's appearance and ministry. *Coram Christo*, as *coram Deo*, I must say: if *this* man should exercise or wish to exercise sovereignty by meticulous control, I shall not brandish before him a freedom of my own which he must respect. Nor, on the other hand, shall I instruct him in what is appropriate to deity, should he indicate an indeterminate space for my freedom. The sole point of what I have said is that we should keep asking what God or what Jesus we have before our eyes when we raise the question of sovereignty in its relation to freedom and control. It is a plea for perspective.

The Holy

My discussion hitherto has been geared not to the contours of the scriptural witness but to standard responses to the language of sovereignty. But the sovereign God of Scripture is Father, Son, and Spirit, and the nature of divine sovereignty is revealed in the economy. Should we not, then, explore sovereignty in this light? Joachim of Fiore, developing a strand of patristic thought, has attracted modern as well as medieval attention in speaking of three kingdoms: that of the Father, the Son, and the Spirit. Jürgen Moltmann has done as much as anyone in modern theology to rehabilitate Joachim, Moltmann being himself a leading exemplar of a trinitarian-economic approach to the doctrine and sovereignty of God. Moltmann is critical, however, of Joachim's tendency to interpret the three kingdoms in terms of successive eras, and we might add that Joachim's talk of the kingdom of the Spirit is altogether questionable, along with any strict dispensational ordering of the kingdoms, to the extent that Joachim advances this.[12] But it is hard to gainsay the positive significance of the general point in these contributions, which is that our eyes are rightly trained in a biblical direction if we think of sovereignty in trinitarian and economic terms. Many questions might be profitably considered in this connection: What are the meaning and significance of the handing over of the kingdom to the Father, of which Paul speaks in 1 Corinthians 15, and its relation to the visions conveyed in the book of Revelation? What is the relation of the kingship of Christ

12. Jürgen Moltmann, *The Trinity and the Kingdom of God*, trans. Margaret Kohl (London: SCM, 1981), 203–9; *History and the Triune God: Contributions to Trinitarian Theology*, trans. John Bowden (London: SCM, 1991; New York: Crossroad, 1992), 91–109.

to the kingship of God? What is the relation of the authority of the exalted Christ to the governments of this world and aeon? A dogmatic treatment of the sovereignty of God is bound to pursue such questions as long as its agenda is the unfolding of biblical theology. Such a treatment, however, would lead us into discussions of eschatology or political authority, and I wish to remain in the orbit of questions already touched on. It is instructive that Moltmann's laudable ambition to gain a biblical orientation returns us to these questions. How so?

Moltmann's insistence that the trinitarian history of God must inform us about the nature of divine sovereignty has taken the form, at least mainly, of a running battle with Karl Barth. Whether or not we award him the palm or are partial to Moltmann's dynamic theism/panentheism, Moltmann is right to insist that we must interpret the sovereignty of the Triune God with reference to the form that His rule actually takes in history. Yet in the execution Moltmann either deploys a faulty principle or wrongly applies a defensible principle.[13] It concerns the relation of the economy to the "immanent" Trinity:

> It is impossible to say, for example, that in history the Holy Spirit proceeds from the Father "and from the Son," but that within the Trinity he proceeds "from the Father alone." God's truth is his faithfulness. Consequently we can rely on his promises and on himself. A God who contradicted himself would be an unreliable God. He would have to be called a demon, not God.[14]

This is way off the mark.[15] Just possibly, we might reach tentatively from the economy to the *Filioque* as the latter is traditionally conceived in the West. But Moltmann uses dangerously inflated language: there is no contradiction in putatively different orders ("immanent" and "economic," to use traditional terminology) or shadow cast on God's character if we cannot read off the one from the other. It is an entirely different matter, however, if a benign economic appearance masks a malevolent immanent reality, and here we find reflection on the trinitarian economy veering back toward our earlier concerns over control and freedom. For the economy reveals to us the *kind* of God that is sovereign over us and the *kind* of salvation that his eschatological kingdom brings about. Love is at the heart of this sovereignty; freedom is at the heart of salvation; so, at

13. I am leaving this issue open only because it would be a distraction to go into greater detail.

14. Moltmann, *The Trinity and the Kingdom of God*, 154.

15. For all his differences with Moltmann, Robert Jenson makes a mistake inspired by the same use or misuse of theological principle when he seriously entertains the notion of intradivine reconciliation. See "Reconciliation in God," in *The Theology of Reconciliation*, ed. Colin Gunton (London and New York: T&T Clark, 2003), 159–66.

least, Moltmann believes and so, despite differences, does Pannenberg, an equally eminent exemplar of a trinitarian-economic approach to the question of God.[16]

"In the kingdom," Moltmann says, dwelling on Jesus's proclamation, "God is not the Lord; he is the merciful Father," and we are not servants, only children; we love in freedom; we do not submit to rule.[17] He is scarcely alone in adopting such a viewpoint. But this is irresponsible language for anyone who wishes to make broad biblical categories constitutive for theology. Why not integrate talk of lordship, almightiness, love, fatherhood, servanthood, friendship, freedom, and obedience instead of forcing antitheses? The question shows how a claim about theological method—the need to derive our idea of sovereignty from the trinitarian economy—is swiftly returning us to issues of love and control, freedom and reciprocity. Barth is surely very impressive here. The first two volumes (or half-volumes) of the *Church Dogmatics* announced the centrality of divine lordship in his thought even before he arrived at the specific treatment of God as the One who loves in freedom. Once he arrives there, he succeeds remarkably in keeping before our eyes, in a single vision, oneness and threeness, transcendent fatherhood and humble sonship, "immanence" and "economy," if I may use the terms rather lazily.[18] His christocentric theological sense enables him to do so.

It is thus ironic when John Frame, in a detailed treatment of the doctrine of God that takes sovereignty as its key theme and emphasizes the almighty control that Moltmann repudiates, repeatedly accuses Barth of being unbiblical.[19] On the various points under consideration, Barth may or may not deserve the stick. But he is clear where the Bible is clear, namely, on the fact that Jesus Christ is the fullest revelation of the Father, the light of world and mind, through whom we are to interpret the law and the prophets, which are the preparatory witness to him. Yet Frame does not understand God supremely through Jesus Christ; the Father is not understood most luminously through the Son. We are well more than four hundred pages into *The Doctrine of God* before the author touches on the fact that God's love involves humility and before Frame confesses, "There is something mysterious here, but as I grope for words, I would conclude that Jesus's self-abasement reveals something about the very

16. Pannenberg, who argues more rigorously than does Moltmann, finds an idea of lordship such as we meet in Barth less emotionally and theologically distasteful than does Moltmann. A perusal of *Systematic Theology*, vols. 1 and 3, reveals this; see esp. vol. 1, chs. 5 and 6, and vol. 3, chs. 12 and 15.

17. Moltmann, *The Trinity and the Kingdom of God*, 70.

18. Karl Barth, *Church Dogmatics* (Edinburgh: T&T Clark, 1957), II/1.

19. John M. Frame, *The Doctrine of God: A Theology of Lordship* (Phillipsburg, NJ: P&R, 2002).

lordship of God."[20] What Frame has to say on this point is exhausted in just eleven lines whereas we have learned of authority, control, and power for hundreds of pages before this. In an early footnote he defends (against Moltmann inter alios) the fact that he will treat the Trinity at the end of his volume. Order is a secondary and relatively unimportant matter: "In a systematic theology, every part should presuppose every other, so that it does not much matter what is discussed first."[21] But the nonchristocentric treatment of authority and control that governs the volume does not in any obvious way presuppose that Jesus's "self-abasement reveals something about the very lordship of God." Frame does not think it even worth considering whether the humble form in which Jesus exercised his lordship might figure at the heart of the revelation of the lordship of God. I regret the need to be negative and polemical at this point, but it is a point of religious importance and anything but purely academic. Jesus Christ, the center of God's economic dealings with His creation, himself one with the Father, in whom, if we have seen him, we have seen the Father—it is with supreme reference to him that we must understand the sovereignty of God. We are safe in our thought only when it is centered on the one through whom all things were made, the royal man who hung on the cross and was exalted to universal authority, given to us as Lord of the church whose kingdom shall have no end, Jesus Christ, our Lord.[22]

Naming the name of Christ does not resolve disagreement over the question of whether sovereignty is either love or control or both love and control, whether it is either determination or bestowal of freedom or both determination and the bestowal of freedom, and so forth. It is to be feared that in arguments over the nature and form of God's sovereignty, we are prone to appear like prosecuting and defense attorneys squabbling before the judge's bench—the judge's character being the

20. Ibid., 442.
21. Ibid., 15n32; cf. 620n3.
22. Frame's defense of his approach, as stated in the footnotes cited above, is that he is following the order of Scripture itself, which starts out, in the Old Testament, with the "primarily . . . singular being," God (ibid., 620). But there is a logical hiatus here. We are to approach God through Christ in thought as well as in worship; we are not authorized to worship God without reference to Jesus Christ because the Old Testament figures did so; no more so with our thought. This is not to demote but just to contextualize the Old Testament. On a more abstract plane, both Frame's view of triunity as an "attribute" of God and his description of God as "a person" are extremely problematic. "It is not evident to me why triunity should not be considered an attribute of God" (228). What is the referent of "God" here? Presumably it cannot be either "the Father" or "Father, Son, and Spirit." So it must be the divine nature, considered in abstraction from any person. That is scarcely biblical usage. For the averment that God is *never* thought of under the indefinite article (e.g., "a Person") in traditional theism, see T. F. Torrance, *God and Rationality* (London: Oxford University Press, 1971), 80.

subject of dispute. But we are always treading on holy ground. We are concerned with that greatest of all questions, knowing God. We ask the question *coram Deo*. Here, if anywhere, we need to be prepared for extreme correction even if we have prayed and worshiped, preached or written with confidence for years. Are most of us not in need of constant purging and correction of our ideas, present writer in the forefront? More specifically, are we not all too prone to flee from one of God's perfections (or attributes) to another? I simply do not see the depths of my sin, and so the absolutely unlimited right God has over me as Creator, let alone Redeemer, is concealed from my sight. So I flee to divine love, which tenderly connotes sympathy and relational give-and-take. Alternatively, I simply do not see the immense depth of God's love, His stooping to wash my feet, and the unbounded humility of His self-sacrifice. So I flee to an authority that I unimpeachably honor by declaring that He is in absolute sovereign control. Perhaps in both cases our vision is unduly constrained. Would a focus on divine holiness help us overcome the impasse that we reach when we square up to each other over matters of freedom, love, sovereignty, and control? An example from the recent debate on "open theism" explains this suggestion.

Heated debate on open theism has gone on in North America for a number of years, and the nature of sovereignty is at its heart. What appears to be novel in open theism is the denial, on the part of thinkers in the evangelical theological community, of exhaustive divine foreknowledge. It is argued that exhaustive foreknowledge robs humans of their freedom of will and action and thus destroys the divine-human relationship rooted in God's love. Exhaustive foreknowledge entails absolute control. My interest here is not in the open-theist case as such. But is this just about control? Clark Pinnock, the leading proponent of open theism, has written that "to work with a history where the outcomes are not predetermined and with creatures that are able to resist him is a challenge and, no doubt, a source of great delight even for God."[23] Consider this statement. Biblically and theologically, resistance to God is nothing other than sin, and sin is *the* problem of the human race, diametrically and infinitely opposed to God's holiness, bringing upon us defilement and condemnation. God "delights" in my ability to sin? I do not see how this can be said without ridding sin of its heinous quality. In defense, it might be claimed that God delights in the *use* of my ability in order to obey ("ability" is not used here in a theologically aligned way) and also that I have this ability only because I have a contrary ability. God delights in the situation that He has created. But whatever we make of this reasoning, what we can-

Not!

---

23. Clark Pinnock, *Most Moved Mover: A Theology of God's Openness* (Grand Rapids: Baker Academic; Carlisle, UK: Paternoster, 2001), 95.

not conclude is that God delights in my ability to sin. To speak of God's delight in working with creatures able to sin, in terms that seem to imply God delighting in this actual ability, is very dangerous.

It may be that Clark Pinnock does not mean what I take his words to imply and that he would be horrified if he thought that saying what he does say entails going easy on sin. Yet what is striking is that the formulation does not so jar him that he distances himself from its apparent implications. I have labored over his remark in order to show how the desire to combat *control* means that what is effectively (though not designedly) going by the board is *holiness*. Is it not the awesome holiness of God that prevents our speaking easily of give-and-take or reciprocity in the divine-human relationship? This rhetorical question is not designed to foreclose a number of questions about the nature of the relationship between God and humans, often focused, for example, on the question of prayer. But as soon as we add, "who are in heaven, hallowed be your name" to "Our Father," divine holiness is brought to the forefront of our minds. If divine sovereignty is a sovereignty of love, it is a sovereignty of holy love or the sovereignty of the love of the Holy One. Love cannot really be conceived apart from holiness.

This cuts both ways and not simply against those who protest against divine control. Remembrance of divine holiness decisively modifies any contrasting theological elevation of divine control as well. The standard difficulty with "control" is with the way power seems to be conceived in relation to deity. It is a difficulty associated more with the Calvinist than with any other tradition; indeed, the very phrase "sovereignty of God" will suggest Calvinism to many people. Calvin himself was anxious to divest interlocutors of the belief that he conceived of divine sovereign power independently of wisdom, justice, and goodness. However successful or unsuccessful he was, the problem with emphasizing sovereignty in terms of control is that it runs the risk of depriving God of being intrinsically worthy of worship. We truly worship God not because He has the sheer power to command it, like King Nebuchadnezzar, but because, in commanding it, He reveals Himself for who He is, in holy sovereignty "compassionate and gracious, slow to anger, abounding in love and faithfulness, maintaining love to thousands, and forgiving wickedness, yet not leaving the guilty unpunished" (Exod. 34:6–7). The sovereignty of *control* is the aspiration of any despot; the sovereignty of *holiness* is the actuality of God alone. Moreover, we are to worship God in the *beauty* of His holiness, an idea that starkly contrasts with the assertion that "the Lord is totalitarian."[24]

24. Frame, *The Doctrine of God*, 89. If there is a sense in which this is the case, it must be a sense acquired by giving revelation in Christ its due place in theology.

Dogmatics has sometimes given pride of place to divine holiness when treating *de Deo*, including in the twentieth century. Brunner wrote that "from the standpoint of revelation the first thing which has to be said about God is his Sovereignty. But this first point is intimately connected with a second one—so closely indeed that we might even ask whether it ought not to have come first: God is the Holy One."[25] Hugh Ross Mackintosh, in his volume on God, orders his chapters with reference to "the holiness of God," then "the love of God," and then "the sovereign purpose of God" after establishing the "personality of God," although I think it was because he found this a felicitous rather than a necessary order.[26] So, if we center our thinking about divine sovereignty on divine holiness, it is not purely under the constraints of contemporary discussion. And if it seems that I have spiraled off into complete forgetfulness of the Trinity and the economy, we should simply remember that the kingdom of God is the sphere or place where holiness is (prominently) perfected. I have already alluded to Peter's reaction to the holiness of Jesus. We also speak of the *Holy* Spirit, employing the only adjective standardly used in Scripture for any trinitarian person. The last solemn warnings in the last chapter of the Apocalypse are directed to those from whom God will take away the share in the tree of life and in the holy city (Rev. 22:19). The sovereignty of God, who bestows upon His servants their own perpetual reign, is above all a sovereignty of holiness in the climax of the book of Revelation. Granted, any thought of playing off one divine perfection against another, singling out one over the other for special praise, must be anathema. But in our present context, it may be salutary to introduce talk of holiness into a scene where almighty power and fatherly love are so construed that they are pitted in opposition to each other. It reminds us peerlessly of what it is that evokes our worship, and worship is the proper soil from which springs appropriate talk of God. "Worship the Lord in the beauty of His holiness."[27]

In Broader Context

Robert Letham observes, with some dismay, that in his *Systematic Theology* Charles Hodge "does not get around to suggesting that God

25. Emil Brunner, *The Christian Doctrine of God* (London: Lutterworth, 1949), 157.

26. Hugh Ross Mackintosh, *The Christian Apprehension of God* (London: SCM, 1929). It should be noted that Frame wants to put holiness at the forefront of his discussion of lordship (*The Doctrine of God*, 15).

27. I am not defending this translation of, e.g., 1 Chron. 16:29, but quoting the familiar words to make a theological point. Cf. Pss. 29:2; 96:9.

is triune until after 250 pages of detailed exposition of the doctrine of God," and he protestingly proceeds to ask how this helps us in an encounter with Islam.[28] I must disclaim any particular competence in this area; nevertheless, it may be helpful to conclude by reflecting on divine sovereignty in the light of the teaching of the Qur'an in particular.[29]

The existence and sovereignty of the one God and the revelation vouchsafed to His prophet, Muhammad, are the grand themes of the Qur'an. Although it contains both a record of mighty works and portions of narrative, the Qur'an does not describe to us the unfolding of an economy such as we find in Scripture. If the Qur'anic account of God reminds us of any part of Scripture, it is likely to be the Pentateuch, particularly the repeated "I am the Lord" in Leviticus and the intense reiterative clauses that pervade Deuteronomy. Allah is the most Beneficent, most Merciful. He is All-Knowing, Aware, Strong, Severe in punishment. He is entirely Just: "Allah wrongeth not mankind in anything" (Qur'an 10:45).[30] He is All-sufficient, Wise, Truth-telling, and "of infinite bounty" (8:29). He is alone, God transcendent, infinitely great. Spiritually, we are obligated to journey unto Him, for we all come from Him, by creation.

It is impossible that Allah should have partners, a point that is at first made occasionally in the Qur'an but becomes increasingly insistent as it proceeds: trinitarian thought is not only mistaken; it is offensive. It appears that Christianity is misunderstood as claiming a trinity of God, Jesus, and Mary (5:114), but it is the alleged divine sonship of Jesus which is particularly rejected. Allah has no son because He has no needs and He has no consort either. To ascribe partners to Allah is more than intellectual error in religious belief; it is ingratitude for life and deliverance; it denies the beneficence of Allah.[31] One interesting and significant reason for this assertion is that nature itself testifies to the existence of the one God: how can we gaze upon it without due adoration and acknowledg-

28. Robert Letham, review of *The Triune Creator* by Colin Gunton, *Westminster Theological Journal* 62/1 (2000): 146–48.

29. Colin Gunton's book indirectly indicates directions in which we might go in exploring the contrasts between Christianity and Islam, in particular by the use that he makes of Irenaeus's trinitarian theology of creation. Both constraints of space and the focus of this essay prevent my pursuing them. In *Church Dogmatics* II/1:448–49, Barth expresses his conviction that nothing separates Islam and Christianity "so radically as the different ways in which they appear to say the same thing—that there is only one God"—and that Islamic monotheism is "the religious glorification of the number 'one.'"

30. I use what I believe to be the first English "translation" of the Qur'an by an English Muslim: Mohammed Marmaduke Pickthall, *The Meaning of the Glorious Koran* (New York: Mentor, 1953). The very title indicates that, strictly, the Qur'an is untranslatable, but its "meaning" may be rendered in translation.

31. Qur'an 6:63–64, 101; 10:35, 69; 19:35, 92–93.

ment? More than purely intellectual acquiescence, a religious response in the form of monotheistic confession is required by creation.[32]

Intellectual principle and religious existence are not the same thing, and I do not comment on the latter. But in principle, it is not difficult to see what might be attractive about the sovereign Allah, and without indulging in willful triadic perversity, three things may be enumerated in this connection. First, there is a loftiness to the conception: we are in the presence of the transcendently great compared with ourselves and all that is created. Second, one can see how love and warmth might be evoked by Allah, to which there has been ample testimony in the history of Islamic thought. "Those who are with thy Lord are not too proud to do Him service, but they praise Him and adore Him" (7:206). "His are the most beautiful names" (17:110). "Almost might the heavens above be rent asunder while the angels hymn the praise of their Lord and ask forgiveness for those on the earth" (42:5). Third, there seems to be a fundamental justice that characterizes the being and doings of Allah. He bids us to believe aright; we are to repent if we have not; we are to be obedient and do the right; we shall be rewarded if we do.

In comparing the sovereignties of the Qur'anic Allah and the biblical God in light of issues that have occupied us here, one theme that invites thought is the relation of sovereignty to mercy. Allah's mercy is sovereign and He can sovereignly withhold it; there is something mysterious about it.[33] However exactly this sits with the reliability and safety of His justice and goodness, the questions that arise here appear similar to those that arise most especially in Reformed Christianity, where the divine justice, goodness, and love of God sit starkly alongside the sovereign prerogative of God in showing or withholding mercy and ordaining all human actions. But how should Christians understand the relation of God's mercy to His nature or character? It is often said that salvation by sovereign grace entails that God need not have saved or displayed mercy toward anyone. For God, merciful behavior is a contingent possibility of will, not a necessity of nature.[34] But is this really so? If God is love, is mercy only a *possible* form of divine action in history whereas justice is a *necessary* form? It is indeed the case that we have no claim on God's mercy. God owes us nothing. Grace must remain grace. But are there no relevant constraints of the strongest kind from within the divine nature? Are we

32. There is a considerable amount of material to which we could refer here. Note, e.g., Qur'an 13:16–17, but the whole sura ("The Thunder") or, e.g., sura 10 ("Jonah") is instructive.

33. For example, Muhammad is dismayed by clearly culpable unbelief, and yet "if thy Lord willed, all who are in the earth would have believed" (Qur'an 10:100).

34. This is rather loosely phrased; the sense in which we ascribe contingency to God's will requires a more detailed formulation than we need to offer here.

really to say that the exhibition of mercy is a matter of indifference to God, as far as His nature is concerned, that nothing in Him impelled the salvation of the ruined soul to the point of *necessitating* action? Is mercy not a compulsion of love? Supposing I visit you in the hospital, though it is not convenient and I do not know you well. You might say to yourself, "That was nice of him; he didn't have to do it; if he hadn't, there could be no cause for complaint." Supposing, however, a mutual friend responded, "You don't understand; he had to do it. That's the kind of person that he is." The second is a "higher" commendation of character than the first, and yet nothing is legitimately claimed by or owed to another. It appears to me that we might conceive of mercy in relation to divine sovereignty along such lines where we have a God who knows us rather well and trades in far weightier merchandise than "convenience." Adumbration is not possible here. But the question arises whether this kind of position distinguishes a Christian from a Muslim conception of the nature and the sovereignty of God.

The sovereign mercy of which Christians speak is exercised in a humility of a depth and quality that defies and transcends our understanding. Kenneth Cragg tells the story of how a Muslim son rethought the nature of greatness when his widowed father humbly fulfilled the responsibilities traditionally thought of as the domain of the mother.[35] The son perceived that condescension and humility of this nature were a sign, not a denial, of greatness in the father. So might not condescension and humility be a sign of greatness in One far greater than the father? The Qur'an occasionally and allusively directs the mind toward the beauty of Allah by bidding it reflect on the wonders of nature. The connections between natural wonder, natural beauty, and divine beauty are too intricate to be considered here. But where Christians speak of sovereignty, they cannot dissociate it from beauty, and the beauty of which they speak includes not only the beauty of holiness but the beauty of merciful humility as well. When the eyes of the heart perceive this, adherence to the conviction that God is sovereign becomes more or other than a dutiful confession flecked with pious and sometimes authentic confession of wonder. It becomes instead the passion of a soul ravished by the actuality of Father, Son, and Spirit, the union of goodness, truth, and beauty.

---

35. Kenneth Cragg, "Conversion and Convertibility—with Special Reference to Muslims," in *Down to Earth: Studies in Christianity and Culture*, ed. John Stott and Robert Coote (London: Hodder & Stoughton, 1981), 193–208.

10

The Actuality of God

Karl Barth in Conversation with Open Theism

BRUCE L. MCCORMACK

For nearly two decades now, the evangelical churches in America have been the scene of a polarizing debate between defenders of classical theism and the proponents of what is typically referred to as "open theism." After reading through the growing literature generated by both sides, my own conclusion is that each has something important to say; each has "theological values" which would need to be preserved in any truly adequate doctrine of God. The trouble is that both sides are actually occupying a *shared* ground on which no resolution of the debate is thinkable. It is clearly time for some fresh thinking.

As the subtitle of this essay makes clear, the goal here is to bring Karl Barth into conversation with the open theists. The decision to treat Barth in relation to open theism rather than classical theism is not based upon a belief that he stood closer to the former than the latter. Far from it. As I have already suggested, both sides to the current debate stand finally upon the same ground—a ground which would have to be abandoned if the values now contained in each model were to be brought into a single, unified conception. Barth occupies a very different ground, and as we shall see, it is because he does so that he is able to take up and preserve the values set forth in each of the other two models. In any event, Barth does not stand closer to the open theists than he does to the classical theists. The decision to bring Barth into conversation with open theism is based simply upon the perception that open theism is attracting a great deal of attention—to the point of disturbing the peace of the churches—and the belief that it is not dealt with adequately where it is met by power plays (e.g., attempts to exclude its proponents from membership in the Evangelical Theological Society). The only adequate response is to provide an alternative which is demonstrably superior to it—something today's defenders of classical theism have consistently failed to do.

In what follows, I am going to begin with a brief typology of under-standings of the being of God in relation to the world. To do so will help me to make clear why it is that open theism is far too indebted to classical theism to offer effective resistance to it. It will also enable me, at a later point in the essay, to make clear why Barth's doctrine of God cannot be found within this spectrum but rather constitutes a break with it—which is also why he is able to take up the theological values resident in both models and reorder them into a coherent whole. I will then look closely at central elements of open theism, followed by a consideration of the aspects of Barth's doctrine of God which correspond to these elements. I will conclude with a brief statement of what evangelicals can learn from this comparative study.

A Brief Typology of Treatments of the Being of God in Relation to the World

The significance of the proposal being made by open theists will be most easily grasped by locating it on a spectrum of beliefs about God and the world which range from classical theism, on the one side, to process theism, on the other. Because they appear on this spectrum at the furthest possible remove from each other, the impression is easily given that classical and process theisms could scarcely be more different. As we shall see, however, this impression misleads; the two positions do, in fact, belong to one and the same spectrum of thought. Still, the differences are not unimportant.

Classical theism presupposes a very robust Creator-creature distinc-tion. God's being is understood to be complete in itself with or without the world, which means that the being of God is "wholly other" than the being of the world. Moreover, God's being is characterized by what we might think of as a "static" or unchanging perfection. *All* that God is, he is changelessly. Nothing that happens in the world can affect God on the level of his being. He is what he is regardless of what takes place—and necessarily so, since any change in a perfect being could be only in the direction of imperfection. *Affectivity* in God, if it is affirmed at all, is restricted to dispositional states which have no ontological significance.

Process theism, by contrast, understands the being of God and the being of the world to stand in a relationship of continuity. Process theologians will typically make appeal to the image of head and body to describe a relationship which, in their view, allows God to remain superior to the world even as God is deeply affected by everything that happens in the world. As the "head" which "directs" the activities which take place in the world which is his "body," God is "more" than the world. And yet God's "directive" activity is said to be limited to creating conditions which would steer outcomes in a desired direction. Outcomes are not predetermined. God is responsive to what happens in the world, and such responsiveness does indeed have ontological significance. That is to say, the being of God grows, develops, changes, evolves through the history of his interactions with the world. This organic conception of the God-world relation is often personalized at the point at which God's interaction with free rational creatures comes into view. God seeks to encourage or perhaps persuade such creatures to do his will, which certainly gives the impression of rational and purposive activity. The additional thought that creation is, for God, a *necessary* activity (a thought which is found in virtually all process theologies) might well seem to make God less personal than his free creatures. But whether process theism succeeds finally in constructing a fully personal conception of God or not, the decisive point for our purposes here is that God's will is not understood to be fully formed before the creation of the world (any more than God's being is characterized by static perfection). The will of God is a work-in-progress, something that is constantly being adapted to changing circumstances which lie beyond God's control.

In spite of these rather significant differences, what classical theism and process theism have in common is far more important. What they have in common, in the first place, is the belief that the "order of knowing" runs in the opposite direction to the "order of being." That is to say, though the being of God is above and prior to the being of all else that exists (and therefore first in the "order of being"), our knowledge of God proceeds from a prior knowledge of some aspect or aspects of creaturely reality (and therefore the knowledge of God follows knowledge of the self or the world in the "order of knowing"). The consequence of this methodological decision is that the way taken to knowledge of God controls and determines the kind of God-concept one is able to generate; thus, epistemology controls and determines divine ontology.

It follows, in the second place, that both conceptions are the result of an exercise in *metaphysical* thinking in the strict sense of the term. Whether one seeks to *liken* God to some aspect of creaturely existence ("personhood" on the creaturely level, perhaps) or to *deny* to God any similarity to created reality through a process of negating the limits thought to belong to the creaturely does not really matter at the end of the day. Both are exercises in metaphysics because both take up a starting point "from below" in some creaturely reality or magnitude and proceed through a process of inferential reasoning to establish the nature of divine reality.

And this means, third, that both claim to know *what* God is before a consideration of Christology. At the point at which Christology is finally introduced, its central terms ("deity" or "divinity," the divine "nature" or "person") have already been filled with content. The result is that the content of Christology will be made to conform to a prior understanding of God. By its very nature, then, metaphysical thinking is an exercise in *abstractive* reasoning in a twofold sense; first, in the sense described in the second point above (abstracting from a prior knowledge of the creaturely to arrive at a concept of divine being) and, second, in the more important sense of looking away from the knowledge of God given in Jesus Christ.

Fourth and finally, both conceptions rely heavily on an *independent* doctrine of creation. Classical theism is buttressed by the notion of a *creatio ex nihilo*; process theism, by a return to the ancient idea, found among the pagans, of divine emanation. Both concepts of creation are—in their actual use if not inherently—"independent" in the specific sense that like the doctrines of God they support, their content has been filled out without reference to Christology. The consequence is that such teleology as can be found in either conception of creation will (where consistency prevails) be elaborated without reference to God's reconciling and redeeming activity in Jesus Christ.

It is my conviction that open theism belongs to the spectrum of opinions established by the elements I have just described as being common to classical theism, on the one side, and process theism, on the other. Where it is to be found on this spectrum will perhaps occasion some surprise. Evangelical opponents of open theism have typically sought to lump it in with process theology. But the truth is that open theism is far closer to classical theism than most realize. Karl Barth's doctrine of God, on the other hand, is not to be found anywhere on this spectrum—for the simple reason that he rejects the metaphysics embodied in all of the approaches belonging to it. His is a strictly *christological* approach—which means that it constitutes a fairly radical departure from all other existing options. And this means that even at the points where he seems to stand far closer to open theism than to classical theism, it must not be forgotten that the ground on which he stands is quite different.

Armed with the tools provided by this brief typology, we are now ready to turn more directly to a consideration of open theism.

Open Theism

Introduction

The origins of the theological movement known today as open theism have been traced by Roger Olson to the mid-1970s, to the publication of essays by James Daane and Nicholas Wolterstorff which challenged, respectively, traditional assumptions of God's aseity (or "self-sufficiency") and timelessness.[1] The big step, however, was taken in 1986 when Clark Pinnock published an essay in which he claimed that "God limits himself in relation to creation so that he does not know the future exhaustively and infallibly."[2] Though Pinnock was not the first to make such an assertion, his prominence in the evangelical world made him a lightning rod. Others quickly joined themselves to his cause.[3] In 1994, Pinnock and his friends released what amounted to a manifesto entitled *The Openness of God*.[4] The positive echo this book found and the backlash to which it gave rise were both considerable. Since that time, further works have poured forth from the presses—though without adding a great deal in the way of a substantive deepening of the perspective.[5] Open theism today

1. See Roger Olson, "Theism," in *The Westminster Handbook to Evangelical Theology*, ed. Roger Olson (Louisville and London: Westminster John Knox, 2004), 275–76. For the articles mentioned by Olson, see James Daane, "Can a Man Bless God?" in *God and the Good: Essays in Honor of Henry Stob*, ed. Clifton Orlebeke and Lewis Smedes (Grand Rapids: Eerdmans, 1974), 165–73; Nicholas Wolterstorff, "God Everlasting," ibid., 181–203.

2. See Olson, "Theism," 276. In lifting up Clark Pinnock, "God Limits His Knowledge," in *Predestination and Free Will: Four Views of Divine Sovereignty and Human Freedom*, ed. David Basinger and Randall Basinger (Downers Grove, IL: InterVarsity, 1986), 143–62, as a pivotal moment, I am simply following Olson's lead. It should be noted, however, that Pinnock's thesis was not wholly new at that time, having been largely anticipated by Richard Rice, *The Openness of God: The Relationship of Divine Foreknowledge and Human Free Will* (Nashville: Review and Herald, 1979); repr. as *God's Foreknowledge and Man's Free Will* (Minneapolis: Bethany House, 1985). For more on Pinnock's early formulations of the open theistic position, see Clark Pinnock, "Between Classical and Process Theism," in *Process Theology*, ed. Ronald Nash (Grand Rapids: Baker Academic, 1987), 313–27.

3. See esp. William Hasker, *God, Time and Knowledge* (Ithaca, NY: Cornell University Press, 1989); Gregory A. Boyd, *Trinity and Process: A Critical Evaluation and Reconstruction of Hartshorne's Di-polar Theism towards a Trinitarian Metaphysics* (New York: Peter Lang, 1992); idem, *Letters from a Skeptic* (Wheaton, IL: Victor Books, 1994).

4. Clark Pinnock, Richard Rice, John Sanders, William Hasker, and David Basinger, eds., *The Openness of God: A Biblical Challenge to the Traditional Understanding of God* (Downers Grove, IL: InterVarsity, 1994).

5. Among the most important are the following: David Basinger, *The Case for Free Will Theism: A Philosophical Assessment* (Downers Grove, IL: InterVarsity, 1996); John

is pretty much what it was in its origins: a highly aggressive, missionary movement in theology which seeks to convert the evangelical churches to what it alleges to be a more "biblical" understanding of God.

Underneath it all, open theism is a rather narrowly defined project. If we thought that open theists attend exclusively to the doctrine of God to the exclusion of all other doctrines which are impinged upon by the moves they make, we would be guilty of a half-truth. The truth is that what these theologians are interested in is basically two things: the will of God as it relates to free rational creatures and the question of what God knows and when he knows it. So open theism has to do, above all, with the doctrines of providence and divine foreknowledge. Other aspects of the doctrine of God are mentioned only in passing (e.g., the belief that God is truly "other" than the world because he creates *ex nihilo*). No attempt is made to offer a fully integrated doctrine of God such as would allow it to compete with other "theisms." It is, to a large degree, parasitic upon classical theism in that it draws its life from the negations it registers over against aspects of the latter. These negations become immediately apparent in the meaning assigned to "openness."

The basic intuition is that the future is "open" not only for us but also for God—"open" because God has chosen not to control the decisions made by free rational creatures. God may indeed have a "central" purpose which he determines "from eternity" (i.e., before creating) to bring to fruition. But *how* God brings this purpose to fruition in time is itself conditioned by free acts which God does not control and—precisely because he does not control them—cannot foresee. The latter point is the one that attracts the most attention on the part of opponents. Open theists hold (for reasons we will consider in a moment) that an exhaustive divine foreknowledge is logically incompatible with human freedom, and so they conclude that God's foreknowledge is *limited*. God may know in advance that which *he* will effect, acting alone and without the cooperation of his creatures. But God does not know in advance what the outcome of any cooperatively produced effects will be. To put it this way is to suggest that what is most basic to open theism is not its position with regard to divine foreknowledge but rather its take on the divine

---

Sanders, *The God Who Risks: A Theology of Providence* (Downers Grove, IL: InterVarsity, 1998); Gregory Boyd, *God of the Possible: A Biblical Introduction to the Openness of God* (Grand Rapids: Baker Academic, 2000); idem, *Satan and the Problem of Evil: Constructing a Trinitarian Warfare Theodicy* (Downers Grove, IL: InterVarsity, 2001); idem, "Neo-Molinism and the Infinite Intelligence of God," *Philosophia Christi* 5 (2003): 187–204; Clark Pinnock, *Flame of Love: A Theology of the Holy Spirit* (Downers Grove, IL: InterVarsity, 1996); idem, *Most Moved Mover: A Theology of God's Openness* (Grand Rapids: Baker Academic; Carlisle, UK: Paternoster, 2001).

concursus. The doctrine of *concursus*, or "cooperation," is that aspect of the doctrine of providence which addresses itself to the question of *how* God interacts with rational creatures in order to ensure that his will is done. Classically, Christian theologians have typically said that God acts upon and "in" his rational creatures by means of some sort of infused causal power. Open theists prefer to explain *concursus* along the lines of an influence that is personal in nature; hence, the preferred image is that of *persuasion*. In any event, the result of these twin positions with respect to *concursus*, on the one hand, and divine foreknowledge, on the other, is a view of God's providence which is quite similar to that found among process theists. God's will, as I have already observed, is a work-in-progress, one which evolves in response to changing circumstances and conditions. If open theists insist, nevertheless, that they are not guilty of the process "heresy," they do so because they continue to hold to the traditional conception of a *creatio ex nihilo* and, with that, to a robust Creator-creature distinction.

There are other implications from the foregoing which will emerge in the course of the exposition which follows—for example, the rejection of a putative divine timelessness and impassibility. But what we have said to this point is sufficient by way of introduction. What we need to do now is examine how open theists seek to support these conclusions with arguments drawn from the spheres of biblical studies, systematic theology, and philosophy. We will conclude with a brief attempt to assess the implications of open theism for ecumenical unity.

The Biblical Case for Open Theism

HERMENEUTICAL CONSIDERATIONS

To the extent that the New Testament comes into play in the attempt made by open theists to provide biblical warrants for their conclusions, it is above all the Johannine affirmation that "God is love" which is made to be decisive. As we shall see, the incarnation does not have a constitutive role to play in "defining" God. Virtually the whole of the open theistic understanding of God has been fully elaborated on the basis of the Old Testament *before* the incarnation comes into view. Or more accurately, passages are collected from the Old Testament which, in the eyes of the open theists, conform most closely to the requirements of 1 John 4:8 (as interpreted by them).

That such a "hermeneutical key" is needed is based on the observation (as Richard Rice puts it) that "the Bible contains an enormous range of material, and on almost any significant topic we can find diverse statements if not diverse perspectives as well. This is certainly true of the idea of God. Thousands of texts refer to God, but they are immensely

THEOLOGICAL PERSPECTIVES

varied."[6] All language employed to speak of God, it is asserted, is to some extent metaphorical. Those metaphors are rightly understood to be "controlling metaphors" which stand "closer, so to speak, to the intended object." Of these, the most important is the word "love."[7] "The statement *God is love* is as close as the Bible comes to giving us a definition of the divine reality."[8] While it is unquestionably true, in my view, that the Johannine phrase is telling us *something* absolutely basic about God, the meaning of the statement is anything but obvious. At the end of the day, it is not the meaning we assign to such statements which defines the being of God; it is the being of God which must give meaning to them. Rice, however, takes the meaning of the statement as fairly obvious and straightforward.

> The view of God and his relation to the world presented in this book . . . expresses two basic convictions: love is the most important quality we ascribe to God, and love is more than care and commitment; it involves being sensitive and responsive as well. These convictions lead the contributors of this book to think of God's relation to the world in dynamic rather than static terms. This conclusion has important consequences. For one thing, it means that God interacts with his creatures. Not only does he influence them but they also exert an influence on him. As a result, the course of history is not the product of the divine action alone. God's will is not the ultimate explanation for everything that happens; human decisions and actions make an important contribution. Thus history is the combined result of what God and his creatures decide to do.[9]

We may leave to one side the question of whether the conclusions drawn for the nature of history are a wholly necessary consequence of the basic affirmation that love entails sensitivity and responsiveness on the part of God. The more basic issue is surfaced when we realize that Rice takes it as self-evident that the definition of the word "love" which he believes appropriate for describing human-to-human relations must apply with equal validity and force to the relation of God to the human. What is happening here is that a definition of a term devised originally for speaking of love on the plane of human relations is being applied in a rather straightforward fashion to the being of God—without any sense that an illegitimate anthropopathizing of God might be taking place. Is it really true that the reciprocal relations proper to the human experience of love may be taken, without further ado, to be characteristic of

6. Richard Rice, "Biblical Support for a New Perspective," in Pinnock et al., *The Openness of God*, 16.
7. Ibid., 17.
8. Ibid., 18.
9. Ibid., 15–16.

the divine "love" as well? Are we justified in making God to be "like" us in this way? Does the statement "God is love" justify us in doing so? For Rice and his colleagues, such questions are not asked because they apparently do not believe that humans have any alternative, hermeneutically, but to begin with concepts that have their home originally in the sphere of human experience and thinking and to apply them more or less directly to God. The only question for them is which, among the many candidates, is to be chosen. I think myself that they are altogether wrong to make this assumption—and wrong not to recognize that it at least needs to be discussed and defended. There is, as we shall see, an alternative.

In any event, the Johannine axiom—and the meaning assigned to it— provides the open theists with (1) a criterion of selectivity for identifying passages in the Old Testament which are supportive of their claims and (2) a hermeneutical key for ordering these passages to other, more problematic passages.

THE OLD TESTAMENT

The open theists are well aware that there are biblical passages which set forth a strong view of divine immutability as well as passages which lend support to the thought of an exhaustive divine foreknowledge of future contingent events. Under the heading of immutability, classical theists often refer to the following: "God is not a human being, that he should lie, or a mortal, that he should change his mind. Has he not promised, and will he not do it? Or has he spoken, and will he not fulfill it?" (Num. 23:19); "Moreover the Glory of Israel will not recant or change his mind; for he is not a mortal, that he should change his mind" (1 Sam. 15:29); "For I the Lord do not change" (Mal. 3:6); "Every generous act of giving, with every perfect gift, is from above, coming down from the Father of lights, with whom there is no variation or shadow due to change" (James 1:17). Under the heading of an exhaustive foreknowledge are the following: "Even before a word is on my tongue, O LORD, you know it completely. You hem me in, behind and before, and lay your hand upon me. Such knowledge is too wonderful for me; it is so high that I cannot attain it. . . . Your eyes beheld my unformed substance. In your book were written all the days that were formed for me, when none of them as yet existed" (Ps. 139:4–6, 16); "And before him no creature is hidden, but all are naked and laid bare to the eyes of the one to whom we must render an account" (Heb. 4:13). Such passages provide the bedrock of the biblical case for classical theism.

But the open theists prefer to treat such passages as a problem to be solved while the "fixed pole," if you will—that which is thought to lie closest to divine reality—are those passages which speak of God changing his mind or repenting of a decision already made. Since all such passages are, without exception, to be found in the Old Testament, it is not surprising that the Old Testament should play such a massive role in the defense of open theism. And in truth, passages in which "God does in fact repent of having promised, threatened or even done something, and in which He in a sense retracts either once or many times, and sometimes goes on to retract the retraction, returning to what He had originally said or done"[10] are not few in number. Genesis 6:6 sounds a note that would recur here and there throughout the Old Testament: "And the LORD was sorry that he had made humankind on the earth, and it grieved him to his heart." In addition, one might consider the following: Genesis 18:20–33 (God makes concessions, where his judgment on Sodom and Gomorrah is concerned, in response to the entreaties of Abraham); Jeremiah 18:1–10 (God promises to repent of the evil he would do to a nation if that nation should turn from its evil); Amos 7:1–6 (God repents of sending a plague of locusts in response to the intercessory prayer of his prophet); and Jonah 3:10 (where it is said, rather strikingly, that "when God saw what they did, how they turned from their evil ways, God changed his mind about the calamity that he had said he would bring upon them; and he did not do it"). For their part, classical theists are well aware of the existence of these passages. But they tend to treat *them* as the problem to be solved, regarding the "immutability" passages as the fixed pole.

Some degree of harmonization is possible starting from either pole of this debate. Starting from that which constitutes the fixed pole for classical theists, it is possible (up to a point) to insist that what changes in the case of "divine repentance" are not God's *ultimate* intentions but the direction taken by God in fulfillment of them because of a change of behavior on the part of God's people. Starting from the other end, it is possible (again, up to a point) to insist that God "essentially" is *love* and that God therefore remains essentially unchanged (and the purposes dictated by his loving nature remain unchanged) even as his intentions change from situation to situation. But there is a real question here of whether it is really necessary to seek any final harmonization between the sets of *Old Testament* passages regarded by each side of the controversy as fixed poles in the hermeneutical process. The choice of either is predicated finally upon a presupposed metaphysical construct (in the one case, the metaphysics of pure being and, in the other case, the metaphysics of love). Given that this is so, it is very questionable whether either procedure can finally be justified.

10. Barth, *Church Dogmatics* (Edinburgh: T&T Clark, 1956), II/1:496.

Perhaps it would be better to allow such passages to simply stand in an unresolved tension—in the realization that perceptions of God's intentions (and the understanding of God's character and even his "essence") would quite naturally undergo a certain amount of growth and development, advance and retreat, in response to shifts in national fortune until the Definitive had come and the people of God were at last in a position to understand that God's ultimate intentions had to do, from the very beginning, with the sending of his eternal Son into this world and not with the political fortunes of the nation to whom he is sent. Such an understanding of growth and development in the *reception* of revelation, it has to be said, will be threatening only to those who presuppose an understanding of biblical inspiration which would require that all biblical statements ultimately find their source in a single Author. On this basis, one could, I suppose, imagine that all Old Testament passages must be capable of *complete* harmonization. But evangelical theology surrendered the notion of mechanical dictation a long time ago, and it is hard to imagine any other explanation of the process of inspiration which would allow for and require a single-Author theory. Most today are quite content to acknowledge that inspiration is wrongly construed where divine authorship excludes or even only suppresses human activity in the production of biblical writings. And given the diversity of human writers, their varied backgrounds educationally, their differing historical and social locations, most evangelicals readily allow for differing styles, differing genres, and—dare I say?—differing perceptions of revelation on the part of God's people in the Old Testament economy. All of this would, I suspect, be immediately granted not only by the open theists but by a fair number of the defenders of classical theism today as well. The problem is that both sides to this controversy function hermeneutically and exegetically in a way that would truly be necessary only on the supposition that the Bible ultimately has but a single Author. And where this supposition is allowed to hold sway (however unconsciously), one must inevitably appeal to one or the other metaphysic in order to justify one's choice of a fixed pole.

If both sides were to cease treating either set of passages as a fixed pole—recognizing that the decision to do so must rest inevitably on a metaphysical theory whose validity is taken for granted in advance of exegetical practice—then the passages could stand in a tension and our attention would necessarily shift (as it ought, in my view) to God's self-revelation in Jesus Christ, wherein alone his ultimate intentions are made known. Where open theism is concerned, failure to make such a decision must inevitably mean that it is not Christology which finally grounds their understanding of the divine reality but a metaphysics of love. That this is so helps us to understand why it is that open theists

generally treat the incarnation as an afterthought, a topic that is introduced only to confirm a case that has already been made in its entirety
without its help.

THE NEW TESTAMENT

The open theists are not at all willing to concede the charge that the
New Testament differs from the Old Testament in offering no support for
their "dynamic portrait" of God's relation to the world and to humans.
Richard Rice has the New Testament case for open theism rest on four
basic elements: the incarnation (and with that, the identification of God
with Jesus); the general portrayal of God in Jesus's ministry; Jesus's teachings about God; and the nature of Jesus's death.[11] As the first and fourth
of these elements are closely connected and possess an importance of
which the open theists seem only dimly aware, I will treat them at length.
The second and third elements can be dealt with more briefly.

By the "portrayal of God in Jesus's ministry," Rice wishes to point to
Jesus's style of relating to others: "His life was characterized by *service to*
and *suffering with* rather than power over human beings."[12] The logic of
the argument is that if this is how Jesus behaves, then this must also be
how God behaves, since Jesus is God. The weakness in the argument—
where the case for open theism is concerned—is that "service to and
suffering with" are behaviors which carry no necessary implications
for one's understanding of the being and essence of God. Such observations are suggestive only; they tell us *something* about God's "nature,"
but no firm conclusions can be drawn from them for God's will and the
relation of that will to the divine being. The same is true of observations
drawn from Jesus's teachings about God. The joy expressed by God at
the return of a wayward son or daughter could just as easily support a
Calvinist conception of double predestination and limited atonement as
the positions taken by open theists.

The concept of incarnation is passed over rather quickly by Rice. He
finds in it a single thought, namely, that Jesus is the definitive revelation
of God. This much is certainly true, but it invites the question of *how*
it is true. That Jesus is the definitive revelation of God means, for Rice,
that the human experiences of Jesus bring to expression the "nature"
of God.

> The fact that God chose to express himself through the medium of a
> human life suggests that God's experience has something in common
> with certain aspects of human existence. If human life in its fullness

11. Rice, "Biblical Support for a New Perspective," 39.
12. Ibid., 40.

and complexity, with social, emotional and volitional dimensions, represents the supreme expression of God's own nature among the creatures
(Gen. 1:26–7), it is reasonable to infer that the distinctive features of
human experience are most reminiscent of the divine reality. It would
seem that God, like us, is personal existence. If so, then God enjoys
relationships, has feelings, makes decisions, formulates plans and acts
to fulfill them.[13]

Nothing that is said here moves beyond the realm of divine *experience*,
of dispositional states (i.e., the "psychological" realm) and "faculties"
(e.g., volition). The Subject of these dispositional states and faculties
remains hidden in the background, so that it is impossible to guess what
ontological significance, if any, these experiences might have.

Now, one might have thought that Rice's treatment of the death of
Jesus would bring us somewhat nearer to an understanding of God's
being and essence. And Rice does indeed say that "God was in Christ,
himself enduring the agony that Christ underwent."[14] But it is not at
all clear what is meant by this. *Himself* enduring? How? By being an
empathetic presence to the human Jesus in his sufferings? By feeling
"grieved" by the spectacle of the sufferings of the human Jesus? Or by
being himself the Subject of those human sufferings? The latter claim
might well have put us on the road to understanding something important about the being of God—not only in time but also in eternity.
The former claim would leave us with a hidden divine Subject and an
equally hidden divine being, lying somehow in back of the experiences
of empathy and grief. But Rice leaves completely uncertain as to which
view he really intends.

No doubt, Rice would say that, as a New Testament scholar, it is not
his task to reflect upon divine ontology. That is the concern of the systematic theologian or perhaps the Christian philosopher. If this is the
reason for his silence, it would have a *relative* justification. The problem
is that New Testament scholars, too, need to keep at least one eye on the
work of systematic theologians even as they do their exegesis. If they
do not, the hermeneutical strategies by means of which they approach
the task of exegesis will all too easily be controlled by nontheological
factors. And this, in my judgment, is what finally happens with Rice.
His exegesis is controlled by a hermeneutic which finds its ground in
the metaphysic of love which he seeks to validate by reference to 1 John
4:8. Jesus Christ is introduced in an attempt only to provide validation
for a conception of God that has been worked out without reference
to him.

13. Ibid., 39.
14. Ibid., 45.

Theological Considerations

At the heart of the open theistic project lie the twin doctrines of fore-knowledge and providence. But the effort to limit divine foreknowledge in order, on that basis, to revise the traditional conception of how God interacts with his creatures is accompanied by an assault upon two elements central to classical theism, namely, the attribution to God of impassibility and timelessness. One might have thought that a well-ordered Christology and a doctrine of the Trinity commensurate with it would be necessary for achieving these ends. The open theists, however, approach the matter differently. Abandonment of the ideas of impassibility and timelessness is thought to be the necessary consequence of a limited divine foreknowledge and a mode of divine relating to the world that is characterized by affectivity and reciprocity. The net effect of these methodological decisions is that Christology, when it finally puts in an appearance, is simply adapted to the needs and requirements of the "open" God. I say "when it finally puts in an appearance" because Christology has little or no role to play in open theism's programmatic volume, *The Openness of God*.[15] Christology is finally treated only in subsequent volumes. And when it is, the model adopted is a highly popularized (and truncated) version of the kenotic Christologies which originated in mid-nineteenth-century Germany.[16]

In what immediately follows in this section, I want to begin with the subject of Christology (with a sidelong glance at the doctrine of the Trin-

15. Strangely enough, Clark Pinnock, "Systematic Theology," in Pinnock et al., *The Openness of God*, 101, begins with the claim that he will be reflecting on the divine perfections "on the basis of God's self-disclosure in Jesus Christ." But if we expected to find, on the basis of this statement, that Christology would provide the starting point for the reflections which follow, we would be very much mistaken. Pinnock treats the doctrines of the Trinity and creation and the themes of divine power, immutability, impassibility, eternity, and knowledge without any sustained reflection on Christology. The incarnation is mentioned in passing at various points, but no attempt is made to articulate the ontological conditions in the incarnate one which would make sense of the attribution to him of suffering, etc. See ibid., 110, 117–18. This procedure is repeated in *Most Moved Mover*. Here again Pinnock tells us that "for Christians the knowledge of God comes through his self-disclosure in: (1) the history of Israel" and "especially" in (2) "the life, death and resurrection of Jesus Christ" (p. 26). But all the themes proper to the doctrine of God which then pass in review (Trinity, transcendence and immanence, creation, the relation of God to Israel, the nations and individuals, divine knowledge and sovereignty) are all treated without reference to Christology. And when finally Pinnock turns to the subject of the passion of Christ, it is only to provide a final illustration of that "passion" which God necessarily experiences in relation to all human beings as a consequence of his decision to grant them a relative autonomy. See *Most Moved Mover*, 58–59.

16. See Gottfried Thomasius, "Christ's Person and Work, Part II: The Person of the Mediator," in *God and Incarnation in Mid-Nineteenth-Century German Theology*, ed. Claude Welch (New York: Oxford University Press, 1965), 31–101.

ity). I do so because it seems to me that what is said about Christology and the Trinity by the open theists reveals commitments which threaten to unravel the open theistic project, commitments which show that they have not really broken free of classical theism at all but are merely seeking to limit aspects of it.[17] I do not want to ignore the theological elements the open theists think to be of paramount importance, however. So I will return to a discussion of divine providence in a second subsection.

CHRISTOLOGY

Already in his contribution to *The Openness of God*, Clark Pinnock had suggested that "in becoming flesh the logos underwent change."[18] On the face of it, this is a very strong claim indeed. The grammatical subject of the sentence is the Logos (which, classically, was directly equated with the eternal Son, the second Person of the Trinity). It is this subject which "underwent change." But what kind of "change" did he have in view?

The greatest surprise, after following Pinnock through the thickets of his critique of classical theism in that early volume, is that he was still committed to a fairly classical understanding of immutability and even of impassibility. Consider, for example, the following statements. "God is immutable in essence and in his trustworthiness over time, but in other respects God changes."[19] "God is unchanging in nature and essence but not in experience, knowledge and action."[20] "What does it mean to say that God suffers? . . . What we should say is that God sympathizes in his relationship with us."[21] And, finally, "impassibility is a subtle idea with a grain of truth. We have to distinguish ways in which God can suffer from ways in which God cannot suffer. God is beyond certain modes of suffering, just as he is beyond certain modes of change. We could say that God is impassible in nature but passible in his experience of the world."[22] The effect of such statements would appear, on the face of it, to be a restriction of divine "suffering" to an experience without significance for the divine being. *What* God is, it would seem, is something that is complete in itself, above and prior to any *experience* by God of suffering or pain. And certainly, Pinnock believes that to be true of the Father and the Spirit. "Father, Son and Spirit both [?] suffer, though in different ways. The

17. In fairness, it has to be acknowledged that this is precisely what Pinnock, at least, has set out to do: "Let us seek a way to revise classical theism in a dynamic direction without falling into process theology" (Pinnock, "Systematic Theology," 107).

18. Ibid.

19. Ibid., 117.

20. Ibid., 118.

21. Ibid., 119.

22. Ibid.

Father suffers the death of his Son and the Spirit feels both the Father's
pain and the Son's self-surrender."[23] Here the suffering of the Father and
the Spirit are clearly reduced to psychic states without any discernible
ontological significance. The only question is: does the Son experience
"change" on the level of *his* being? What really is the meaning of "the
logos underwent change"? No answer was forthcoming in this essay.

Some light—not much!—is shed on the question by Pinnock's musings
on Christology in his later book, *Flame of Love*. In this book, Pinnock looks
away from questions posed by the hypostatic union in order to focus his
attention on the work of the Holy Spirit in the life, death, and resurrection
of the human Jesus. So what we have before us is, at best, an incomplete
Christology. Still, what Pinnock does say is sufficient to indicate that he
is committed to a version of kenotic Christology. "The Son," he writes,
"decided not to make use of divine attributes independently but experience what it would mean to be truly human. Therefore he depended on
the Spirit for power to live his life and pursue his mission."[24] What is in
view here would seem to be a *kenōsis* (or "self-emptying") by means of
a freely willed non-use of certain divine attributes. But willed non-use
is not the same thing as the surrender or divestment of anything proper
to deity. And because it is not, it would not justify the earlier claim that
"the logos underwent change."

It is precisely at this point that Pinnock finds himself in a dilemma.
On the one hand, the logic of his case against classical theism seems to
press toward affirming divine mutability in the strong sense of a change-
ability in God on the level of his being. On the other hand, his concern
to uphold the full divinity of Jesus Christ leads him to regard a voluntary
non-use of certain divine attributes as an act without ontological significance. Gregory Boyd and Paul Eddy, who treat kenotic Christology
more fully than does Pinnock, put the matter this way: "The most frequent objection raised against kenotic Christology is that it undermines
Jesus' divine nature. While this objection applies to the views of certain
liberal kenotic theologians who argue that Jesus actually *extinguished*
his divine attributes, it does not apply to the evangelical kenotic theory,
which simply asserts that Jesus willingly gave up the *use* of those attributes that would have conflicted with his human nature."[25] Understood
in this way, the Logos might conceivably be in a position to have human

23. Pinnock, *Most Moved Mover*, 58.
24. Pinnock, *Flame of Love*, 88.
25. Gregory A. Boyd and Paul R. Eddy, *Across the Spectrum: Understanding Issues in
Evangelical Theology* (Grand Rapids: Baker Academic, 2002), 109–10. It should be noted
that the work in which this consideration of kenotic Christology appears is a textbook in
which the editors have chosen not to reveal their own position(s). It may well be the case
that neither would finally affirm kenotic Christology. But the passage remains relevant for

experiences (though much more attention would need to be given to the classical problem of the "communication of attributes" to explain it adequately); but such experiences would not have any impact on that which the Logos is *essentially*.

The truth is that kenotic Christology in the form in which it is advocated by Pinnock and discussed by Boyd and Eddy leaves completely untouched the *essentialism* that made classical theism possible in the first place. "Essentialistic" are all ways of thinking which would treat the ontological "otherness" of God as something that can be defined and established by human beings without respect for the incarnate life of God and, therefore, as something complete in itself apart from and prior to all acts of God. What is God for Pinnock? God is triune: a "community of persons," an "open and dynamic structure"[26] of eternal relatedness— "open" because God can freely choose to include humans in those relations but is not compelled to do so. That is what God is *essentially*. "The Trinity is unchangeably what it is from everlasting to everlasting—*and nothing can change that.*"[27] Pinnock takes obvious satisfaction in the fact that he has substituted a doctrine of relationality for the doctrine of substance which governed much early church thought about the Trinity.[28] But to substitute a doctrine of relationality for a doctrine of substance in this way is simply to replace one form of metaphysical essentialism with another. And at the end of the day, the choice between them will be an arbitrary one where it is made without respect for the concrete reality of the incarnate life of God. It will most certainly give expression to the tastes and preferences of the age in which it is made but no more than that. *I regard the lack of an adequate Christology—i.e., one which gives comprehensive attention to the problem of the ontological constitution of the Mediator—to be the single biggest defect in open theism; one which threatens to undermine the entire scheme and render its justified protest against classical theism ineffectual.*

DIVINE PROVIDENCE (OR, THE ACTS OF GOD IN HISTORY)

The theological root of the open theistic doctrine of providence is to be found in the understanding of conversion shared by all members of the movement. The open theists are self-styled "Arminians"—even "consistent Arminians."[29] But their radicality finally emerges only in

an estimation of what kenotic Christology might look like, when done by an open theist. Certainly, it seems to describe Pinnock's leanings quite well.

26. Pinnock, "Systematic Theology," 108.

27. Ibid., 117 (emphasis mine).

28. Ibid., 108.

29. Pinnock, *Most Moved Mover*, 12: "We have made Arminian thinking sharper and clearer. . . . Our Calvinist critics call it 'consistent' Arminianism, a judgment I am not

relation to the question of divine foreknowledge, a question on which their opinions diverge rather dramatically even from those held by James Arminius himself. In relation to the process of conversion, though, their views are consistent with traditional Arminianism. For this reason, open theists also refer to their perspective as "free will theism."[30]

How does God convert the sinner? Through an offer of the gospel of saving grace which the individual must freely accept. "Love woos—it does not compel. Conversion is not coerced. We are saved by grace through faith; a response is involved. . . . God convicts and moves us toward intimacy. His Word is powerful, but there must be a response to it. God does not overpower but saves those who yield to his persuasion. God lays hold, but sinners must also consent to be laid hold of. They must let God renew them."[31] And again: "God can have our love only if we decide to give it. God made us to love him, and the key issue is what we decide to do with that freedom. God empowers but does not overpower. Grace works mightily but does not override. God is a loving parent, not a tyrant."[32] And: "Even Jesus' miracles could not compel faith in people with no openness."[33]

That such a conception of the workings of grace entails a conception of human sinfulness is clear. For his part, Pinnock says that being "dead in our sins and trespasses" (Eph. 2:1) does not mean that we have no capacity to respond to the overtures of grace. Our "deadness" is not an "inability to believe" but an "inability to merit God's favor."[34] And in any case, Pinnock affirms the Tridentine concept of a "prevenient grace, which assists sinners to conversion if they assent and cooperate with it."[35]

---

inclined to reject." Cf. p. 106: "The open view of God grows out of the ideological, if not the ecclesiastical, soil of Wesleyan-Arminianism." See also Pinnock's autobiographical account of his journey from Calvinism to Arminianism in Clark Pinnock, "From Augustine to Arminius: A Pilgrimage in Theology," in *The Grace of God and the Will of Man*, ed. Clark Pinnock (Minneapolis: Bethany House, 1989), 15–30.

30. William Hasker, "A Philosophical Perspective," in Pinnock et al., *The Openness of God*, 150.

31. Pinnock, *Flame of Love*, 157.

32. Ibid.

33. Ibid., 158.

34. Ibid., 160.

35. Ibid., 161. On a personal note, when I was a student at Covenant Theological Seminary in the late 1970s, Pinnock's newly edited volume on the universality of grace and the conditionality of election provided me with arguments which helped me to withstand the Calvinist perspective which was dominant there. It was not until I had transferred to my denominational seminary, Nazarene Theological Seminary, that I experienced a "second conversion"—one which moved me from a Wesleyan-Arminian perspective to a Reformed outlook. The occasion was a paper I wrote on John Wesley's doctrine of prevenient grace. The disappointment I experienced as a consequence of close study of

This account of free will is the motor which drives the open theistic account of divine providence. Open theists do not deny that God works, on many occasions, *monergistically* (i.e., without cooperation). The raising of Jesus from the dead is a good example. But their claim is that the way God works in converting sinners to himself is typical of the way God works with human beings generally. "Though no power can stand against him, God wills the existence of creatures with the power of self-determination. . . . By willing the existence of significant beings with independent status alongside of himself, God accepts limitations not imposed from without."[36] That is to say, the limits imposed on God's use of power are self-imposed. God did not have to create at all, and having decided to create, God did not have to create free rational creatures. But the decision to do the latter is itself an act of self-limitation. Omnipotence therefore "does not mean that nothing can go contrary to God's will . . . but that God is able to deal with any circumstance that may arise."[37] "God has to be resourceful, because the world is an open project."[38] Quite clearly, God's will is a work-in-progress—and on this point, open theism is in agreement with process theology. "God has the power and ability to be (in Harry Boer's words) an 'ad hoc' God, one who responds and adapts to surprises and to the unexpected. God sets goals for creation and redemption and realizes them ad hoc in history. If Plan A fails, God is ready with Plan B."[39]

Consistent with this view of the evolution of the will of God in history, open theism denies that the eternity of God is rightly thought of

---

this doctrine was tremendous. I regarded it then (and continue to do so to this day) as a sophistical attempt to overcome the doctrine of "total depravity"—a doctrine to which Wesley was theoretically committed—by means of a "grace" which is alleged to restore in all just enough freedom so as to put every human being in the position of being able to accept or reject "saving grace" when it is "offered." The problem for me did not lie simply in the fact that such a view only pushes the logic of irresistible grace back one step (since the liberty which is restored in all must be the work of God alone if the affirmation of total depravity is seriously meant). It did not even lie in the fact that the net effect of Wesley's teaching was to make his affirmation of total depravity meaningless, since the totally depraved turn out to be an empty-set. The real problem for me lay in the fact that there is not a hint, so far as I can see, of such a concept of grace to be found in Holy Scripture. Having said that, I should add that I do understand the allure of Arminianism, for I too was once an Arminian.

36. Pinnock, "Systematic Theology," 113.

37. Ibid., 114.

38. Pinnock, *Most Moved Mover*, 102.

39. Pinnock, "Systematic Theology," 113. Pinnock's more outrageous formulations arise out of this conception of the divine will and activity. Cf. ibid., 114: "God does not go in for power tactics." And p. 116: "God . . . is flexible and does not insist on doing things his way." In relation to such statements, it can only be said that it would be rather awkward if they were true, for it would make it very hard indeed to explain, for example, the plagues of Egypt or the deaths of 50,070 Bethshemites in 1 Sam. 6:19.

as timelessness. Since God experiences "temporal passage,"[40] eternity must be redefined. Pinnock's definition is this:

> When I say that God is eternal, I mean that God transcends our experience of time, is immune from the ravages of time, is free from our inability to remember, and so forth. I affirm that God is with us in time, experiencing the succession of events with us. . . . God's eternity embraces time and takes temporal events into the divine life. . . . God is not temporal as creatures are, however, but can enter into time and relate to sequence and history.[41]

Notwithstanding the elements which open theism shares in common with process theology, however, the differences are significant. Pinnock and his colleagues affirm the doctrine of a *creatio ex nihilo* and, on this basis, reject the idea that God and the world are ontologically continuous and that God is therefore "ontologically dependent upon the world."[42] As already noted, open theism stands closer to the classical pole of the spectrum than it does to the process pole. What open theists share with process theologians is simply this notion that God's preferred mode of interaction with human beings is that of persuasion. But the ontological presuppositions of this claim differ in each case.

When we turn to the problem of God's knowledge, however, we enter onto terrain on which the open theists find it much harder to defend their claim to orthodoxy. And it has to be said that the key argument advanced in support of their rejection of an exhaustive divine foreknowledge is strictly philosophical in nature. This being the case, it is time that we turn to philosophical considerations.

The Philosophical Case for the Rejection of an Exhaustive Foreknowledge

At the heart of the argument against exhaustive divine foreknowledge is the claim is that such knowledge is logically incompatible with genuine human freedom. The reasons given are as follows:

> If God knows already what will happen in the future, then God's knowing this is a part of the past and is now fixed, impossible to change. And since God is infallible, it is completely impossible that things will turn out differently than God expects them to. But this means that the future event God knows is also fixed and unalterable, and it cannot be true of any human beings that they are both able to perform a certain action and able not to

40. Ibid., 120.
41. Ibid., 120–21.
42. Pinnock, *Most Moved Mover*, 145; cf. idem, "Systematic Theology," 112.

perform that action. If God knows that a person is going to perform it, then it is impossible that the person fail to perform it—so one does not have a free choice whether to perform it or not.[43]

The Achilles heel of this argument lies in the fact that it confuses "certainty" with "necessity." As William Lane Craig has observed, certainty is a predicate of persons, of knowers. Necessity is (or is not) a predicate of the events known. God's foreknowledge, in other words, gives him certainty with regard to what will happen. Whether the events God knows with certainty take place necessarily or contingently is a function of the natural and historical conditions under which they take place.[44] This argument seems to me to be irrefutable. Because this is so, the whole of the open theistic case for a new understanding of God's knowledge seems to be in jeopardy. For in the event that Hasker's philosophical argument fails, all that the open theists are left with are the Old Testament passages touching on divine repentance—passages which, as we have already seen, are read in the light of a metaphysical conception of God grounded in observations made with respect to the requirements of love on the human plane.

But now notice: it is not just the case against an exhaustive divine foreknowledge that is in jeopardy. For virtually the whole of the open theistic case against divine timelessness, too, rests finally upon the claim that God's knowledge is discursive. Because God experiences past, present, and future successively, God finds things out as they happen. God "learns"—and a learning God is clearly a God whose being is structured by time.[45] But if this is not the case, then a successful case has not yet been made against timelessness.[46] Here again the need for an adequate Christology is clear.

43. Hasker, "A Philosophical Perspective," 147.

44. William Lane Craig, "The Middle Knowledge View," in *Divine Foreknowledge: Four Views*, ed. James K. Beilby and Paul R. Eddy (Downers Grove, IL: InterVarsity, 2001), 127–28.

45. Pinnock, *Most Moved Mover*, 97.

46. We saw earlier that, in spite of himself, Pinnock leaves room for an essential impassibility. Here, too, he is anything but sure-footed. He says, for example, "We can only speculate what things would be like apart from the world and before it existed—perhaps then God experienced a kind of timelessness because there was nothing to measure temporally. . . . We cannot know how it is with God to exist in eternity without a creation. Maybe that involves a relative timelessness" (ibid., 98–99). Leaving aside the fact that it is not at all clear what a "relative timelessness" might mean, what Pinnock really seems to want to say is that there is a kind of temporality that is proper to God. And so he can say that "time is not a 'thing' that God may or may not have created. Time is the concomitant of God and personal life. It exists because of God's nature" (ibid., 98). But what kind of temporality this is and how it relates to time as we humans know and experience it is apparently beyond our knowing. Here, too, it seems to me, we catch sight of a residual essentialism in Pinnock's thinking which threatens to undermine his case against a putative divine timelessness.

Final Assessment: Just How Orthodox Is the Open Theistic Proposal?

A large part of the motivation which has led to the elaboration of the "open view" of God is to be found in the desire of its proponents to address the threat posed (as they believe) by "theological determinism" to human freedom and dignity. The polemical horizon against which the work of open theists is directed is everywhere the same: the Augustinian/ Calvinist tradition. Historically, attempts to engage this tradition critically have typically focused on the doctrine of predestination/election. The open theists have tried instead to undermine theological determinism through an attack on traditional conceptions of divine foreknowledge. But the doctrine of predestination/election is always lurking in the background. Thus any final assessment of open theism should take into account all of these elements and not be focused exclusively on the issues posed by divine foreknowledge. And it is fortunate for the open theists that this should be so—fortunate because the orthodoxy of some elements in their program are more easily defended than others. To put a finer point on it: their Arminianism stands more clearly within the bounds of orthodoxy than does their position on divine foreknowledge (which goes well beyond anything that traditional Arminianism would have been willing to grant).[47]

What counts as "orthodox" teaching is disputed, and how one would decide what counts equally so. That it has something to do with the scriptural warrants for any doctrinal proposal is clear. But Scripture must be interpreted, and some interpretations weigh more heavily than do others for the great majority of Christians throughout the world. For most, it is the ancient creeds and conciliar decisions which are the most important. This is true even for Protestant churches, though most would add that the doctrinal basis for ecclesial authority is not to be found in them alone—or in them at all unless and until they are interpreted under the guidance of the Reformation-era confessions, which alone are constitutionally binding in those churches.

Where the doctrine of predestination/election is concerned, the early church was able to arrive at a fairly high degree of agreement as to the

---

47. The open theists are well aware that their proposal radicalizes evangelical Arminianism. Pinnock, for example, readily admits that neither Arminius nor Wesley had any hesitation in accepting "traditional definitions of unchangeability, eternity, and omniscience" (*Most Moved Mover*, 13). It is because of this that he is far more worried when a Wesleyan-Arminian such as Thomas Oden characterizes open theism as heretical than he is when Calvinists such as R. C. Sproul and Roger Nicole do so. And so he says, "I suspect that a wave of Arminian criticism is yet to come. This outcome concerns me because, if the Arminian evangelicals decide to line up with the Calvinistic evangelicals in opposition, there is little future for the open view in evangelicalism" (14).

limits of orthodoxy. After close study of the issues raised by the dispute which had raged in southern Gaul between the strict followers of the later Augustine and the "semi-Augustinian"[48] followers of John Cassian and Vincent of Lérins, the Council of Orange decided not to come down firmly on either side but sought instead to keep them together within the bounds of a single, united church. Thus *both* unconditional election *and* a conditional election based upon God's foreknowledge of who would believe and make proper use of the sacraments were upheld as orthodox. The effect of this decision was to ensure that both views would survive within the Catholic Church of the West throughout the Middle Ages and into the Reformation period. Augustine's doctrine of predestination was ably defended by Thomas Aquinas, Luther, and Calvin; the idea of a conditional election was supported by Alexander of Hales and Bonaventure, among others.

When later the Reformed churches made the Augustinian/Calvinist doctrine alone to be authoritative teaching, they were most certainly narrowing the limits of what might be regarded as orthodox by their own members. But it is important to remember that the other Protestant churches did not follow them in this. To this day, agreement as to what constitutes orthodoxy in this area of doctrine is lacking. This being the case, it seems to be the better part of wisdom to recognize both of the options allowed by Orange as orthodox. Certainly, the evangelical movement in America has never made adherence to a Reformed confession a test of whether one can be truly "evangelical" or not. Thus the open theists are on solid ground, ecumenically speaking, where the evangelical Arminian elements in their program are concerned.

The same cannot be said for their stance on divine foreknowledge. Granted, there is a precedent for bringing the subject of divine foreknowledge to center stage in the debates over predestination. This much had already been accomplished by Luis de Molina in *Liberi arbitrii cum gratiae donis, divina praescientia, providentia, praedestinatione, et reprobatione concordantia* (The Compatibility of Free Will with the Gifts of Grace, Divine Foreknowledge, Providence, Predestination, and Reprobation), published in the year 1588.[49] But Molina did not deny to God

---

48. Since the Reformation, Protestants have typically referred to Cassian's position as "semi-Pelagian." In the twentieth century, however, historical theologians came to the conclusion that "semi-Augustinian" would be a more accurate description. See, e.g., Bernhard Lohse, *A Short History of Christian Doctrine* (Philadelphia: Fortress, 1980), 123.

49. The English translation of part 4 of this work (which touches directly on the subject of divine foreknowledge) is Luis de Molina, *On Divine Foreknowledge*, trans. Alfred J. Freddoso (Ithaca and London: Cornell University Press, 1988). Molina divided God's knowledge into three different classes: "natural knowledge" (by which God knows all metaphysically necessary states of affairs); "free knowledge" (by which God knows all that which he has freely willed to be); and, standing between them, "middle knowledge" (by which God knows

an exhaustive foreknowledge of future contingent events. His goal was simply to show how such knowledge could be compatible with free will and therefore with a conditional election. Given Molina's concern to uphold a conditional election and the fact that he also affirmed a robust doctrine of providence (in accordance with which all that takes place in nature and history has been "specifically decreed" by God),[50] it is not surprising that the teaching office of the Roman Church should have decided that Molinism fell within the bounds of acceptable Catholic teaching and that it should, as a consequence, have called upon both sides in the dispute created by his work to cease and desist from labeling their opponents heretics. Thus, to the extent that evangelical Protestants are willing to recognize the Council of Orange as bearing at least some degree of ecclesial authority, Molinism must count as orthodox (even if, in the final analysis, better options are available). The great difficulty, where open theism is concerned, is that its proponents are not Molinists. Open theism does what Molinism refused to do: it denies to God an exhaustive foreknowledge of future contingents.

Pinnock in particular tries to defend the orthodoxy of this move by arguing that divine foreknowledge has never been made the subject of a church council. "In raising the issue of divine foreknowledge, we have not transgressed some rule of theological discourse and placed ourselves outside the pale of orthodoxy. Why can an evangelical not propose a different view of this matter? What church council has declared it to be impossible?"[51] I suspect that Pinnock's appeal here is to the ancient councils, perhaps on the grounds that only those councils could be said to have expressed the mind of an undivided church. In a situation in which the

---

eternally how things would have turned out had spatiotemporal relations been arranged differently than God willed them to be). In accordance with the latter, God knows "from eternity" whether the incarnation would have taken place even if Adam had not sinned. God knows "from eternity" what would have happened had President Kennedy not been assassinated—whether, for example, the United States would have committed itself to a full-scale war in Vietnam (as it did, in fact, do under President Johnson). It should be noted that the subject at issue in the debates between the Thomists and the Molinists was not whether God has foreknowledge of future contingent events; this much was granted by both sides. The question was whether such knowledge was prevolitional or volitional. If the latter, then God's foreknowledge of future contingent events is a function of God's will (or "decree"), and there really are only two classes of knowledge in God—"natural knowledge" and "free knowledge." This was the position of the Thomists (and of the Reformed, who followed them). If, however, such knowledge is prevolitional, then it cannot be brought under the heading of "free knowledge." And it cannot be brought under the heading of "natural knowledge" either, since the objects of this knowledge are not metaphysically necessary. Thus there must be three classes of knowledge in God. This is the position of Molina (and of the Lutherans and the Remonstrants, who followed him).

50. Alfred J. Freddoso, introduction to *On Divine Foreknowledge*, 3.
51. Pinnock, *Most Moved Mover*, 110.

Christian churches are deeply divided, no council convened by one church alone or confession adopted by one church alone can be authoritative for all. But the logic of such a view would make it impossible to test the orthodoxy of any proposal made since the Reformation. The truth is that the doctrine of an exhaustive divine foreknowledge enjoys fairly widespread ecumenical support, having been affirmed by both the Reformed and the Roman Catholics. The Westminster Confession says, "In his sight all things are open and manifest; his knowledge is infinite, infallible, and independent upon the creature; so as nothing to him is contingent or uncertain."[52] And in its Dogmatic Constitution on the Catholic Faith, the First Vatican Council declared, "By his providence, God watches over and governs all the things He has created, reaching from end to end with might and disposing all things with gentleness (see Wisd. 8:1). 'All things are exposed and open to His eyes' (Heb. 4:13), *even those things that are going to occur by the free action of creatures.*"[53] Pinnock would, no doubt, dismiss the Westminster Confession as a Presbyterian confession without significance for his church and the churches of his allies. But given the radically divided nature of Protestantism in the West today, it seems to me—once again—the better part of wisdom to grant to the teaching office in Rome relatively binding authority on questions in relation to which no existing Protestant confession has taken a different position. I am well aware that such an argument will have little meaning for strict Presbyterian (or Lutheran) confessionalists, but I think it should carry at least some weight with Pinnock. His position enjoys no ecclesial support, and there is a fair bit of ecumenical support for the position he rejects.

Provisional Conclusions

What is valuable in the open theistic proposal is its critique of a putative divine impassibility and timelessness—though the attempt made to ground that critique in a metaphysic that is every bit as essentialistic as that which funded classical theism has caused the critique to misfire at the decisive point. As we have seen, Pinnock winds up affirming a "kind of impassibility" and a "relative timelessness" in God, which means that his proposal is anything but stable and consistent. If impassibility and timelessness are indeed problematic concepts, they will be shown to be so on the basis of a well-ordered Christology and that basis alone.

52. See "The Westminster Confession of Faith," in *The Creeds of Christendom*, ed. Philip Schaff (Grand Rapids: Baker Academic, 1990), 3:607.
53. H. Denzinger and A. Schönmetzer, eds., *Enchiridion symbolorum*, 32nd ed. (Freiburg: Herder, 1963), no. 3003 (new numbering), 587; cited by Freddoso, introduction to *On Divine Foreknowledge*, 30.

On the other hand, the thought of an exhaustive divine foreknowledge enjoys fairly widespread ecclesial support. And, as we shall see, it is not at all inconsistent with a christologically grounded doctrine of God. This is one theological value in classical theism, certainly, which must be upheld.

Karl Barth's Doctrine of God

Preliminary Observations

It has been a long-standing contention of mine that Karl Barth's theology experienced a final clarification and critical correction as a consequence of his revision of the doctrine of election in 1936 and following.[54] At the root of this revision lay the idea that the primary object of election is God himself. The content of God's "primal decision" was his determination to be God in the covenant of grace and to be God in no other way. What makes this decision truly "primal" is that there is no other being of God standing in back of it, hidden in the shadows, so to speak. "There is no height or depth in which God can be God in any other way."[55] The eternal event in which God chose to be "God for us" is, at the same time, the eternal event in which God gave (and continues to give) to himself his own being—and vice versa. So there are not two eternal events, one in which God gives being to himself and a second (following "after" the first) in which he enters into a relationship with the human race; these are, in fact, one and the same event. Thus divine election stands at the root of God's being or "essence."[56] That is the revolutionary insight set forth in Barth's doctrine of election.

The impact which this final adjustment had on Barth's thinking as a whole was both subtle and profound. Its subtlety had to do with the fact that virtually all of the building blocks needed for the new doctrine of election were already in place as early as 1924/1925, in Barth's first

54. Bruce L. McCormack, *Karl Barth's Critically Realistic Dialectical Theology: Its Genesis and Development, 1909–1936* (Oxford: Clarendon, 1995), 453–63.

55. Barth, *Church Dogmatics*, II/2:77.

56. Among the many passages which substantiate the point of view set forth in this claim, the following may be considered: "If we are to lay hold of the concept of the true God, we shall do so only as we conceive of Him in His *Dominium*, in His actuality as Lord and Ruler. We shall do so only as we conceive of Him in the determination and limitation which are peculiar to Him, which He has *not* taken upon Himself *as something additional*, in His relationship with the world or as an accommodation to it, but which are characteristic of His presence and activity in the world because they are the determination and limitation proper to His own eternal being [*seinem eigenen ewigen Wesen*], so assuredly has He decided for them by the decree of His eternal will" (ibid., II/2:50; lightly revised, emphases mine); cf. Barth, *Kirchliche Dogmatik*, II/2:53.

cycle of lectures on dogmatic theology in Göttingen—so that the final step was a wholly natural one to take. The profundity of this final adjustment will be seen where it is recognized that prior to it Barth's thinking about the being of God still gave expression to a residual commitment to aspects of classical metaphysics; after the adjustment, his thinking about the being of God became more consistently "postmetaphysical."[57] Put another way, the fundamental problem addressed by Barth's doctrine of God—before and after this shift—was the same problem faced by classical metaphysics: how do you talk about God without talking about something else instead? But the answer Barth gave to this question was quite different from the classical one, and it was an answer which became more radicalized as a consequence of the development I have described.

Traditional metaphysics held that it is not possible to speak of God without first speaking of something else. All talk of God begins as talk about something else—as talk about the cosmos, perhaps, or as talk about what it means to be a "person" on the human plane. And the hope was that through a series of negations (removing from divine being the imperfections proper to creaturely being) and a series of analogies (making God to be *like* us in that he "has" certain qualities or attributes that we also have but has them perfectly), one would eventually arrive at talk about God that was really talk about *God* and not just an endless chain of self-referential statements. Barth held that on the basis of metaphysical reasoning, such a hope was bound to end in disappointment; one can never truly talk about *God* by speaking first of himself or herself, or his or her experiences. Talk that begins with the creaturely must also end with it. If talk of God is really to be possible, then it must begin and end with the event in which God gives himself his own being—as Jesus Christ, in the power of the Holy Spirit. In putting it this way, what I am suggesting is that human language and divine being must inevitably fall apart where the event in which God gives himself being and the event in which our language finds its ground are conceived of as two distinct events. Where, on the other hand, the event in which God gives himself being *is* the event which founds our knowledge of him, there divine reality and human language do not fall apart. And so Barth holds that God is the self-constituting, self-speaking, self-*interpreting* God whose "talk" of himself *is* the event in which responsible human speech about him

57. The language employed here has been chosen carefully: "*more consistently* 'postmetaphysical.'" I am not suggesting that Barth was ever absolutely consistent with the line I am taking, only that he was more consistent with it after having written *Church Dogmatics*, II/2. What I offer in the pages that follow is a reconstruction—what Barth ought to have said, had he followed through, of the ontological implications of his revised doctrine of election with complete consistency.

is made possible. How does one talk about God without talking about something else? By resolving never to speak about God on any other basis than that of the incarnation. To speak of Barth's doctrine of God as "postmetaphysical" and to speak of it as christologically based are to say one and the same thing.

Now, admittedly, the foregoing description of Barth's doctrine of election in *Church Dogmatics*, II/2, has required some smoothing out of Barth's own reflections in the direction of what I believe to be his best and most important insights. The truth is that Barth was not always consistent with the vision I have just set forth—even as the shift I have described was taking place and afterward.[58] But part of the argument for this reading of Barth is that it helps to make sense of moves he makes subsequently that would have been unthinkable on the basis of any residual elements of classical metaphysics still remaining.

In any event, I will begin, in the section that immediately follows, with material that has provided the customary jumping-off point for all previous treatments of Barth's doctrine of God in *Church Dogmatics*, II/1, namely, section 28, "The Being of God as the One Who Loves in Freedom." Most of what is said here is easily adjusted to the requirements of Barth's later doctrine of election—though some statements would have to be challenged. This material is also compatible with Barth's mature Christology, which has a large significance where a challenge to the classical concepts of divine timelessness and impassibility are concerned. So in the second half of this section, I am going to jump ahead to Barth's mature Christology as found in *Church Dogmatics*, IV/1, in order to show why Barth's challenge to classical theism in relation to impassibility and timelessness succeeds where the challenge of open theism failed. I am then going to turn, in a third section, to a brief consideration of Barth's treatment of the divine *concursus* in *Church Dogmatics*, III/3. Written after the final clarifications achieved in Barth's doctrine of election, the material found here belongs to what I think of as Barth's most mature theology. My goal here will be to think through Barth's understanding of *how* God's will is made effective in relation to rational creatures possessed of a relative autonomy. That the answer to this question depends on the content assigned to God's "will" ought to be obvious. The result is a distinctively postmetaphysical account of providence. I will then return in a fourth section to speak briefly of Barth's treatment of divine immutability, power, knowledge, and will in *Church Dogmatics*, II/1, in order to show why some of the things

58. I have treated the problems which arise in relation to Barth's inconsistencies elsewhere. See Bruce L. McCormack, "Grace and Being: The Role of God's Gracious Election in Karl Barth's Theological Ontology," in *The Cambridge Companion to Karl Barth*, ed. John Webster (Cambridge: Cambridge University Press, 2000), 92–110.

Barth says here would need to be revised in order to be brought into line with his later doctrine.[59]

The Eternal Being of God

GOD'S BEING AS *ACTUS PURUS ET SINGULARIS*

There is a tension that cuts through the heart of Barth's treatment of the being or "essence" of God in *Church Dogmatics*, II/1, which makes itself felt right away. Barth writes, "When we ask questions about God's being, we cannot in fact leave the sphere of his action and working as it is revealed to us in His works." But in the very next sentence, Barth does precisely what he says we must not do—he leaves the sphere of God's action: "He is the same even in Himself, even before and after and over His works, *and without them*."[60] How Barth could in any way know that God would be "the same" in himself "without His works" without resorting to a form of metaphysical essentialism is anything but clear. Still, in the first statement, we do indeed catch sight of a possible line of thought which will achieve all that the open theists hoped to achieve—without the problems that attended their efforts. It is a line of thought which would be taken up with renewed energy and increasing consistency in *Church Dogmatics*, II/2, and subsequent volumes. But for now we will stay with *Church Dogmatics*, II/1.

It is of the greatest significance that Barth believes that *what* God is can be known, for the following reason: For classical theology, the "essence" of God had been universally regarded as unknowable. But this commitment was not without its problems. On the one hand, classical theologians wanted to say that God would have been the same in himself without his works—a claim that would make sense only if it could be known what God is in himself. On the other hand, they wanted to

59. It was not until Barth began to lecture on the material contained in *Church Dogmatics*, II/2, in the winter semester of 1939–1940 that his mature doctrine of election finally emerged. Even his 1936 Debrecen lecture on *Gottes Gnadenwahl* constitutes but an intermediate step on the way which led from his older conception to his mature view— which helps to explain why some of the material found in the doctrine of God on which he lectured from the summer semester of 1937 through the summer semester of 1939 had yet to benefit from the clarity he would later attain in working through election. To say this much is to admit that the picture I drew in my book, of a sudden shift in Barth's doctrine of election which was alleged to have taken place immediately after hearing Pierre Maury's lecture on Calvin's doctrine of predestination at the International Calvin Congress of 1936, needs to be revised a bit. The change was not immediate but gradual. The steps involved in this process have been more accurately set forth in Matthias Gockel, "One Word and All Is Saved: Barth and Schleiermacher on Election" (PhD diss., Princeton Theological Seminary, 2002), 199–204. Gockel's dissertation is now published as *Barth and Schleiermacher on the Doctrine of Election* (Oxford and New York: Oxford University Press, 2006).

60. Barth, *Church Dogmatics*, II/1:260 (emphasis mine).

say that what God is "essentially" is unknowable. The same is true of all those who subsequently have thought about the being of God on the basis of alternative forms of metaphysical essentialism. Barth clearly would like to overcome this ambivalence, and it is the way in which he tries to overcome it that is of interest here. "What God is as God, the divine individuality and characteristics, the *essentia* or 'essence' of God, is something which we shall encounter either at the place where God deals with us as Lord and Savior, or not at all."[61] That we encounter God in his "essence" is guaranteed by the fact that "God is who he is in the act of His revelation."[62] When Barth speaks of God's being as a being-in-act, he is not speaking of a being in the act of a dynamic relationality that is the immanent Trinity in and for itself without regard for God's works. God's being-in-act is, rather, his being in a most concrete and definite act *in history*. It is his being, as Barth puts it, *in the act of his revelation*. God's being-in-act is a being in *this* act and not some other. If we thought that God's being-in-act were a being in any act other than this one, it would not (and could not!) be the "essence" of God which we encounter in his act of self-revelation. "We are dealing with the being of God: but with regard to the being of God, the word 'event' or 'act' is *final*, and cannot be surpassed or compromised. To its very deepest depths, God's Godhead consists in the fact that it is an event—not any event, not events in general, but the event of His action, in which we have a share in God's revelation."[63] And "God's being is *absolutely* His act."[64]

Barth further explains the significance of this claim by means of a concept found in Augustine, Thomas Aquinas, and Amandus Polanus, namely, the concept of God's being as *actus purus*. "It was quite right when the older theology described the essence of God as *vita*, and again as *actuositas*, or more simply as *actus*. What was meant was: as *actus purus*, indeed, *purissimus*."[65]

God is indeed "pure act." But we must be very careful, when we say this, not to assume that we can know what is meant on the basis of what actuality means elsewhere. "In speaking of the essence of God we are concerned with an act which utterly surpasses the whole of the actuality that we have come to know as act, and compared with which all that we have come to know as act is no act at all, because as act it can be transcended. This is not the case with the act of God that happens in revelation."[66] And so "*actus purus* is not sufficient as a description of God.

---

61. Ibid., 261.
62. Ibid., 262.
63. Ibid., 263.
64. Ibid., 272 (emphasis mine).
65. Ibid., 263.
66. Ibid.

To it there must be added at least '*et singularis.*'"[67] God's being-in-act is a being in a "particular event"[68]—an event whose singularity consists in the fact that its basis is different from all other events in history. "It is a definite happening within general happening: so definite that, while it takes part in this [general] happening, it also contradicts it, and can only be seen and comprehended together with it in its contradiction."[69] What Barth is saying here is not simply that the self-revelation of God takes place *in* history as we know it while not being *of* that history; he is not simply saying that history does not produce an event of this nature. That, too, is true, of course. But with the *et singularis* he is saying something rather more than this. "No other being exists *absolutely* in its act. No other being is *absolutely* its own conscious, willed and executed decision."[70] *This* is why God is *actus purus et singularis*. The eternal act in which God determines to be God-for-us in Jesus Christ and the act in time in which this eternal act reaches its (provisional) goal are a "singular" act, an act utterly unique in kind. God is what he is in this act—which is not true of anyone or anything besides God.

Barth does seem at times to contradict this, his best and most important insight, in those places where he speaks as if God's triunity were something complete in itself, apart from and prior to the eternal act of self-determination to be God-for-us in Jesus Christ.[71] But this is not a path he should have entered. Granted, to say that God would still be God without us is something that needs to be said by anyone desirous of honoring the divine freedom in God's act of eternal self-determination. But if we wish to pass beyond such limit-language, if we think ourselves to know precisely *what* God would be had he not determined himself to be God-for-us in Jesus Christ, if we think ourselves to know *how* his being would have been constituted in the absence of his relation to us, then we have looked away from God's being in the act of his self-revelation

67. Ibid., 264.
68. Ibid.
69. Ibid.
70. Ibid., 271 (emphasis mine).
71. We have already considered one such example: "God is who He is in His works. He is the same even in Himself, even before and after and over His work, and without them. They are bound to Him, but He is not bound to them. They are nothing without Him. But He is who He is without them." See n. 57 above. To this example might be added the following: "As and before God seeks and creates fellowship with us, He wills and completes this fellowship in Himself. In Himself He does not will to exist for Himself, to exist alone. On the contrary, He is Father, Son and Holy Spirit and therefore alive in His unique being with and for and in another. The unbroken unity of His being, knowledge and will is at the same time an act of deliberation, decision and intercourse. He does not exist in solitude but in fellowship. . . . That He is God—the Godhead of God—consists in the fact that He loves, and it is the expression of His loving that He seeks and creates fellowship with us" (ibid., 275).

and have made ourselves guilty of thinking on the basis of some form
of metaphysical essentialism. God might still have been triune—though
what precise form that might have taken is impossible to say. When
we look away from the eternal act of self-determination in which God
determined to be God-for-us, we are directing our attention to possibilities which were not realized and, for that very reason, are *unreal*. Any
attempt to think about that which has no reality must inevitably land
us in the realm of speculation.

One of the consequences of the line of thought I am pursuing here
is that what it means to be a divine "person" is something that can be
known, if at all, only on the basis of God's being in the act of his self-
revelation. If we think that we can arrive at a satisfactory conception of
divine "personhood" on the basis of a phenomenological consideration
of personhood on the human plane, we are deluding ourselves. "No
other being exists absolutely in its act. No other being is absolutely its
own conscious, willed and executed decision. Only in the illusion of sin
can man ascribe this being to himself or to the content of the world as a
projection of himself. . . . Now, if the being of a person is a being in act,
and if, in the strict and proper sense, being in act can be ascribed only
to God, then it follows that by the concept of the being of a person, in
the strict and proper sense, we can understand only the being of God."[72]
And so "the real person is not man but God. It is not God who is a person
by extension but we."[73]

It follows, second, that we can know what is meant by the statement
"God is love" only when we have before us the divine "person" and not
human persons. "God is love" does not mean simply that God is well
disposed toward us, that God has strong feelings of affection for us, and
so forth. It is not merely a question of dispositional states, though this
is certainly included. Rather, fundamentally, "God is love" is a statement
which describes the nature and meaning of the act in which God gives
himself his own being. The act in which God gives to himself his own
being is an act of love. God "does not will to be God for Himself nor as
God to be alone with Himself. He wills as God to be for us and with us
who are not God. . . . He does not will to be Himself in any other way
than He is in this relationship. His life, that is, His life in Himself, which
is originally and properly the one and only life, leans toward this unity
with our life."[74] The life which is God's "originally and properly" leans
toward unity with our life! So when Barth speaks of an "overflow" of
God's love in his turning toward us, he is not speaking of a secondary act,

---

72. Ibid., 271.
73. Ibid., 272.
74. Ibid., 274.

an act which merely *expresses* God's true being. He is speaking of what God is essentially. "It implies so to speak an overflow of His essence that He turns to us. We must certainly regard this overflow as itself matching His essence, *belonging to His essence.*"[75] To say that "God is love" means all of this, and it is something that could not be learned on the basis of what "love" means on the human plane.

> The tempting definition that "God is love" seems to have some possible support in 1 John 4:8, 16. . . . But it is a forced exegesis to cite this sentence apart from its context . . . and to use it as the basis of a definition. We read in v. 9: "In this was manifested the love of God towards us, because that God sent His only-begotten Son into the world, that we might live through him." . . . The love of God, or God as love, is therefore interpreted in 1 John 4 as the completed act of divine love in sending Jesus Christ. If we want to follow Martin Dibelius in describing v. 8 and v. 16 as an "equation of God," we must at least go on to say that as such (as the equating of God with an abstract content of God's act as such) it is at once resolved again, being replaced by a declaration of God's act as such.[76]

"God is love" is not an axiom whose meaning is self-evident. It is "a declaration of God's act as such." To try to understand this passage without reference to Christology is to miss its meaning altogether. The correction offered here to open theistic exegesis is obvious. Ironically, the open theists would really like to be in a position to say what Barth says. They would like to say that love is the "essence" of God. On the basis of their metaphysical essentialism, however, they are only finally able to speak of dispositional states. Clearly, Barth's christologically based divine ontology allows him to say much more.

In sum, God's being-in-act is his being in the eternal act of turning toward the human race in the covenant of grace, and as a direct consequence, it is his being in history as incarnate Lord and outpoured Spirit as the completion of this eternal act. *The root of Barth's actualism is to be found in this eternal act of self-determination and in it alone.* His actualistic ontology is not philosophical in nature; it is strictly theological. If we thought that Barth's actualism could be grounded in any other way—in a metaphysical essentialism characterized by dynamic relationality, for example—we would be giving an altogether different account of actualism than Barth gives.

It remains only to say a brief word with regard to what Barth adds to this line of reflection in *Church Dogmatics*, II/2. What happens in *Church Dogmatics*, II/2, is that Barth introduces a critical correction into

75. Ibid., 273 (emphasis mine).
76. Ibid., 275.

his earlier doctrine of the Trinity on the basis of the line of reflection
we have been following. He does so by means of an astonishing claim:
"Jesus Christ is the electing God. We must not ask concerning any other
but Him. *In no depth of the Godhead shall we encounter any but Him.*"[77]
In *no* depth of the Godhead! We saw earlier that the first and primary
object of election is God himself. God chose eternally to be God-for-us
in Jesus Christ. This much is sufficient to explain how it could be that
Jesus Christ is the object of election. But Barth also wanted now to say
that Jesus Christ is the Subject of election.[78] But what sense does that
make? How can being Jesus Christ be the *consequence* of an eternal act
if the One performing this action already is Jesus Christ? Logically, the
"transformation" of a Subject into another mode of being cannot be carried out by a Subject who already is that mode of being; otherwise no
"transformation" has taken place at all. In truth, however, Barth's claim
will never be understood where we rest content with playing with the
logic of Subject-object relations. What is happening here is quite simply
a refinement of Barth's earlier doctrine of the Trinity.

Barth's basic model of the Trinity was (and would remain) that of a
Single Subject in three "modes of being." One Subject three times, "an
eternal repetition in eternity"[79]—this is the basic structure of the triunity
of God as Barth understands it. God is the same Subject as Father and as
eternal Son.[80] And because God is the same Subject in both modalities,
it is the same Subject who makes the eternal decision to be God-for-us
in Jesus Christ and who as a consequence is Jesus Christ. So whether
we say that the Father is the electing God or the eternal Son is the electing God, we are really speaking of one and the same Subject. The only
real question is, Why say "Jesus Christ" instead of "the eternal Son"?
And the answer is that this eternal act of choosing to be God-for-us in
Jesus Christ is the very act in which God constitutes himself as triune.
Again, there is only one eternal act, not two. To speak of Jesus Christ
as the electing God, then, serves the purpose of reminding readers that
the Second Person of the Trinity is not the "eternal Son" in abstraction
from the humanity he would assume. The eternal Son has a name and
his name is Jesus.[81] Any talk of the eternal Son in abstraction from the

77. Ibid., II/2:115 (emphasis mine).
78. Ibid., 106.
79. Ibid., I/1:350.
80. Ibid., 439.
81. Ibid., II/2:4: "Theology must begin with Jesus Christ, and not with general prin-
ciples; however better, or, at any rate, more relevant and illuminating, they may appear
to be: *as though He were a continuation of the knowledge and Word of God, and not its root
and origin, not indeed the very Word of God itself.* Theology must also end with Him, and
not with supposedly self-evident general conclusions from what is particularly enclosed
and disclosed in Him: as though the fruits could be shaken from this tree; *as though in*

humanity to be assumed is an exercise in mythologizing; there is no such eternal Son—and there never was.[82]

We are now ready to consider the implications of Barth's mature Christology for his treatment of a putative divine timelessness and impassibility.

THE ETERNAL BEING OF GOD IN THE LIGHT OF BARTH'S MATURE CHRISTOLOGY (*CHURCH DOGMATICS*, IV/1–3)

Barth's mature Christology consists in an "actualizing" of the two-natures Christology of the Chalcedonian Formula. The justification for this actualizing is to be found, above all, in a faithful following through of the ontological implications of his doctrine of election. But such internal requirements should not prevent us from seeing that *some* adjustment of the formula would have been needed regardless, due to problems resident within the formula itself.

The Chalcedonian Formula was written under a twofold pressure. On the one hand, the bishops were as committed as ever Arius had been in the previous century to the notion of divine impassibility. Even Cyril of Alexandria's paradoxical claim that the Logos "suffered impassibly"[83] testifies to the tremendous influence which the idea of impassibility had at that time. On the other hand, the majority of the bishops were just as committed to the soteriological concept of *theōsis*, "divinization."

The effect of the first commitment was to keep the divine and human natures as far apart as possible. God, it was believed, cannot suffer. Therefore the sufferings of Jesus had to be restricted to the human nature only—which meant that the divine nature could not come into direct contact with the human nature. Later orthodox thinkers such as John of Damascus explained this "separation" by treating the person in whom both natures subsist (the Logos) as a kind of mediating principle, something that stands "between" the natures, effectively holding them apart.[84] But if the Logos could perform this role, if the Logos could be so

---

the things of God there were anything general which we could not know and designate in addition to and even independently of this particular" (emphases mine).

82. I have treated the implications of the significance of Barth's claim that Jesus Christ is the Subject of election more extensively elsewhere. See Bruce L. McCormack, "Karl Barth's Christology as a Resource for a Reformed Version of Kenoticism," *International Journal of Systematic Theology* 8 (2006): 243–51; idem, "Seek God Where He May Be Found: A Response to Edwin Chr. van Driel," *Scottish Journal of Theology* 60/1 (2007): 62–79.

83. See John Anthony McGuckin, introduction to *On the Unity of Christ*, by Cyril of Alexandria (Crestwood, NY: St. Vladimir's Seminary Press, 1995), 44.

84. John does not express himself quite so baldly. What he does say, however, leads quite naturally to that conclusion: "Therefore, when we speak of the divinity, we do not attribute the properties of the humanity to it. Thus, we never speak of a passible or created divinity. Neither do we predicate the divine properties of the flesh, for we never speak

distinguished (conceptually) from his divine nature that the former was thought to be capable of acting upon or with respect to the latter, then the Logos was being treated as an absolute metaphysical Subject—that is, one without the qualities or predicates we associate with his divine "nature." The truth, of course, is that the Logos would not be the Logos in the absence of his divine nature (his qualities and predicates) and could not function as a Subject otherwise than as the Logos clothed in his divine nature. But the pressure created by the thought of impassibility was leading the orthodox into incoherence; the Logos was being asked to perform actions with respect to its divine nature rather than in and through its divine nature. That the commitment to impassibility also had the unintended effect of driving even the most ardent defenders of a single-Subject Christology in the direction of Nestorianism is equally clear. Where the sufferings of Jesus are assigned to the human nature alone, there the human nature is being treated as if it were a Subject in its own right—which has to render incoherent the commitment to a single-Subject Christology.

Even Cyril, the greatest proponent of a single-Subject Christology, was only able to point out the direction in which a real solution could be found with his talk of "suffering impassibly"; he was not able to arrive at the solution himself. What was right in this phrase was its first half. The Logos does indeed suffer. How could it be otherwise? If the human nature assumed by the Logos "subsists" in the Logos (i.e., has reality only to the extent that it is the nature of *this* Subject), then there is no other Subject to whom suffering might be assigned than the Logos. But even Cyril was not finally able to break free from the spell cast by the thought of impassibility. All of this is on the one side.

On the other side was the soteriological commitment. The pressure which this second commitment placed on orthodox Christology was exactly the opposite of the first. The effect was to bring the two natures into the most intimate communion conceivable. In that the orthodox were thinking along this line, their reception of the Chalcedonian Formula experienced a dramatic reversal. No longer was the Logos treated as an absolute metaphysical Subject. It was precisely because the Logos

---

of uncreated flesh or humanity. In the case of the person, however, whether we name it from both of the parts or from one of them, we attribute the properties of both natures to it. And thus, Christ—which name covers both together—is called both God and man, created and uncreated, passible and impassible" (John of Damascus, "An Exact Exposition of the Orthodox Faith," in *Writings*, trans. Frederick H. Chase Jr. [Washington, DC: Catholic University of America Press, 1958], 276). To the extent that human predicates (and experiences) can be ascribed to the person of the union (the Logos) *without ascribing them at the same time to the divine nature*, the person is being treated as something that can be abstracted from the divine nature and stand "between" (so to speak) the natures, mediating between them.

was divine in nature and possessed the attributes of incorruptibility and immutability that the Logos was thought capable of infusing his life into the crucified Jesus. Whatever the shortcomings of the idea of *theōsis* when assessed in the light of the New Testament, it has to be said that the formula was being employed with far greater coherence when it was understood as providing a basis for this soteriology than was the case when it was being used to defend divine impassibility.

But now we need to take a final step. What made possible the incoherent use of the Chalcedonian Formula to defend impassibility in the first place was a third commitment—that to the Greek notion of "substance." The word "substance" was meant to point to the *whatness* of a thing, that which made it to be what it is. The effect of the doctrine was to treat the whatness of a thing as something complete in itself without regard for its actual existence. Applied to the concept of a "nature," the doctrine of "substance" had the effect of making what a nature is to be something that is complete in itself apart from and prior to all the acts and relations which make up the lived existence of the individual person in which this nature is instantiated in time. In taking this step, the Greeks were also controlling the meaning that could be assigned to the word "essence." The most basic meaning of the word "essence" is (or should be) the self-identical element proper to a thing or person which perdures through all outward changes of circumstance and so forth. Controlled by the doctrine of "substance," however, the "essence" of a divine person was not controlled by an eternal act, a decision for historical existence in time; rather, it was defined in abstraction from that decision and that history. And this is how it came about that the Logos could be treated on occasion as an absolute metaphysical Subject. It was the shadow cast by the idea of "substance" which gave such a move a relative plausibility. Moreover, it was the idea of "substance" which, more than any other single idea, made a commitment to divine impassibility seem to be a necessary one. The abstract definitions assigned to substances were themselves timeless and unchanging. It was but a short step to treat the perfect spiritual substance (divine "being") itself as absolutely timeless and unchanging.

If the problems resident in the nexus of ideas which made the Chalcedonian Formula possible in the first place are to be overcome without setting aside the theological values contained in that formula, then, clearly, a different set of ontological commitments are needed. And this is what Karl Barth sought to provide. The values resident in the formula are three in number. Chalcedon committed the church to (1) a single-Subject Christology, one in which both (2) the full divinity and (3) the full humanity of Jesus Christ could be upheld. As we have seen, it is the single-Subject Christology which is imperiled by a commitment to impassibility (because it steers this Christology in the direction of Nestorianism). Addressing this problem would mean replacing the doctrine of "substance" with a rather different understanding of "essence"—one that is both actualized and historicized. In the process, the thought of a divine timelessness and impassibility is rendered completely untenable. That is Barth's contribution.

For Barth, Jesus Christ *is* his history. He *is* the history set in motion by an eternal act of self-determination; hence, the history that he is finds its root in election. This is what he is "essentially." Jesus Christ is what he is in his eternal act of self-determination and in its outworking in time. The implications for a putative divine timelessness should be clear. Already in *Church Dogmatics*, II/1, Barth had treated "eternity" as something that is defined by God's being. The concept is used illegitimately where it is filled with content drawn from some other quarter and then applied to God. Moreover, Barth had already claimed that eternity is that which founds time, that which provides time with its basis. And it would be hard to see how it could be anything else. If God's eternal act of self-determination is a determination for existence as a human being in time, then it is the eternal decision itself which founds time. And if God's being is, on the basis of this decision, a being-for-time, then clearly God's being cannot be timeless. We would do better to understand the decision in eternity and its outworking in time to be a single activity, one which originates in eternity and is completed in time. But this then also means that time is not alien to the innermost being of God.

The critique of impassibility requires a further step. Who, we might well ask, is the Subject who suffers in Jesus of Nazareth? We have just seen how a commitment to impassibility led to an understanding of the Logos as an absolute metaphysical Subject, with the consequence that it became necessary to treat the human nature as a Subject in its own right, capable of a suffering which had no ontological implications for the Logos. That such a conception tilts in the direction of Nestorianism is clear. What Barth has done, however, is to insist that a single-Subject Christology such as Chalcedon's *cannot* make this move. There can be only one Subject of the human sufferings of Jesus, and this Subject is the Logos. That the Logos suffers *humanly* goes without saying. Suffering is made possible only through the *assumptio carnis*. But it is the Logos who suffers, for there is no other Subject. Even more important where the concept of impassibility is concerned, Barth has also closed the gap between the Logos and his divine nature. If the Logos is the Subject of the human sufferings of Jesus, then suffering is an event which takes place *within the divine life*—which also means that the divine "nature" cannot be rightly defined in abstraction from this event. The divine nature can rightly be defined only by this event. The net consequence of this move is that *Barth is able to advance an understanding of divine immutability which is no longer controlled by the further thought of impassibility*. If becoming human, suffering and dying, and so forth, are the content of the eternal decision in which God gives himself his being, then no change is introduced into the being of God when this becoming and so forth take place in time. And if God is immutably determined for suffering, then the concept of immutability has been cut loose from impassibility.

THE WILL OF GOD AND DIVINE CAUSALITY IN BARTH'S DOCTRINE OF PROVIDENCE (*CHURCH DOGMATICS*, III/3)

In the history of Christian reflection on questions surrounding the relation of divine sovereignty and human freedom, the doctrine of providence has played a much larger role than is often realized. To see why this should be so, one need only recall what was said earlier about foreknowledge and necessity. One can indeed say that God knows *all* that will happen in the world even before he creates the world, and one can even say that God knows all that will happen precisely because he has *willed* all things (thus making foreknowledge to be dependent upon foreordination), and still not make all events to be necessary. As we have seen, foreknowledge does not, in and of itself, necessitate anything. Granted, it does give to the One who foreknows certainty with regard to what is to come. But certainty is a predicate of persons. Necessity, on the other hand, is (or is not) a predicate of events. All of this is true on the level of a formal analysis of concepts at the very least. But for it also to be true *materially*, God's way of ensuring that his eternal will is fulfilled in this world must leave room for the *autonomy* that is proper to the creature. If necessity is indeed a function of how events take place, then contingent events must truly be contingent—which means that the autonomy of the human must be honored. So everything depends here on one's understanding of God's providential activity. The open theists, I would suggest, have been looking in altogether the wrong direction by concentrating their attention almost exclusively on foreknowledge. What they should have been looking at more closely is the doctrine of providence. How is God's eternal will made effective in this world? This is the central problem in the doctrine of providence.

According to the Thomistic/Calvinistic doctrine of providence, every event that takes place in nature and in history was "specifically decreed"[85]

85. See n. 50 above.

by God before the world was made.[86] That God "wills all things" means, quite literally, that God wills every individual event precisely in its particularity. Nothing falls outside the eternal will of God. To ensure that God's will is actually carried out, God was further understood to be causally involved in every event. *How* God acts in relation to a particular event was seen, in turn, to depend on the mode of operation proper to the variety of creatures upon which or whom God acts. Where God's interaction with rational creatures is concerned, Thomas Aquinas put it this way: "By reason of their own nature, some beings are autonomous agents, having control over their own acts; these are governed by God not only by their being moved by him working interiorly in them, but also by their being drawn towards the good and restrained from evil through commandments and prohibitions, rewards and punishments."[87] It was further stipulated that such interior operation as might be involved was not coercive. God knows how, Thomas maintained, to move the free choice of the human without suppressing or nullifying it. Judged by today's standards, Thomas was a "compatibilist," that is, one who held that divine determination is fully compatible with human freedom.

Whether compatibilism is a fully coherent position is a subject which philosophers of religion love to debate. My own view is that, in Thomas's hands at least, it is indeed coherent. The explanation why this is so would, however, take us too far afield and is not finally relevant to the point which needs to be made here.[88] The decisive point, where a conversation between Barth and open theism is concerned, is that Barth did *not* follow Thomas or the later Calvinists in making the efficacy of God's eternal will depend on a work that God does *in* human beings. He thoroughly revised the Thomistic/Calvinist understanding of God's providential activity so that the autonomy proper to the creature could be fully honored.[89] And the consequence was that he was also in a posi-

86. Before divine providence is the actualization, in time, of God's relation to the cosmos, it is a set of "providential decrees" in eternity which set forth the ends of all things. On this point, see Thomas Aquinas, *Summa theologiae* Ia, q. 22, art. 3, ed. Thomas Gilby (London: Blackfriars in conjunction with Eyre & Spottiswoode; New York: McGraw-Hill, 1967), 5:99: "There are two sides to providence, namely the idea or planned purpose for things provided, and its execution, which is called government."

87. Aquinas, *Summa theologiae* Ia, q. 103, art. 5, ed. T. C. O'Brien (London: Blackfriars in conjunction with Eyre & Spottiswoode; New York: McGraw-Hill, 1975), 14:23.

88. A full account of Thomas's doctrine of *concursus* would require that we treat the anthropology which it presupposes, the nature of "grace," how it is made effective, and so forth—which cannot be undertaken here. I regard Thomas's version of compatibilism as far more coherent than, for example, the versions set forth by Calvin, on the one hand, and the later Calvinists, on the other. But this is a subject for another essay.

89. Barth, *Church Dogmatics*, III/3:xii: "In the doctrine of providence, . . . I have found it possible to keep far more closely to the scheme of the older orthodox dogmatics (*conservatio, concursus, gubernatio*) than I anticipated. The radical correction which I

tion to show why God can have an exhaustive foreknowledge of future events that are truly contingent in nature.

For Barth, no adequate solution to the problem of *concursus* can be had unless we keep in mind the content of God's eternal will. "When we say 'the will of God' we have to understand His fatherly good-will, His decree of grace in Jesus Christ, the mercy in which from all eternity He undertook to save the creature, and to give it eternal life in the fellowship with Himself. . . . And when we say 'the work of God' we have to understand the execution in history of the covenant of grace upon the basis of the decree of grace."[90] The content of the eternal will of God is the covenant of grace made with all men and women in Jesus Christ. The eternal will of God is not "all things" considered as ends in themselves but "all things" only in their relation to the covenant. In other words, God does not specifically decree an earthquake here, a tsunami there, as particular events; God wills this world and its history *as the context* in which the covenant of grace is played out. In willing this world and its history, it goes without saying that God has willed the kind of world in which earthquakes and tsunamis take place. But it is in that sense only that God wills "all things." This is the first thing to be borne in mind.

How, then, is God's eternal will made effective in this world? Barth makes it clear that we cannot completely avoid the concept of "cause" if we wish to speak of God's activities in this world. The Thomists were not wrong to take up this term. But he also insists that certain conditions have to be met if the term is to be used rightly of God. He names five such conditions.

First, the term "cause" as applied to God "must not be regarded as the equivalent of a cause that is effective automatically. If we had no choice but to think of *causa* as the term is applied in modern science, or rather natural philosophy, with all its talk about causality, causal nexus, causal law, causal necessity and the like, then clearly it is a concept which we could not apply either to God or to the creature of God, but could only reject."[91] The free actions of persons—whether divine or human—cannot be conceived of as merely mechanical in nature. To the extent that such actions take place in and through material elements, there is a mechanical aspect to them, but this is not what is basic. One thinks here of the bodily resurrection of Jesus—a free act of God, to be sure, but one with decidedly material consequences.

Second, if the term "cause" is to be employed correctly, "care must be taken lest the idea should creep in that in God and the creature

---

have also undertaken will not be overlooked." What I would like to do here is make clear the nature of this radical correction.

90. Ibid., 117.

91. Ibid., 101.

we have to do with two 'things.' . . . The human thinker and speaker
is in constant danger of forgetting the inconceivable mystery of their
existence and being, their presence and operation, and of imagining
that he can think and speak about them directly, as though both they
themselves and their relationship to each other were somehow below
him."[92] The point here is simply that the knowledge of persons is quite
different from the knowledge of things. In knowing things, the knower
stands above the object to be known as one who would master the object through knowledge of it. In knowing persons, this is impossible. If
persons are to be known, they must choose to reveal themselves. "A true
theological realism consists primarily in a constant awareness of the
fact that neither God nor the creature is a 'thing,' that on the contrary,
to those who really want to think and speak about them . . . they must
be *self*-revealed."[93]

The third condition is the most important. I noted earlier that talk
of God which really intends to be talk of *God* must begin with God—
and end with him. It cannot begin as talk of something else. But this
is what always happens in a metaphysical thinking which takes its
starting point in the realm of the creaturely. And so Barth says, "If the
term *causa* is to be applied legitimately, it must be clearly understood
that it is not a master-concept to which both God and the creature are
subject, nor is it a common denominator to which they may both be
reduced. . . . It must be clearly understood that when the word *causa*
is applied to God on the one side and the creature on the other, the
concept does not describe the activity but the active subjects, and
it does not signify subjects which are not merely not alike, or not
similar, but subjects which in their absolute antithesis cannot even be
compared."[94] Whatever the "infinite qualitative distinction" between
God and the human might have meant to Barth in the period in which
he wrote his famous commentary on Romans,[95] it is clear that it has
become a *content-specific idea*. It is not a distinction whose goal is
simply to promote an abstract conception of the absoluteness of God.
Barth specifies what it means:

> They are unlike because their basis and constitution as subjects are quite
> different and therefore absolutely unlike. . . . The divine *causa*, as dis-
> tinct from the creaturely is self-grounded, self-positing, self-conditioning
> and self-causing. . . . The creaturely *causa* is not grounded in itself but

92. Ibid., 101–2.
93. Ibid., 102.
94. Barth, *Church Dogmatics*, III/3:102.
95. See Karl Barth, *The Epistle to the Romans*, trans. Edwyn C. Hoskyns (London:
Oxford University Press, 1960), 10.

absolutely from outside and therefore not at all within itself. It owes the fact that it is a *causa* and is capable of *causare*, not to itself but to God, who created it and as the Creator still posits and conditions it, and then to the other *causae* of its own order, without whose conditioning or partial conditioning it would not exist. This is how the creature is a subject. And this is how it is a *causa*.[96]

But if, as subjects, God and the human are so utterly different, then it will not do to begin with the human subject in an effort to understand what it means to be a divine Subject. For it is God who is a Subject in the most proper sense, not we. Therefore God is not to be likened to us. We may well find, once we have understood something of what it means to be a divine Subject, that we are like God in certain respects. But if we try to reverse this epistemic relationship, if we try to begin with the human and reason from there to God, we will inevitably wind up simply projecting our highest ideals onto God. We will have spoken of ourselves and not of God. Again, knowledge of God must begin with God—and end with him. In the light of the knowledge acquired in this way, we can then understand ourselves. Barth concludes by saying that this rule was not observed where—with Aristotle—Thomas (and the later Protestant orthodoxy) sought to understand the problem of *concursus* in terms of the relationship between "primary" and "secondary" causality. For here the understanding of "primary causality" was built on a foundation laid in a knowledge of "secondary causality," and the absolute difference between God and the human was not safeguarded.

The fourth condition follows directly from the third. "When the causal concept is introduced, it should not be either with the intention or the consequence that theology should be turned into philosophy at this point, projecting a kind of total scheme of things."[97] This point should be easily comprehensible in an age such as our own, in which the efforts of nineteenth-century philosophers such as Hegel to provide an "explanation of everything" are in such widespread disrepute. Such efforts are possible only on the basis of some form of foundationalist thinking. It should be added that Barth intends no disrespect to philosophy here. But he is insisting that, at the end of the day, a theology which is truly Christian will honor the autonomy that is proper to it.

The first four conditions were negative in character. The fifth has something positive to say: "As the doctrine of *concursus* . . . is expounded, there must be a clear connexion between the first article of the creed

96. Barth, *Church Dogmatics*, III/3:103.
97. Ibid., 104.

and the second."[98] The first question cannot be, How does God act? but, rather, Who is the God who acts? And the answer to this question is: The God and Father of our Lord Jesus Christ, the God who revealed himself in Jesus Christ to be the God of the covenant of grace.

> Basically the doctrine of *concursus* must be as follows. God, the only true God, so loved the world in His election of grace that in fulfilment of the covenant of grace instituted at the creation He willed to become a creature, and did in fact become a creature, in order to be its Saviour. And this same God accepts the creature even apart from the history of the covenant and its fulfilment. . . . He co-operates with it, preceding and accompanying and following all its being and activity, so that all the activity of the creature is primarily and simultaneously and subsequently His own activity, and therefore part of the actualisation of His own will revealed and made triumphant in Jesus Christ.[99]

It is of the utmost importance to remember here the *content* of God's eternal will. God's will, I noted earlier, is not each and every event that takes place in nature and history as an end in itself. The eternal will of God is the covenant of grace. *Concursus*, then, rightly understood, is the doctrine which seeks to explain how it is that God executes *this* will in time. And so Barth says, "Therefore His *causare* consists, and consists only, in the fact that He bends their activity to the execution of His own will which is His will of grace, subordinating their operations to the specific operation which constitutes the history of the covenant of grace."[100] It remains to us now only to show how God does this.

So, what view of the divine *concursus* fulfills all five of these conditions? How is the eternal will of God made effective in this world in and through all creaturely occurrence? Barth's answer to this question is deceptively simple: God makes his will effective through Word and Spirit. "The operation of God is His utterance to all creatures of the Word of God which has all the force and wisdom and goodness of His Holy Spirit. Or, to put it another way, the operation of God is His moving of all creatures by the force and wisdom and goodness which are His Holy Spirit, the Spirit or His Word. The divine operation is, therefore, the fatherly operation."[101] What this answer says, in the first instance, is that we are not to look for an answer to the question of how God works by looking first at cosmic occurrence in general and then turning to an evaluation of God's activity in a particular event. Rather, we are to look

98. Ibid., 105.
99. Ibid.
100. Ibid.
101. Ibid., 142.

to the one particular event in which alone the meaning of the whole is enacted, namely, the event of God's self-revelation in Jesus Christ. Having understood how God operates here, we can then widen the lens in order to comprehend how God operates in relation to cosmic occurrence generally. And what is it that we learn when we look first to this event? "This is how God works in the specific event which forms the center and meaning and goal of all creaturely occurrence: objectively, proceeding from God by His Word; and subjectively, moving towards man by His Holy Spirit. For everything that happens here, no matter how great or small, does so in the relation of claim and response, of speaking and hearing, of command and obedience."[102] How does God work? By speaking. God speaks—and worlds come into existence.

But there is even more to this answer than appears here in the context of Barth's treatment of *concursus*. To fully grasp the significance of the answer given here, we would have to look ahead to his elaboration of the work of Christ in *Church Dogmatics*, IV/1–3. And when this is done, what we find is that God's eternal will has been *fully and completely* realized in Jesus Christ. It is not only the case that the work of the Holy Spirit does not complete a work of Jesus Christ which was incomplete without it; the work of the Holy Spirit does not even make effective a work of Jesus Christ which is ineffective without it![103] Whereas traditional theology held that the redemption accomplished in Jesus Christ needs to be applied to the individual through the Holy Spirit's work *in* him or her, Barth holds that the Holy Spirit's work consists in awakening the individual to the truth that Christ's work is *already effective* for him or her. That God works by Spirit refers, above all, to this work of awakening. But notice: the work of the Spirit does not consist in a work done *in* the human. Granted, the *effects* of this work are indeed realized in the individual. But the Holy Spirit does not need to perform a sort of divine surgery on a will which itself has been construed as an isolable element (as a "faculty") in human nature. What is required is simply that the Holy Spirit reveal Christ. In confronting the fallen human with the truth of his or her being in Christ, the Holy Spirit reorients the sinner, disclosing to him or her a new possibility, namely, the possibility of living a life in conformity to the truth of his or her being in Christ. Knowing this much about Barth's doctrine of reconciliation, we are better able to understand Barth's solution to the problem of *concursus* in *Church Dogmatics*, III/3.

102. Ibid.
103. I treat Barth's christocentric soteriology more fully in Bruce L. McCormack, "*Justitia aliena*: Karl Barth in Conversation with the Evangelical Doctrine of Imputed Righteousness," in *Justification in Perspective: Historical Developments and Contemporary Challenges*, ed. Bruce L. McCormack (Grand Rapids: Baker Academic, 2006), 167–96.

What Barth sets forth in *Church Dogmatics*, III/3, is a christologically grounded conception of the divine providence. The effect of this
christological grounding is to completely reorient the problem of *concursus*. From being a solution to a question arising in cosmology (the
divine government of the world), it has now been rendered the reflex
of a christologically grounded soteriology with a very definite content.
The significance of this move can be further illustrated by reference to
the concept of "irresistible grace." *What Barth has done is transfer the
concept of irresistible grace out of the realm of the Holy Spirit's work in
calling, justifying, and regenerating the individual into the realm of Christ's
work.*[104] As a consequence, the activity of the Holy Spirit in relation to
the activity of free rational creatures is not to be understood in terms
of "the imparting of a quality or quantity of the divine essence or operation to the creature and its activity, as a kind of infusion of divine love
or divine power or divine life into the essence of the creature."[105] God
"does not subtract anything from the creature or add anything to it,
but allows it to be just what it is in its creaturely essence. Even in the
union of the divine activity and creaturely occurrence there remains a
genuine antithesis which is not obscured or resolved either by admix-
ture or transference, either by divine influence or infusion. There is still
a genuine encounter, and therefore a genuine meeting, of two beings
which are quite different in type and order."[106] The image employed in
this passage of an "encounter" is an extremely important one. Barth does
not think of the Holy Spirit's work organically, as it were—in terms of a
quasi-physical surgery. And in any case, he does not share the substan-
tialist anthropology which would make such a conception viable. Barth
thinks of the Holy Spirit's work in terms of an existential *encounter*. The
decisive point in all of this is that the work of the Holy Spirit does not
alter what we are as creatures. And given that a relative autonomy (i.e.,
an autonomy whose meaning and significance is everywhere relativized

104. Barth, *Church Dogmatics*, III/3:144: "The Word of God is omnipotent, and His
Holy Spirit is eternal and omnipresent. Again, on this presupposition, we can gladly and
unhesitatingly ascribe to the divine work the honour which is due to it. It is an unconditioned and irresistible work."

105. Ibid., 136. Cf. p. 137: "Our older divines . . . used the (in this context) ambiguous
expression *influxus* far too readily and freely. . . . In this respect caution must also be
exercised in relation to the intrinsically attractive power-terminology of the 18th century,
in which especially the South German theology deriving from J. A. Bengel and developed
mainly by F. C. Oetinger and later J. T. Beck . . . came to speak about the reality, substan-
tiality and dynamic of the activity of God in creaturely activity. But from this it is only a
short step and we are suspiciously close to gnostic and gnoticising theories of emanations
and infusions. Again, it is only a step and we are involved in dangerous affinities to the
Roman Catholic conception of the impartation of grace."

106. Ibid., 136–37.

by God's activity) is proper to the creature as such, the work of the Holy Spirit does nothing to change that. Rather, the Holy Spirit encounters human individuals precisely in their freedom.[107] In doing so, the Holy Spirit gives to them "new potentialities"[108]—uses for their freedom which to that point in time were completely unavailable to them.

Can, then, the grace of God in Jesus Christ be resisted? The traditional formulation of the problem would need to be revised in the light of Barth's solution to the problem of *concursus*. What is beyond question is that the work of Christ is *finished*. It is in this that its irresistibility is to be found. In truth, then, it is only those who are awakened to the reality of their being in Christ who are capable of resisting in the strict sense. "Resistance" here would mean knowing the truth—and acting in ways contrary to it. But such resistance does not and cannot overturn the finished work of Christ.

In sum, the concern of the open theists to preserve and protect the relative autonomy proper to the creature has been upheld by Barth. But he has upheld it without surrendering an exhaustive divine foreknowledge. God knows all things because he wills all things; this much Barth shares with the tradition. But God wills "all things" only in relation to a covenant of grace which is made efficacious in and through all creaturely occurrence without detriment to the relative autonomy of human beings. This is not sleight of hand; it makes eminent sense on the soil of a theological ontology which finds its ontic ground in election and its noetic ground in Christology.

DIVINE IMMUTABILITY, POWER, KNOWLEDGE, AND WILL IN *CHURCH DOGMATICS*, II/1

At no point in his *Church Dogmatics* does Karl Barth come closer to sharing the concerns of Clark Pinnock than he does in his treatment of God's "holy mutability" in *Church Dogmatics*, II/1. Like Pinnock, Barth holds that

> it is not possible . . . to distil a motionless *ipsum ens* out of the "I am that I am" of Exodus 3:14, as if the divine self-affirmation expressly stated in

---

107. Ibid., 144: "If the supremacy of this [God's] work is the supremacy of Word and Spirit, it does not prejudice the autonomy, the freedom, the responsibility, the individual being and life and activity of the creature, or the genuineness of its own activity, but confirms and indeed establishes them." Cf. p. 145: "Even under this divine lordship the rights and honour and dignity and freedom of the creature are not suppressed and extinguished but vindicated and revealed." Barth goes so far in this context as to suggest that the "specific concern" of the Lutherans and the Jesuits (for human freedom and dignity) needs to be upheld, though he quickly adds that it cannot be upheld by "dissolving the divine *praedeterminatio* into a mere *praevisio*" (ibid.).

108. Ibid., 137.

these verses took place and could be understood apart from the fact that it is the self-affirmation of the God who approaches Moses and Israel and deals with both in a very definite manner. There is such a thing as a holy mutability of God. He is above all ages. But above them as their Lord, as the "King of the ages" (1 Tim. 1:17), and therefore as One who—as Master and in His own way—partakes in their alteration, so that there is something corresponding to that alteration in His own essence. His constancy consists in the fact that he is always the same in every change. The opposite of His constancy, that which is ruled out by it, is not His holy mutability, but the unholy mutability of men.[109]

Like Pinnock, Barth refuses to allow talk of divine repentance in the Old Testament to be treated figuratively: "It would be . . . foolish to try to see in the alteration which is certainly contained in the idea of repentence only an alteration in man in his relation to God, but not an alteration in God in His relation to man. . . . It would not be a glorifying, but a blaspheming and finally a denial of God, to conceive of the being and essence of this self-consistent God as one which is, so to speak, self-limited to an inflexible immobility, thus depriving God of the capacity to alter His attitudes and actions."[110] Like Pinnock, Barth protests against the concept of immutability found in Protestant orthodoxy: "If it is true, as Polanus says, that God is not moved either by anything else or by Himself, but that, confined as it were, by His simplicity, infinity and absolute perfection, He is the pure *immobile*, it is quite impossible that there should be any relationship between Himself and a reality distinct from Himself—or at any rate a relationship that is more than the relation of a pure mutual negativity, and includes God's concern for this other reality. . . . The pure *immobile* is death. If, then, the pure *immobile* is God, death is God. . . . And if death is God, then God is dead."[111] The understanding of "immutability" along the lines of the pure *immobile* is a "pagan idea."[112]

And yet this proximity to Pinnock is to be explained, in part at least, by the fact that Barth has not yet arrived at his most mature conception of the being and essence of God. Granted, he is already feeling his way toward this later perspective. Here and there he will speak of the becoming of God in history as something essential to God.[113] But Barth can also speak in a quite different way, as though the "constancy" of God refers solely to his fidelity to purposes established in election, as though

109. Ibid., II/1:495–96. I have here used the NRSV translation of 1 Tim. 1:17 in place of the Greek found in Bromiley's text.
110. Ibid., 498.
111. Ibid., 494.
112. Ibid., 495.
113. See n. 111 above.

such fidelity is *also* a fidelity to himself but only because his purposes are somehow consistent with a being that is complete in itself above and prior to the decision which gives rise to those purposes. What Barth has not yet seen is the possibility that God *is* the purposes established in his electing grace, that fidelity to his purposes simply *is* fidelity to himself. Christology appears here only on the margins, only after the concept of "immutability" had been fully elaborated without its help. It is introduced as the "confirmation and manifestation" of God's "immutable vitality,"[114] but God's "immutable vitality" has yet to be clearly grounded in God's eternal act of self-determination precisely for a "holy mutability" that consists, finally, in the history of the one God-human (rather than in the dialectic of mercy and wrath manifested in relation to Israel).

It is very instructive to compare Barth's understanding of humiliation and exaltation in *Church Dogmatics*, II/1, with that found in IV/1. Here, in *Church Dogmatics*, II/1, the "self-emptying" spoken of in Philippians 2:7 is explained solely in terms of a concealing or hiding of the divine Subject in the form of the servant. Consistent with this move, the "exaltation" is explained as movement out of concealment, a revelation of the divine Subject which had hitherto been hidden.[115] All of this belongs to a quite traditional reading of the Christ Hymn in Philippians 2: a humiliation followed by an exaltation on the part of the Logos, who hides himself in order, finally, to reveal himself. In *Church Dogmatics*, IV/1, however, the divine self-humiliation clearly has ontological significance: "The New Testament describes the Son of God as the servant, indeed as the suffering servant of God. Not accidentally and incidentally. Not merely to prove and show His mind and disposition. Not merely to win through by conflict to a concrete goal. Not merely as a foil to emphasize His glory. But necessarily and, as it were, essentially."[116] No longer is "holy mutability" treated alongside the concept of an "immutable vitality" which remains complete in itself, so that the former has to be assigned to the attitudes and actions of God and the latter to his true being and essence. Now, in *Church Dogmatics*, IV/1, humiliation is made to be "essential" to the eternal Son, with the further result that exaltation is no longer the revelation of the true identity of the God hidden in Jesus Christ in the days of his earthly ministry but the creation of a new humanity in the human "nature" of Jesus which is made possible by the humiliation of the eternal Son. Humiliation and exaltation are now seen to take place not successively but simultaneously—in the one history of the one God-human, which finds its ontic root in the electing grace of God.

114. Barth, *Church Dogmatics*, II/1:512.
115. Ibid., 516–18.
116. Ibid., IV/1:164.

At the heart of the tensions resident in Barth's doctrine of God in *Church Dogmatics*, II/1, then, lies the fact that Christology does not yet control his theological ontology. For this reason, he is able to speak of the work of reconciliation and redemption as a "fundamentally new work"[117] in comparison with the work of creation—an impossible thing to say had Barth already become a supralapsarian of the kind he would become in *Church Dogmatics*, II/2. For this reason, too, Barth cannot stabilize and render meaningful the dialectic of mercy and wrath in the Old Testament otherwise than by means of providing a starting point and a telos for it in election understood as a divine activity with no ontological implications.[118]

It is for all of these reasons that Barth was never closer to Pinnock than he was in *Church Dogmatics*, II/1. Pinnock, too, as we have seen, tried to distinguish an essential immutability from a mutability in relation to the world of human beings. But Barth is also reaching forward to a better understanding when he says, "We cannot and should not form any conception of God in abstraction from what He has effected, His reality in Jesus Christ. . . . God has limited Himself to be this God and no other." Truly a harbinger of things to come.

Turning, then, to the concept of divine power found in *Church Dogmatics*, II/1, much that is said there could still be said subsequent to Barth's revision of his understanding of election. It is the being of God which defines power in him. "To define the subject by the predicate instead of the predicate by the subject would lead to disastrous consequences. . . . To define Him in terms of power in itself has as its consequence, not merely the neutralization of the concept of God, but its perversion into its opposite. Power in itself is not merely neutral. Power in itself is evil. It is nothing less than freedom from restraint and suppression; revolt and domination. If power by itself were the omnipotence of God it would mean that God was evil, that He was the spirit of revolution and tyranny *par excellence*."[119] God's power is not power in the abstract; it is the omnipotence of grace and holiness, mercy and righteousness, patience and wisdom. To define God's power in the abstract (by means of a process of inferential reasoning—the *via negativa* perhaps) is to allow a concept of power to define the being of God, rather than allowing God's being to define the limits of power. The root meaning of omnipotence, for Barth, is that God "is able to do what He wills."[120] It is as "the constant One"[121]— the God of the covenant—that he is omnipotent.

117. Ibid., II/1:510.
118. Ibid., 505.
119. Ibid., 524.
120. Ibid., 522.
121. Ibid.

But then the dialectic takes one more turn, this time in a less than helpful way. Barth describes God's power as a power "over everything that He actually wills *or could will*."[122] The distinction made here between that which God actually wills and that which He could have willed allows Barth to then assert that

> the confession of God's omnipotence involves a statement about God which, although like every such statement it refers to what, according to His Self-revelation, God has done, does and will do in His actual work, is not actually exhausted in content by an affirmation and description of this work. It is not the case that this work coincides with the omnipotence and therefore with the essence of God, because it takes place by His will and in virtue of His perfect power. In that case, God's omnipotence would simply be his omnicausality and the latter the divine omnipotence. Of course it is God, and God alone, who is active in His work. . . . We have neither to fear nor to hope nor in any sense to expect that He will be different, and not the Shepherd of Israel and Lord of the Church, in any other work not known to us or in His divine essence. Nevertheless we must reject the idea that God's omnipotence and therefore His essence resolves itself in a sense into what God actually does, into His activity, and that it is to be identified with it. It is not the case that God is God and His omnipotence omnipotence only as He actually does what He does. Creation, reconciliation and redemption are the work, really the work of His omnipotence. He is omnipotent in this work. Loyally binding Himself to this work He does not cease to be omnipotent in Himself as well as in this work. He has not lost His omnipotence in this work. It has not changed into His omnicausality in this work, like a piece of capital invested in this undertaking, and therefore no longer at the disposal of its owner. The love with which He turns to us in this work, and in which He has made Himself our God, has not made Him in the least degree poorer or smaller. It has its power and its reality as love for us too in the fact that it continues to be free love.[123]

122. Ibid.
123. Ibid., 526–27. I regard all talk of "omnicausality" of the sort that emerges in this passage as dangerous and as qualified by the doctrine of providence set forth in III/3. Examples of a positive use of the term abound in II/1, however; see in II/1: 528, 529, 531, 532, 539, 544, 564, 575, 578, 587, 604, and 619. The term is used only five times after Barth revised his doctrine of election. Of these uses, the first two are clearly ascribed to understandings of God which Barth rejects; see III/3: 28, 32. The third appears in a very complicated section of Barth's treatment of *das Nichtige* ("nothingness"), in which he seeks to occupy a middle ground between saying that God is the cause of evil and saying that the creature is the sole cause of evil; see ibid., 292. The last two are found in the posthumously published volume on baptism. Of these two, the second is decisive for understanding the meaning of the first: "Precisely in the covenant of grace, the house of the Father, the kingdom of Jesus Christ and the Holy Ghost, there can be no talk of divine omnicausality. One is attacking this house at the very foundations if one fails to see that, even if in total subjection to the rule of Him who alone can rule here, there is given to men, to all the men concerned, not merely a place of their own and freedom of movement, but

What is at stake here for Barth is clear. He is concerned to uphold the freedom of God—both in the sense of the independence of his being from the being of the works of his hands and in the sense of the sheer gratuity of God's decision to create, redeem, and so forth. Would that Barth had realized that he could have achieved these ends without the expedient of speaking of a surplus of power which passes beyond the limits of what God actually willed to do. In speaking not only of what God did but of what he could have done, Barth has trespassed against the very core of his methodological commitments. He has opened the door to speculation with regard to what God could have done—thereby looking away from the limits set for us by God's self-revelation in Jesus Christ. As I say, none of this was necessary. Barth could have upheld the divine freedom simply by insisting that the eternal act of Self-determination in which God chose to be God in the covenant of grace and to be God in no other way is itself a free act.

The residue of classical metaphysics which comes to expression in the lengthy passage just cited had to be eliminated. The change Barth introduced with his new doctrine of election in *Church Dogmatics*, II/2, had to be effected if Barth was to be self-consistent. And with this new understanding of election came a new understanding of the relation of election to power as well. Consider, for example, the following rhetorical question: "May it not be that it is as the electing God that He is the Almighty, and not *vice versa*?"[124] It is in the last clause—the "and not *vice versa*"—that the door is firmly closed against the possibility that election (and the work which God does on the basis of it) will be seen as simply one possibility among others available to a God whose omnipotence has been defined in abstraction from what he has actually done in Jesus Christ.

When we turn, finally, to Barth's treatment of knowledge and will in God, we find the same ambiguities which surrounded his treatment of immutability and power. On the one hand, he can speak in ways which seem to limit the knowledge of God to that which God willed and that which, by willing its contrary, he rejected. On the other hand, Barth can speak in ways that suggest that power is basic to both knowing and willing and that the more basic attribute of divine omnipotence is to be

---

also the freedom of decision, with the commission to exercise it. We may thus say that it is in wholly free, conscious and voluntary decision that there takes place in baptism that renunciation and pledge, that No on the basis of the justification of sinful man effected in Jesus Christ, that Yes on the basis of the sanctification accomplished in Him" (ibid., 292, IV/4:163; cf. p. 22). "Omnivolence" is a good word—and would always remain apt for describing Barth's view of God's relation to that which takes place in our world. But a causal relation such as is entailed in the term "omnicausality" is something Barth ought never to have entertained. For Barth's use of the term "omnivolence," see II/1: 555.

124. Barth, *Church Dogmatics*, II/2:45.

understood as God's power to be himself, to be the Triune God whose being is securely established in itself above and prior to the "eternal" act in which God decides to create and redeem.

First, on the side of an equation of knowing and willing with the essence of God, Barth says that God "is omnipotent in His knowing and willing, and His omnipotence is the omnipotence of His knowing and willing. . . . That God's omnipotence is the omnipotence of His knowing and willing is also the basis of the fact that it is not power for anything and everything, but His power with a definite direction and content. It is both His power to will and His power not to will. It is, therefore, His power to know both what has been willed by Him and what has not been willed by Him."[125] So pronounced is the tendency in such statements to make divine willing the basis of divine being—so that God's "constancy" is rooted in his will always to be that which he has willed—that we are not surprised when Barth says, "This also throws light, perhaps, on the reason why the concept of omnipotence occupies a kind of key position for the understanding of all the perfections of the divine freedom and therefore indirectly of all the divine perfections whatsoever—a view which was obviously that of the earliest Christian creeds. It is only retrospectively in the light of the fact that His power is the power of His person, His knowledge and will, His judgement and decision, that we can properly explain what is meant by the constancy of His life."[126] What surprises here is not that Barth could say this. What surprises is that he does not take what he says seriously enough to reorder his treatment. If constancy can be known only on the basis of the divine knowing and willing and if, as Barth surely intends, the order of being has to correspond to the order of knowing and vice versa, then surely constancy is a function of the divine knowing and willing, of the divine judgment and *decision*. So why, then, does Barth treat constancy (immutability) above and prior to knowing and willing? How is he even able to do so?

The answer to the last question has everything to do with the fact that there is an instability at the heart of Barth's treatment of the being of God in *Church Dogmatics*, II/1—an instability which finds its root in the belief that to God's "essence" there belongs *both* a necessary element and a contingent element.

> We have sinned. We are not worthy of His turning towards us. What we deserve is not His turning towards us but His turning away from us. . . . If He turns towards us anyway, then that is an act of His *free Self-determination*. . . . Precisely on the basis of this encounter, every conception of God as the prisoner of His own immutable life is broken open and sublated.

125. Ibid., II/1:543–44.
126. Ibid., 544–45.

He stands before us, much rather, as a free *Person*, who *disposes* of His immutable life, who in His knowledge of Himself and of everything else is bound to the objects of His knowledge only to the extent that He willingly binds Himself to them, so that every possible object of His knowledge is bound first and above all to His will. From this vantage point, it becomes clear that it is not a matter of ascribing to the being and essence of God *necessity* alone and excluding contingency. Just as there is in God the highest necessity, so there is also the highest contingency. And this highest contingency in the essence of God, that which is limited by no necessity, the inscrutable, never ceasing, never to be exhausted, concrete element in His essence, is precisely that which He *wills*.[127]

To define the "essence" of God in terms of *both* necessity and contingency, of immutability and mutability, of absoluteness and concreteness is to allow both elements in these pairs to be canceled out by the other. An essence that is contingent, mutable, and concrete is not and *cannot* be necessary, immutable, and absolute—unless God is necessary, immutable, and absolute precisely *in* his contingency, mutability, and concreteness. Where the two are allowed to fall apart as polar elements, the result can be only incoherence.

It is clear what led Barth into this predicament. He wanted to insist that God is *God* in his self-revelation in time—a concern which had motivated him from the earliest days of his dialectical theology. But he also wanted to preserve in God a triunity that is complete in itself above and prior to the eternal act of self-determination in which God chose himself for the human race. This, at least, is the state of play in *Church Dogmatics*, II/1. The problem is that Barth cannot have it both ways. He has to choose: either necessity (so that power, knowledge, and will in God are limited by his necessary being) or freedom (so that God's essence is *wholly*—not partially—determined by that power and knowledge which find their root in an eternal act of divine will).

It is this instability, then, which allows Barth to say, second, that "God knows Himself, and therefore He knows about us and all things."[128] With regard to its form, this is a very classical statement. On the face of it, its meaning might well be that in knowing himself, God knows all the worlds he might create and all the powers proper to the creatures which inhabit those possible worlds. And indeed, the drift of Barth's claim that God had other possibilities he did not choose lends itself to such a reading of this statement. It is in this context that Barth's position on the Molinist controversy of the late sixteenth and early seventeenth

127. Barth, *Kirchliche Dogmatik*, II/1:616. The translation here is my own. Compare Bromiley's in Barth, *Church Dogmatics*, II/1:547–48.
128. Barth, *Church Dogmatics*, II/1:555.

centuries is explicable.[129] Barth devotes twenty pages of small print to a discussion of the issues raised in that controversy. And he clearly takes the side of the Thomists who held that God's knowledge of what would have taken place had the space-time conditions in the world that God actually chose to create been otherwise is to be reduced simply to God's "free knowledge."[130] For the Barth of II/1, as for the Thomists, there are two kinds of knowledge: necessary and free. There is no "middle knowledge." My only comment on all of this is to point out that if Barth had taken seriously his claim that "everything that God is and does must be understood as His free will,"[131] he would have realized that all divine knowledge—even God's knowledge of himself—ought to be regarded as "free." There is only one kind of divine knowing, the knowing that is rooted in the eternal act of free self-determination in which God gives to himself his own being. It is a reflection of the confusions which lie at the heart of Barth's doctrine of God in *Church Dogmatics*, II/1, that he did not take this step.

Still, Barth anticipates a more mature perspective when he simply says, "God's knowledge does not come about in virtue of a special capacity or in a special act. . . . His being is itself also His knowledge,"[132] and, "God is His own will, and He wills His own being."[133] Even more to the point: "If God's knowledge is God Himself, and again if God's will is God Himself, we cannot avoid the further statement that God's knowledge is His will and God's will is His knowledge. . . . That God's knowledge is His will and His will His knowledge means . . . that His knowledge is as extensive as His will and His will as His knowledge. Everything that God knows He also wills, and everything that He wills He also knows."[134] Surely, if it is the case that God's knowledge is limited to what He wills, then talk of other possible worlds must cease. But to reach that point would require a different understanding of the relation of God's freely willed activity to his being than the one found in *Church Dogmatics*, II/1.

In any event, what is most significant where a conversation with open theism is concerned is that an exhaustive divine foreknowledge is, for Barth, a *necessary* consequence of the fact that God wills all things

129. See n. 50 above.
130. Barth, *Church Dogmatics*, II/1:567–86.
131. Ibid., 548.
132. Ibid., 547.
133. Ibid., 548. In his next statement, Barth reverts very quickly to a completely formal attempt to overcome the instability to which I have been pointing: "Thus will and being are equally real in God, but they are not opposed to one another in the sense that the will can or must precede or follow the being or the being the will. Rather, it is as He wills that He is God, and as He is God that He wills." I would say, on the contrary, "It is as He wills that He is God," and leave it at that.
134. Ibid., 551.

(i.e., God's relation to the world is rightly characterized in terms of an "omnivolence")[135] and that what God wills he knows—and knew it before anything that was made had been made. "God's knowledge does not consist only in His knowing all things before they are and have been, in His actually knowing them when they are still future. It does, of course, consist in this. But the decisive thing is that God and therefore His knowledge of all things is what it is in eternal superiority to all things and eternal independence of all things: a knowledge of them which is complete in every respect; which not only eternally corresponds to them and follows them as human knowledge corresponds to and follows its objects, but is eternally their presupposition. It is not that God knows everything because it is, but that it is because He knows it."[136] In truth, God's knowledge is immediate and direct. God does not know "by the indirect method of the forming of specific concepts of the objects"[137] of his knowledge, for his being is his knowledge.

Conclusion

In this essay, I have tried to do two things. First, I have tried to show that a christologically grounded doctrine of God will accomplish all that is important and legitimate in the open theistic program, namely, the substitution of the living God of the Bible for a timeless, impassible deity. The attack on an exhaustive divine foreknowledge is clumsy at best; everything that the open theists wanted to achieve with it could have been achieved by a different route that would not bring them into conflict with a widespread ecumenical consensus on this question. Second, I have tried to show that a thoroughgoing christological grounding of the doctrine of God is something that could emerge in Barth's thinking only after his revision of election in *Church Dogmatics*, II/2. Therefore those who would make exclusive and uncritical use of *Church Dogmatics*, II/1, in their efforts to elaborate Barth's doctrine of God fail to see that his doctrine of election had ontological implications which brought Barth's thinking into conflict with elements of his exposition of that doctrine in II/1. The doctrine of God that is capable of addressing *all* of the valid concerns of the open theists is a doctrine he never elaborated directly. It is a postmetaphysical doctrine which must be teased out of his mature Christology in *Church Dogmatics*, IV/1, and following.

Only one task remains. One thread was left dangling when I took up the subject of the tension at the heart of the Old Testament between

135. Ibid., 555.
136. Ibid., 559.
137. Ibid., 549.

passages which speak of a divine immutability and passages which speak of a "holy mutability" (as Barth put it). I said earlier that there is a discernible progress in the comprehension of revelation as we move from the Old Testament to the New Testament—a progress which both the defenders of classical theism and the defenders of open theism either miss or ignore in their efforts to make their preferred strand of Old Testament teaching be the basis for a metaphysical construction. The progress in comprehension which I have in mind has everything to do with the concept of election. Election in the Old Testament is a wholly this-worldly, historical activity in which God sets aside for himself a people out of all the peoples of the world to be his people. The locus classicus is Deuteronomy 7:6–8a: "For you are a people holy to the LORD your God; the LORD your God has chosen you out of all the peoples on earth to be his people, his treasured possession. It was not because you were more numerous than any other people that the LORD set his heart on you and chose you—for you were the fewest of all peoples. It was because the LORD loved you and kept the oath that he swore to your ancestors, that the LORD has brought you out with a mighty hand, and redeemed you from the house of slavery, from the hand of Pharaoh king of Egypt." In the New Testament, however, the concept of election is no longer simply historical. It has now become tied to the idea of predestination—an activity of God which took place "before the foundations of the world." Ephesians 1:4 is Barth's favorite instance of this, though it does not stand alone. The passage (Eph. 1:3–4) reads, "Blessed be the God and Father of our Lord Jesus Christ, who has blessed us in Christ with every spiritual blessing in the heavenly places, just as he chose us in Christ before the foundation of the world to be holy and blameless before him in love." With this passage the following should be compared: "You know that you were ransomed from the futile ways inherited from your ancestors, not with perishable things like silver or gold, but with the precious blood of Christ, like that of a lamb without defect or blemish. He was destined before the foundation of the world, but was revealed at the end of the ages for your sake" (1 Pet. 1:18–20); "and all the inhabitants of the earth will worship it [the beast], everyone whose name has not been written from the foundation of the world in the book of life of the Lamb that was slaughtered" (Rev. 13:8); "Then the king will say to those at his right hand, 'Come, you that are blessed by my Father, inherit the kingdom prepared for you from the foundation of the world'" (Matt. 25:34). In each case, we are dealing with an understanding of election as taking place before God created the heavens and the earth. In each case this election is tied to Christ. The elect are chosen in him; the salvation which is made theirs was prepared in him. Whatever influence intertestamental literature may have had on this development, the decisive factor lay in the fact that the earliest Christians felt compelled to worship Jesus as *Lord*. If Jesus Christ is God, if God's salvific purposes could be fulfilled only by God's own appearance in history as a human being, then it becomes necessary to "locate" the history of Israel's election (and the dialectic of divine mercy and wrath to which it gave rise) within a larger narrative whose starting point and telos transcend time and thereby to modify the received understanding of election found in the Old Testament.

It should go without saying that any attempt to elaborate a Christian concept of election on the basis of the Old Testament alone (or even just primarily on the basis of the Old Testament) is bound to fail. But it is also the case that a doctrine of God which chooses the immutability pole of the Old Testament witness over the mutability pole or vice versa—in order then to construct a metaphysical understanding of God's being which comports with the preferred strand—will be sub-Christian at best and probably not Christian at all. In any event, there can be no winner in the debate between classical theists and open theists on the basis of the Old Testament. No progress can be made until each side begins to take Christology more seriously. The best that the tension-filled witness of the Old Testament can give us is the rather formal statement that God remains what he is precisely in the changes he undergoes. *How* God can do this is a question left unanswered until the appearance in history of the One who is both God and human, the living God who remains himself even as he lives a fully human life, suffers and dies, and is raised for our salvation. Abstract doctrines of God have had their day. It is time for evangelicals to take more seriously their affirmation of the deity of Jesus Christ and begin to think about God on a thoroughly christological basis.

PART **4**

Practical
Theology
Perspectives

11

The Doctrine of God and Pastoral Care

Donald Macleod

"Let not your heart be troubled" (John 14:1). It is a danger to which all of us, including pastors themselves, are exposed: anxiety, depression, and even blind panic can overtake us at any time. It may be due to temperament, to circumstances, or to a combination of both, but none of us is immune.

The concern of pastoral care is to deal with the troubled heart, either to prevent it altogether or to soothe it and calm it down. Jesus prescribes only one remedy: "Believe in God [*ton theon*, God the Father]; believe also in me." Pastoral care has to fix the attention of the flock on God himself. But where can we find him? Only God knows God, and we can know only as much as God shares with us of his own self-knowledge. This revelation, in written form, is given to us in the Judeo-Christian Scriptures. From these we derive our doctrine of God, and by this doctrine we shepherd his people. From this point of view, the pastor has no option but to be a teacher (Eph. 4:11), no option, indeed, but to be a *theo*logian.

God as Shepherd

One of the most striking features of those Scriptures is the portrayal of God himself as a shepherd. In the twenty-third Psalm, for example, the psalmist affirms that *"Yahweh* is *my* shepherd" and then goes on to describe the flock on the move, describing in a series of memorable tableaux the ever-changing terrains through which God may lead his people.

Sometimes the scenes are idyllic: lush green pastures and still waters. The flock gazes contentedly, lacking nothing and out of all danger. Sometimes, again, the picture is of respite, renewal, and revival, the flock having negotiated the dangerous, precipitous paths of the mountains and now moving serenely along the straight, smooth paths of plain and plateau, full of hope and vigor. These are more-than-ordinary times: moments in the spiritual life when God leads us along roads where we have a clear view of heaven and an overwhelming sense of his love.

But sometimes the shepherd, this same shepherd, leads us into the valley of the shadow of death: the deep ravine, the dark night of the soul, where predators wait and demons lurk. Any of us may one day face mortal perils. We may have to face a sorrow in itself almost mortal (Mark 14:34). We will have to walk through the valley of bereavement and the valley of the fear of death. And at last we have to taste death itself, be its approach sudden or gradual, expected or unexpected.

But then we have to know that the valley is no cul-de-sac. There is a way in, and there is a way out. We are not there as strays. It is the shepherd himself who leads us in; and he leads us in only because, as Bunyan reminds us, it cannot be circumvented: "Christian must needs go through it, because the way to the Celestial City lay through the midst of it."[1] The same shepherd will take us out ("These are the ones who have come *out* of the great tribulation" [Rev. 7:14]); and while we are in, he is with us, solicitous and encouraging: "Your rod and your staff comfort me." We hear the tap of his staff and feel the reassuring touch of his crook. We know he is there; or rather, we know that when the time comes, he will be there, and we resolve not to fear even though we know that when the time comes, we may find, like David, that we are not as fearless as we had hoped. It is one thing to imagine, another to experience. God forgives when our resolve breaks.

It may be that in the last two verses of the psalm the imagery changes. The shepherd becomes a host, welcoming us to his home and to his table. But whether he is shepherd or host, the care is as real as ever. The welcome is warm, the table lavish, even though it is spread in the presence of the foe, in the very face of the enemy. There may be difficulty and danger all around, but we do not need to wait for changed

---

1. John Bunyan, *The Pilgrim's Progress* (London: Oxford University Press, 1904), 77. Bunyan adds, "Over that Valley hangs the discouraging Clouds of confusion; death also doth always spread his wings over it: in a word, it is every whit dreadful, being utterly without Order."

circumstances to experience the divine blessing. The cup may overflow even in the midst of persecution, loss, stress, and pain. Indeed, at such times it may be especially full.

But at the table we are still pilgrims. In the final scene of the psalm, we have reached the house of the Lord. No longer the steep mountain passes and the deep ravines. No longer are we surrounded by hostile forces. We are safe in the impregnable, lavish home of Yahweh our shepherd—forever. There we sing our hallelujahs! "Only goodness and mercy have followed me all the days of my life; and I will dwell in the house of the Lord for ever" (Ps. 23:6).

The same shepherd image appears in Isaiah 40:11, where the prophet first of all makes the general point that the Lord "tends his flock like a shepherd": he leads, feeds, and protects them and performs all the other tasks of a shepherd. But the passage also speaks of specific personal care. Each member of the flock receives individual attention. He gathers the lambs in his arms and carries them close to his heart, and he leads gently those that are with young. The young lambs seem for a moment to have abundant energy, leaping and frolicking about, but they tire easily and could soon be left behind. The shepherd lifts them. There is a marvelous intimacy to it: he carries them close to his heart. But the personal care is not limited to the lambs. There are also the ewes heavy with lamb. Over the rough terrain and under the desert sun they have to be led gently.

And sometimes the sheep, as well as the lambs, have to be carried. I remember a minister once preaching to crofters[2] and—a risky business— venturing to tell them about the habits of a shepherd. "A shepherd," he said, "may carry a lamb, but he will never carry a sheep." The crofters were not impressed. It was not true, they said, either in nature or in grace.

Yet even in the midst of all this wonderful intimacy, the context provides a clear reminder of the divineness and power of the shepherd. No wonder the flock is safe! This is the sovereign Lord, and the arms that carry the lambs are the very arms that rule the world (40:10), just as the hand that feeds them holds the universe in its palm (40:12).

In the New Testament the primary shepherd passage is John 10:1–21, Jesus's portrayal of himself as the Good Shepherd. Here, of course, there is a change of focus. In the Old Testament passages, the shepherd is Yahweh. Here the shepherd is Jesus, present before his audience in flesh and blood: visible, audible, and vulnerable and yet declaring, "I am the Good Shepherd." This is the one who stopped, weary and exhausted, at Jacob's well (John 4:6), the one who would wash his disciples' feet (13:5)

---

2. In Scotland, crofters are people who rent and cultivate small farms, with much of the work being done communally.

and weep at the tomb of Lazarus (11:35). He is, most manifestly, "flesh" (1:14). Yet we know that he is flesh only because he "became" flesh, and we know that before he *became* flesh, he *was* God (1:1). The person speaking here is the eternal Logos. True, he is the Logos incarnate, but it is never the flesh who speaks. The flesh he took is not itself the shepherd, because it is *anhypostatic*.[3] It is not itself a subject independent of the Logos who took it. We are still dealing with the Lord our shepherd, but now as incarnate, full of grace and truth, and glorious with the glory of the one who alone is God (1:14). The divine shepherd has taken our nature and entered our history in order to save his flock.

Note, too, the price he has paid. He has laid down his life for the sheep (remember the parallel passage, Acts 20:28, where the purchase price is "the blood of God"). And here too, as in Isaiah 40:11, there is an emphasis on the personal nature of the chief pastor's care. He knows his own sheep by name (John 10:14). To most of us, including especially myself, all sheep are the same. They have no faces and no individuality. But to a shepherd, each sheep has a face, a personality, and a name in the notebook. The divine shepherd, too, has his Book of Life (Rev. 21:27). His flock may be a multitude that no one can number (Rev. 7:9), but he knows each one by name. He knows their pasts. He knows their needs. He knows their current circumstances. Each sheep is so important that, should he lose one, he leaves the entire flock and goes off to find it and bring it back to the fold. And there is, of course, but one pen. Everyone who is under this shepherd belongs to the one sheep pen. This is the unshakable foundation of all Christian unity. We all have the same shepherd.

The divine shepherd also appears, appropriately enough, in the vision of the multitude from every nation in Revelation 7:9–17: "The Lamb at the center of the throne will be their shepherd" (7:17). The underlying term here is *poimanei*, the verb corresponding to the noun *poimēn* ("shepherd"), and the literal translation would be, "The Lamb . . . will shepherd them."

The remarkable thing here is the portrayal of the shepherd as a lamb. Nothing could emphasize more clearly the community in nature between shepherd and flock or the empathy between the Lord and his people. No sheep in this flock can bleat and say, "What does he know about sheep?" This is underlined by the brutal image of Revelation 5:6: "a Lamb standing having been slaughtered." It takes us back to the altar—perhaps, indeed, to the abattoir. The Lamb has stood in the queue, waiting to be

---

3. This point will still stand even if we prefer to speak of the human nature of Christ as enhypostatic. What matters is that the human nature is not an independent agent or subject, acting or suffering apart from the person, the Son of God.

shorn and waiting to be slaughtered (Isa. 53:7). Its throat has been cut. It has known the fear of death. It has known the taste of death.

All this community in nature and all this shared experience now go into the shepherding, and far from being merely a future prospect, this shepherding by the slaughtered Lamb is a present reality. Part, at least, of the function of the Apocalypse is to draw aside the curtain and show us what is going on backstage. Onstage are the phenomena of church history: persecution, plagues, war, famine, and triumphant anti-Christianity. But backstage we see the *noumenal*: the throne of God, the sovereign Lamb, the incarnate shepherd. Echoing the table prepared "in the presence of my foes," the shepherd-Lamb, amid all the phenomena besetting the church militant, leads them to springs of living water.

But this does not preclude the extension of divine pastoral care into heaven itself. For the great multitude, the tribulation is now behind them; they carry the palms of victory, and they are before the throne. They will never again hunger or thirst. But this is not due to their having achieved independence, as if, once in heaven, they can now look after themselves. They are sated only because the Lamb is still such a superb pastor and only because he leads them to such rich pastures, pastures where the sun does not beat down on them with a scorching heat, pastures where they drink their fill from the sources of the river of life, pastures where they can roam at will in the very heart of the sovereign will of God (Rev. 7:17 collated with 22:1).

Divine Immediacy of Pastoral Care

What all this points to is a divine immediacy of pastoral care. Christ is the Chief Shepherd (1 Pet. 5:4), and we have a right to go directly to him. We have a right to his personal care. This is an emphasis we need to recover. The burgeoning interest in pastoral counseling and related disciplines can easily produce overreliance on undershepherds. Perhaps, indeed, the undershepherds want it that way. But each of us must know that we can go straight to God, and we should train every member of his flock to do the same. In fact, where there is authentic pastoral care, all it does is convey and administer God's own care. This is just as important as the priesthood of all believers. Indeed, it is part of it. Just as we have no need of a human intermediary to give us absolution, so we have no need of a human intermediary to put us in touch with the divine shepherd. Our "sharing" should be with him. The counsel we take should be his counsel. The confessor we seek out should be our great high priest (Heb. 4:14).

This is not to rule out all human pastoral care. God has made plain that his church is to have undershepherds ("pastors and teachers," Eph.

4:11), and he has made it no less plain that each of us has a responsibility toward the weak, the feebleminded, and those who are out of order (1 Thess. 5:14). But ours is always *under*shepherding: "we are *his* flock, the sheep of *his* pasture" (Ps. 100:3). He may be enthroned and on high, but his ears are open to our every bleat.

God, the Triune Pastor

But what bearing does the doctrine of God have on all this? First of all, we have to take with absolute seriousness the fact that God is triune. The shepherd is the Triune God.[4] The danger that lurks here is that we can all too easily keep the doctrine of the divine attributes and the doctrine of the Trinity in two separate compartments, first laying down the doctrine *de Deo* and then laying down, quite independently, the doctrine *de Trinitate*. To make matters worse, once the doctrine of the Trinity has been "defined," it is seldom allowed to exercise any further influence on either theology or discipleship.[5]

But this is not as straightforward an issue as it sounds. The doctrine of the Trinity is entirely a matter of revelation, and revelation has its own order: first the Old Testament then the New Testament. Furthermore, the triuneness of God comes into sight only in the course of redemption and only toward the end of that course. It cannot be deduced a priori but only a posteriori. In this sense it is empirical. It is given only in the experience of salvation, when it becomes plain that God is Savior in a threefold way. The key element here is the deity of Christ: a fact disclosed only in the incarnation and only after the concept of *theos* had been clarified over the centuries by the earlier revelation in the Old Testament, which had a great deal to say about the attributes of God but nothing about his triuneness. The fact that God is "the Father, the Son and the Holy Spirit" is disclosed only in the fullness of the times (Gal. 4:4–6). It looks very much, then, as if the theological order (first the attributes,

4. This emphasis figures prominently in contributions to this volume, particularly in the chapters on Jonathan Edwards and on the aseity of God.

5. These are the points Karl Rahner was at pains to emphasize in "The Isolation of Trinitarian Doctrine in Piety and Christian Theology," in *The Trinity*, trans. Joseph Donceel (Tunbridge Wells, UK: Burns & Oates, 1970), 10–15. According to Rahner, most Christians, despite their orthodox confession of the Trinity, are in their practical lives almost mere "monotheists" (10). He also suggests that "should the doctrine of the Trinity have to be dropped as false, the major part of religious literature could well remain virtually unchanged" (11). This all arises, according to Rahner, from the fact that "the treatise on the Trinity occupies a rather isolated position in the total dogmatic system. To put it crassly, and not without exaggeration, when the treatise is concluded, its subject is never brought up again" (14).

then the triuneness) is also the order of disclosure, comprehension, and appropriation. The systematic statement of the doctrine of God has to follow the order of biblical theology. In that order, the great Shema (Deut. 6:4), with its emphasis on the unity of God ("Hear, O Israel, the LORD our God is one LORD") has to come before the Great Commission, with its emphasis on the threefold name ("in the name of the Father and of the Son and of the Holy Spirit," Matt. 28:19).

But at our stage in salvation history and church history, one thing is clear: the Lord our shepherd is the Father, the Son, and the Holy Spirit. He is triune, and this has clear pastoral implications.

First, each person of the Trinity is involved in our pastoral care. Apart from all else, this follows from the principle that all God's *opera ad extra* are *opera* of all three persons. They perform them in communion with each other. This is true in creation. It is true in redemption. And it is true in pastoral care. Yet it is equally true that each cares in his own way. The care of each has his own personal stamp. In the valley of the shadow, the Three are there. The Father carries us, the Son is with us, and the Spirit leads us. The ministry of the Son does not preclude that of the Father, nor does the ministry of the Son preclude that of the Spirit. We are temples not only of the Father but of the Trinity. Our Pastor and Bishop is the Triune God.

Second, the love we experience in Christ is the very love of God. In this sense there is no hidden God. There is no Other, no other more ultimate Form, no other and greater glory than we see in the Son. This is why we have to speak not only of the *homoousion* but of the *homoagapē*.[6] The God who is for us in Christ is God as he is in himself. The love we meet in Christ is the very love, as it is the very being, of God: the love of the Father and of the Son and of the Holy Spirit. Christ is the true face of God: the revelation of his heart. Christ's love therefore is a love supported by all the resources of deity. In him, God pledges all that he is to the salvation of his people. But there is paradox here too. What Christ enfleshes is God's love, but it is also love on God's terms. Jesus did not say, "God so loved the world that none will perish, but all will have everlasting life." He said, "God so loved the world that he gave his only Son, so that *whoever believes* should not perish, but should have everlasting life" (John 3:16). Yet there remains the glory of the asymmetry: such a disproportion between the divine input and the human, between what God does and what God requires! He gave his Son, and as our consciences tremble and ask, "How can we possibly match that?" he replies, "I require no matching sacrifice. Believe in my Son." The

6. Though we must also insist that without the *homoousion* there can be no *homoagapē*. If Christ is not one in being with God the Father, he cannot be one in love.

divine love meets the whole cost, and it is a love that never lets go, a love informed with the *ḥesed* of divine fidelity. God the Father, the Son, and the Holy Spirit loves to the end (John 13:1). He never gives up. God never walks out. He never even allows us to walk out. If we try to, he will bring us back—search for us if need be (Luke 15:3–7).

In all pastoral care, this is the first and the last thing: "God loves you." Far from being a trite cliché, it is incredible until God seals it on our hearts.

Third, the triuneness of God is the foundation of the divine compassion. Here we use the word in its strict etymological sense. God feels with us. He suffers with us. He is distressed with us (Isa. 63:9). This is different from mere pity. Pity sees and is moved, but it has not been there. It knows only by observation, not by experience. But compassion has been there. Even for God, the only way to learn sympathy is by experience. He has been there. In Christ, he has not only taken our nature. He has entered our history and lived our human life. He has tasted our vulnerability and pain.

It is true, of course, that the Trinity did not become incarnate. Neither did the Father or the Holy Spirit. Nor, yet again, did the Godhead or the divine essence. It was the eternal Son specifically and exclusively who became flesh; and he, that eternal Son, was the subject of all Jesus's experiences, the agent of all his actions, and the speaker of all his words.

Yet the Son did not become incarnate apart from the Father and the Holy Spirit. This is a clear implication of the *homoousion*. The Son is one and the same in being with the Father and the Spirit. The Logos becomes one with human nature, but he does not cease to be one with God. He is incarnate in fellowship (*koinōnia*) with the Father and the Spirit. Besides, the fact of the incarnation does not undo or undermine the fact of *perichōrēsis*, according to which there is a coinherence of the persons of the Godhead in each other.[7] In the abstract, this means that

---

7. The classic statement of this doctrine is by John of Damascus (*Exposition of the Orthodox Faith* 1.8). Warning against any spatial separation of the persons of the Trinity, John writes, "For with reference to the uncircumscribed Deity we cannot speak of separation in space, as we can in our own case. For the subsistences dwell in one another, in no wise confused, but cleaving together, according to the word of the Lord, *I am in the Father, and the Father in me*. . . . They are made one not so as to commingle, but so as to cleave to one another, and they have their being in each other without any coalescence or commingling. . . . For the deity is undivided amongst things divided, to put it concisely: and it is just like three suns cleaving to each other without separation and giving out light mingled and conjoined into one" in *A Select Library of the Nicene and Post-Nicene Fathers of the Christian Church*, Series 2, ed. P. Schaff and H. Wace (Oxford: James Parker, 1899; repr., Edinburgh: T&T Clark, 1989), vol. 9. Cf. Karl Barth, *Church Dogmatics* (Edinburgh: T&T Clark, 1936), I/1:425: "The doctrine of the *perichōrēsis* . . . asserts that the divine modes of existence condition and permeate one another mutually with such perfection, that one is as invariably in the other two as the other two are in the one."

each person dwells in and around each other person. More concretely, it means that where there is the One there are the Three. In each, the Three come.

The experiences of the incarnate Son must be seen as experiences in which each person of the Trinity shares, even though, again, each person experiences them in his own way. In the light of the *homoousion* and the *perichōrēsis*, the cross cannot be something from which the Father and the Spirit are absent. Nor is it something exterior to God. It is profoundly interior—so interior that the blood which is shed there is the blood of God (Acts 20:28). To put it otherwise, at Gethsemane and Calvary (and even in the dereliction) the Son does not stand alone. In the One, the Three come. In the One, the Three suffer. Christ's suffering and dying cannot be an experience merely of his human nature. It must be an experience of the divine Subject, the Son of God, who is inseparably and always (even when forsaken) one with the Father and the Spirit. Only thus can we say, as we must, that what transpires on the cross reveals God. This does not warrant us to say that the Father and the Spirit *died*. The Three suffer, but each suffers in his own way. The dying is unique to the Son, who offers himself "through" the Spirit and is "given" by the Father. The dying becomes, indeed, an *idiom* of the Son, who even in the midst of the throne is the slaughtered Lamb. But the Father and the Spirit, too, taste death (Heb. 2:9). Each was at Calvary in his own way.

Pastoral Care and the Aseity of God

Two other emphases of the Edinburgh Dogmatics Conference also have clear pastoral implications. First, the aseity of God. This, of course, is simply a Latinate and inelegant expression for "self-existence," and at first sight it seems to offer little by way of pastoral application. But it does remind us of the self-sufficiency and inexhaustibleness of God. The bush burns and burns but is not consumed (Exod. 3:2). Age after age God keeps on being and keeps on giving and keeps on loving. Care does not exhaust him, nor do the passing years render him irrelevant. For all other existences, there is a law of entropy—but not for God.

This is what Isaiah portrays so memorably in his great fortieth chapter. The everlasting God, the Creator of every force on earth, does not become weary or worn out (Isa. 40:28). He suffers no burnout. After thousands of years of shepherding his people, he still cares, he is still committed, and he still remains as constant and resourceful as ever. This is why Christians are indomitable. They are often ordinary and undistinguished, but in a world where the young fail, the strong fall, and the warrior gives up (Isa. 40:30), they simply wait on the Lord, and in and through that dependence, they mount up with wings like eagles, they run and are not weary, they walk and do not faint (40:31).

The Shepherd on the Throne

The conference also focused on the sovereignty of God, another doctrine of clear pastoral relevance. According to Romans 8:28, God works all things together for the good of those he calls. This "good" cannot be reduced to the facile philosophy that "all's for the best." It is a precise and specific good: conformity to the image of his Son (Rom. 8:29). This is God's intended and predetermined outcome of human history: one day we shall be completely Christlike. But God can secure this only if, first of all, he has total control of his universe. This is precisely what Paul affirms in Ephesians 1:11: God works out everything in accordance with the purpose he has willed. It is such language, in turn, that warrants the statement of the Westminster Confession that "God from all eternity did . . . unchangeably ordain whatsoever comes to pass."[8] So defined, God's foreordination is all-embracing: the cast of the dice, the fall of the sparrow, the treachery of Judas, and the death of Jesus are all preordained. But such foreordination is no abstract thing, and this is why it is of such enormous pastoral importance. The *decretum horribile* (not "the horrible decree" but "the decree that causes us to tremble") is the decree *of God*. This means that even in the darkest moments, what we face is the cup given to us by our heavenly Father.

Here once again we have to do justice to the triuneness of God. In the decree, too, there is *koinōnia* and *perichōrēsis*. The Son is a full and equal partner in foreordination; and this means that there cannot be in it or about it anything that is un-Christlike. Nothing in predestination can contradict what God has said about himself in Christ. God does not have either another face or another heart. This is the truth dramatized in Revelation 5:5–10, where it is the Lamb who opens the scroll. The scroll itself is crammed full of writing, even to overflowing, because it contains everything, the whole of history. But to all that is in it, the Lamb has given his consent, and the pages turn only as and when he

---

8. Westminster Confession 3.1. This understanding of New Testament teaching is by no means confined to Westminster Calvinism. See, e.g., the almost casual remark of J. H. Bernard, *A Critical and Exegetical Commentary on the Gospel according to St. John* (Edinburgh: T&T Clark, 1928), 1:115: "The Synoptists and Paul alike share the belief that it is not Fate but Providence that rules the world, that God foreknows each event because He has predetermined it, and that therefore it must come to pass. To reconcile this profound doctrine with human free will was the problem of a later age."

wishes. By the same token, the Book of Life, which contains the names of all those to be admitted to the new Jerusalem, is the *Lamb's* Book of Life (Rev. 21:27). Every aspect of the *decretum* has to be seen in the light of Christology. "His will" is the will of the God and Father of our Lord Jesus Christ.

It was this doctrine of the all-embracing sovereignty of God that William Cowper expressed in these well-known lines:

> Deep in unfathomable mines
> Of never-failing skill,
> He treasures up His bright designs,
> And works his sovereign will.

But we must never invoke this "sovereign will" to absolve ourselves of responsibility. Foreordination does not rule out freedom. We certainly have no right to identify foreordination with determinism. The latter is a philosophical theory; the former is a theological doctrine derived from revelation. It is true that many, perhaps most, advocates of the Augustinian doctrine of predestination have been determinists, but by no means all. Indeed, the Westminster Confession has no sooner laid down that God has foreordained whatever comes to pass than it hastens to add the caveat that "the liberty or contingency of second causes" is not taken away but rather established (3.1). The clear import of these words is not only that foreordination is compatible with freedom (compatibilism) but that foreordination *establishes* freedom. It guarantees it. It might be too much to say that the confession endorses libertarianism (itself only a philosophical theory), but it certainly gives such emphasis to liberty that libertarians have every right to claim that their position is perfectly consistent with Westminster Calvinism.[9]

9. See further William Cunningham, "Calvinism and the Doctrine of Philosophical Necessity," in *The Reformers and the Theology of the Reformation* (Edinburgh: T&T Clark, 1862), 471–524. Cf. A. A. Hodge, *The Confession of Faith: A Handbook of Christian Doctrine Expounding the Westminster Confession* (1870; repr., London: Banner of Truth Trust, 1958), 68–69: "The decrees of God are not the proximate causes of events; they only make a given event certainly future. It [*sic*] provides that free agents shall be free agents, and free actions free actions; and that a given free agent shall exist, and that he shall freely perform a certain free action under certain conditions." Paul Helm does not himself hold a libertarian position, but he does nevertheless acknowledge that "it is possible to hold both to predestination and to libertarian human freedom, providing one sufficiently emphasises the inscrutability and incomprehensibility of such an arrangement." The arrangement may not be entirely "incomprehensible" if, with Hodge, we distinguish between *foreordaining* and *causing*—a distinction which Helm himself appears to use in describing the position of Calvin: "While Calvin holds that God ordains all events and determines many of them, he does not hold that he determines all of them if to determine means to 'efficiently cause'" in Paul Helm, *John Calvin's Ideas* (Oxford: Oxford University Press, 2004), 171–72.

We find this remarkable only because we persist in confusing foreordination with determinism. Determinism describes the relations between events within the created order, arguing (or assuming) that within this order every event occurs within an inexorable causal nexus. Every event therefore has a cause, and this applies not only to physical, chemical, and biological events but no less to psychological and moral events. Our human choices on this perspective are thus determined by other events within the causal nexus: by our genes, by our upbringing and our environment, and by the stimuli and motives which ply our minds in the moments of decision making.

Foreordination, by contrast, is not about the relation of event to event. It is about the relation of God to his world. That God controls that world, there can be absolutely no doubt. But he does not control it by coercion. Nor does he secure his intentions by making our choices the inevitable outcomes of physics, chemistry, psychology, or sociology. Instead, God gives us space to make our own choices. These choices may be influenced by prior events, but they are not determined by them. God foreordained that Judas Iscariot would betray Jesus; he did not foreordain that when the time came, he would *force* Judas to do it. Nor did God trap him in a causal nexus where he had no alternative but to do it. At the crucial moment, Judas was not even the prisoner of his own previous choices: he could have chosen differently, even to the extent of betraying those to whom he had betrayed Jesus. Even less did God make himself part of the causal nexus, as if we could aggregate all the physical, chemical, psychological, and historical factors which were driving Judas and then cap the aggregate by adding "God."

Instead God foreordained that Judas would betray Jesus freely, and because Judas did it freely, he did it responsibly. He practiced his treachery on his own recognizance. God did not allow him to occupy a position where he could say, "I couldn't help it!" He could have helped it. Nothing in the causal nexus constrained him to it, not even his own "character." Judas has absolutely no space to say to God, "You made me do it!"

Today, as never before, we have to give proper emphasis to freedom and responsibility.[10] We have to insist that there is no affinity between foreordination by a loving, intelligent deity and the determinism that underlies the modern behavioral sciences, portraying human beings as the helpless precipitates of heredity, environment, prenatal experi-

---

10. A. A. Hodge was already sounding this warning in 1890: "This matter of free-will underlies everything. If you bring it to question, it is infinitely more than Calvinism. I believe in Calvinism, and I say free-will stands before Calvinism. Everything is gone if free-will is gone; the moral system is gone if free-will is gone; you cannot escape, except by materialism on the one hand or pantheism on the other. Hold hard, therefore, to the doctrine of free-will" (*Evangelical Theology* [London and New York: Nelson, 1890], 157).

ences, and bad parenting. Whatever the forces that beat upon the human psyche, we make our own choices, and each choice is as unpredictable as the trajectory of the individual subatomic particles that give us our television pictures. We are free even to behave out of character, and free, too, to call God to account and tell him that he has no right to blame us because we have done nothing but what he foreordained (including calling him to account). Conversely, even in such a sacred preordained moment as our conversions, God respects our freedom. We owe everything to his initiative, yet he sees to it that we come "most freely, being made willing by his grace" (Westminster Confession 10.1).

It is no wonder that it is in this very context that Paul exclaims, "Oh, the depth of the riches of the wisdom and knowledge of God!" (Rom. 11:33). There can be no greater tribute to the divine wisdom than God's ability to "preserve all his creatures and all their actions" while simultaneously granting these creatures the space to behave freely and contingently.

The Divine Attributes and Pastoral Care

But to what extent can we relate specific divine attributes to pastoral needs? One attribute which Scripture clearly relates to our personal struggles is the divine power, often illustrated and confirmed from God's work in creation. We have already seen this in Isaiah's portrayal of the divine shepherd: the very arms that gather the lambs rule the world, and the hand that feeds the flock holds the waters in its palm (Isa. 40:10, 12). But we see it, too, in Psalm 121:2, where the psalmist finds reassurance in the fact that his safety comes from the Lord, "who made heaven and earth." Key New Testament passages make the same point, though more implicitly, contrasting the divine *dynamis* with the *dynamis* of every potential threat. In the good-shepherd passage, for example, the Lord himself uses this very argument: "my sheep shall never perish and no one shall pluck them out of my hand. My Father, who has given them to me, is greater than all and no man is able to snatch them out of my Father's hand" (John 10:28–29). Here the safety of the flock is guaranteed precisely by the contrast between the divine power and every malevolent force: no one is "able." In the same way, Paul finds comfort in the fact that nothing created "shall be able" to separate us from the love of God (Rom. 8:38–39), and Jude incorporates the same sentiment into the doxology that closes his epistle: "Now to him who is able to keep you from falling away, and with joy to present you faultless before his glory . . . be glory, majesty, power and authority" (Jude 24–25).

Our natural instinct in the presence of divine power is to shrink in terror. It would take so little of it to crush us! But it is precisely this power which, prompted by the divine love, constitutes Augustine's invincible grace (*gratia irresistibilis*). In Paul, indeed, the grace and the power are virtually coordinate: "My grace is enough for you, for my power is perfected in weakness" (2 Cor. 12:9). But these very words make plain that grace cannot work in a context of human self-sufficiency. We cannot rely simultaneously on ourselves and on God. Grace can work only when we are out of our depth, telling God with utter simplicity, "I can't handle it!" Then, and only then, do we become hyperconquerors (Rom. 8:37).

Closely linked to the divine power is the divine presence. God is a very present *help* (Ps. 46:1). Nowhere, unfortunately, did Christian spirituality and Christian theology diverge more radically than in their different approaches to the divine presence. The Scholastic doctrine of omnipresence and the devotional "practice of the presence of God" belong to different universes. The Bible's interest is almost exclusively in the latter, and nothing is of greater pastoral relevance than this doctrine of the nearness of God. It is because God is with us in the valley of the shadow of death that we fear no evil. It is because God is with us all the days to the end of the age that we go forth boldly to evangelize and baptize (Matt. 28:19–20). Here again, of course, the reference is specifically to the presence of Christ, but this serves only to remind us, first, that the divine presence is *his* presence and, second, that the God who is present with us is the Triune God. The Father, the Son, and the Holy Spirit are present with us: each in his own way. This is such a remarkable *plērōma*: the presence of the fullness of the essence and of the fullness of the attributes and of the fullness of the divine personhood. Yet if it is the presence of Christ, it is not simply the presence of the divinely omnipresent. It is the divine presence as *mode*-ified by the incarnation. We cannot say that in the Lord's Supper, for example, the broken body of Christ is present. But we can say that it is the Christ of the broken body who is present, the Christ who took our nature, entered our history, shared our experience, and even now feels with us. There is always a Fourth Man in the fiery furnace (Dan. 3:25). We are never alone.

What of the anger of God? The remarkable thing is that the vast majority of the Bible's references to the divine wrath speak not of his displeasure with reprobates, profligates, and apostates but of his displeasure with his own people. Hence the reality of divine chastisement: in his recoil from sin, "the Lord disciplines those he loves, and he punishes everyone he accepts as a son" (Heb. 12:6).

One of the most helpful statements on this subject is to be found in the Westminster Confession's statement on justification, which affirms clearly that believers can never fall from the state of justification but then affirms equally clearly that when they lapse into sin, they "fall under God's fatherly displeasure" (11.5). The language is carefully chosen, distinguishing clearly between judicial displeasure and fatherly displeasure. God will never revoke the sentence of acquittal and vindication that he pronounces in justification. Even less, having adopted us, will God ever eject us from his family. In these areas we have absolute security. But God has rules for his children. It is true, in the mystery of grace, that neither our "getting in" to the family, nor our "staying in," nor, as far as heaven is concerned, our "getting there" depends on our blameless compliance with these rules. But they are rules nonetheless: God's house-rules. He is indeed our loving heavenly Father, but when we violate his rules, we fall under his *fatherly* displeasure. It is precisely because we call God "Father" that we are to spend our lives here in reverent fear (1 Pet. 1:17). His fatherly displeasure puts us at no risk of a judicial review of our relationship with God, but it does (to use another phrase from the confession) expose us to the risk of having "the light of his countenance" withdrawn from us. We may (to use the parallel biblical metaphors) find ourselves in a fearful pit (Ps. 40:2), in the depths (Ps. 130), or in a darkness without light (Isa. 50:10).

We should not use the distinction between punishment and chastisement to minimize the gravity of God's fatherly displeasure. It is in the very moment of warning that the Lord will judge his own people that the writer to the Hebrews declares, "It is a dreadful thing to fall into the hands of the living God" (Heb. 10:31). If we incur his fatherly displeasure, all joy may depart from our lives, all assurance be lost, and even the strength for ordinary spiritual tasks desert us. For his sin, David suffered the death of his child, terminal strife, and violence in his own family, and for their sins many among the Corinthian believers were weak and sick, and a number had "fallen asleep" (1 Cor. 11:30).

Pastors should be slow to pronounce the sufferings of their flock "chastisement." Such insight requires a prophetic gift not promised to any of us. But we must make crystal clear that when believers do come under God's fatherly displeasure, there is only one way back. We must humble ourselves, confess our sins, beg pardon, and renew our faith and repentance (Westminster Confession 11.5). The words may trip lightly enough off our tongue, but what they describe is the agony of spiritual recovery: a depth of remorse, self-repudiation, and self-denial that may be far more intense and far more traumatic than anything we knew at the time of our first coming to Christ. It is not the novice who goes out and weeps bitterly (Luke 22:62).

Conclusion

In deploying all these considerations, let us bear in mind the words of Hebrews 12:5, which describe Scripture as exhorting us and discoursing (*dialegetai*) with us. This is what doctrine does. It addresses our minds. It makes logical demands of us. It exposes our fallacies and neuroses. It reasons us, with God's blessing, into reverence, confidence, peace, contentment, and hope.

But there is something deeper and more immediate than doctrine: the peace of God that passes all understanding (Phil. 4:7). The doctrine can fight the thoughts and fears that torment us, but the peace of God can stand sentry at the door of our hearts and prevent these thoughts and fears from even entering. How much we need that! It is the most effective of all pastoral care, and it takes us back again to the immediacy of the divine shepherding: the direct personal touch of the Good Shepherd.

We keep our heads in the worst of times because he stands sentry, allowing nothing but peace to enter our hearts.

Scripture Index

Genesis

1:26–27   197
1:31   40
2:17   40
3:4   63
3:5   40
3:11–15   152
4   41
5   41
5:22   157n54
5:24   157n54
6:5   41
6:5–7   153n38
6:6   194
6:8   157
6:9   157
8:21   165n77
9   41, 147n19
18:19   157
18:20–33   194
19   41
20:13   149n24
32:9   160n64
32:22–31   153
32:25–30   38
35:7   149n24
49:10   152n34

Exodus

2:1–21   152n34
3:2   253
3:3–4   158
3:12   156
3:14   161n65, 231
4:14   38
4:24–26   38
15:20–21   149n26
16:7   159, 160
16:10   159, 160
19:5   139

20:2   149n24
20:5–6   163, 164
24:14   148
24:16–17   160
24:18   148
25–31   147, 154n39
25:1–9   148n23
29:46   149n24
30:33   39
30:38   39
31:2   157n50
32   41, 147
32–34   57, 142, 147, 148, 154n39
32:1   148, 148n23
32:1–6   152
32:4   148n23
32:8   148n23
32:8–9   150
32:9   150
32:9–14   152
32:10   150, 151, 152, 158, 162
32:11   152, 153
32:12   153
32:13   153
32:14   153
32:19   149
32:20   150n31
32:21   152
32:22   150, 152
32:25   150, 150n31
32:26–28   150
32:27   150n31
32:29   150n30
32:30   154
32:30–31   150
32:30–33:6   154
32:31   154
32:32   63, 154, 163
32:33   151
32:34   155, 156
32:35   151

33:1–6   156
33:3   150, 151, 154, 162, 165
33:4–6   155
33:5   150, 151, 154, 162
33:7   155
33:7–11   155
33:11   155, 158
33:12   156, 157
33:12–17   156
33:12–23   147, 156n46
33:12–34:9   155
33:13   156, 158
33:14   158
33:15–16   159
33:16   156
33:17   157
33:17–23   162
33:18   147, 161n66
33:18–23   161
33:18–34:4   159
33:19   152, 160, 161, 161n66
33:20   147, 151, 161, 161n66
33:21–22   161n66
33:22   160
33:23   161n66
34   146, 156n47, 162
34:5–6   161
34:5–9   57, 142, 147, 162
34:6   160, 163
34:6–7   8n2, 162n69, 163n71, 164, 180
34:7   163, 164
34:8   164
34:9   150, 162, 165
34:14   161n65
35–40   147, 154n39
35:20–29   147n21
36:2–7   147n21
40:34   147n21

Subject Index